Between Two Seas

Charles Lister was born in 1930 in San Remo, Italy. After Cambridge, he taught in Rome and Naples, then in Africa, before becoming a BBC announcer. He now helps to run an independent sixth-form college in the Midlands, which he founded twenty-five years ago. He and his wife live in Warwickshire; they have two children.

Lalage

Dulce ridentem
dulce loquentem

Between Two Seas

A Walk Down the Appian Way

CHARLES LISTER

Minerva

A Minerva Paperback
BETWEEN TWO SEAS

First published in Great Britain 1991
by Martin Secker & Warburg Limited
This Minerva edition published 1992
by Mandarin Paperbacks
Michelin House, 81 Fulham Road, London SW3 6RB

Minerva is an imprint of the Octopus Publishing Group,
a division of Reed International Books Limited

A CIP catalogue record for this title
is available from the British Library
ISBN 0 7493 9906 6

Printed and bound in Great Britain
by Cox and Wyman Limited, Reading, Berks

I love my kingdom, said Ferdinand, King of Naples;
it's really an island with salt water on three sides
and holy water on the fourth.

Walking is virtue; tourism deadly sin
– Werner Herzog

Minus est gravis Appia tardis
– Horace
The Appian Way should be taken slowly

Acknowledgements

I would like to thank the members of La Scaletta in Matera for their help, both then and now, and particularly Dottor Daniele Cappiello. I am also grateful to Tony Bennett and to Vicki Harris for their patience, diligence, suggestions and excisions in dealing with the tattered manuscript. Finally I apologise to any authors whose ideas I have appropriated or whose words I have bent or bowdlerised.

Contents

ROME
Ariccia ○ Lake Nemi

Fondi
Itri • Sessa
Terracina   Montesarchio
Mondragone Capua (N) Benevento
Capua (o) Caserta Aeclanum
Naples
Frigento

Salerno
Eboli

T y r r h e n i a n
S e a

——— The Appian Way
- - - - The author's route

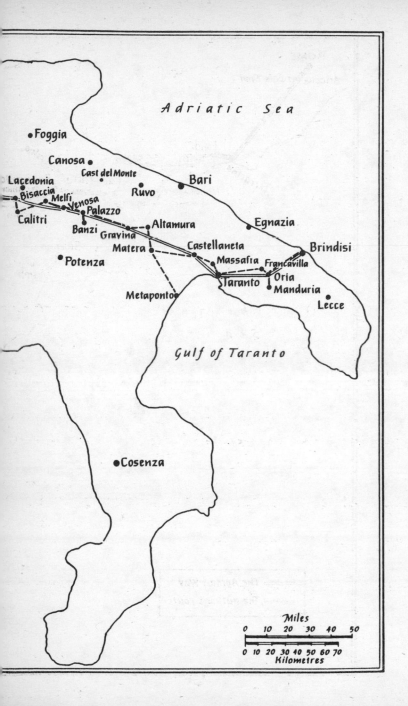

Adriatic Sea

Foggia

Canosa

Cast del Monte

Lacedonia
Bisaccia
Melfi
Calitri
Venosa
Palazzo
Banzi
Gravina
Matera

Ruvo

Bari

Altamura

Egnazia

Castellaneta

Brindisi

Potenza

Massafra

Francavilla

Metaponto

Taranto

Oria
Manduria

Lecce

Gulf of Taranto

Cosenza

Miles

0   10   20   30   40   50

0 10 20 30 40 50 60 70
Kilometres

Introduction

This book was commissioned on 11 May 1960. As contracts were signed the same week, and I then received an advance of £50, I had every reason to be pleased. I knew it wouldn't be hard: the synopsis was fine, I knew the way, I'd looked up bits of history, and better still, I was just married and had a nice London flat and a new enviable job with (seemingly) unlimited prospects, within walking distance of home. Euphoria was an understatement, and no crest of a wave could be higher; my moment had arrived.

There's only one tiny hurdle to be hopped over, I thought: a little leave of absence – but that shouldn't be a problem, not if it's been commissioned. So I made the necessary appointment to meet my un-maker, and at the designated second I knocked on his door, reverentially though barely audibly through the Sten-gun roar of four secretaries clattering out the culmination of his daily workload. I knew I wasn't his favourite person: 'BBC announcers don't wear yellow socks,' he'd growled at me six months ago, 'or desert boots. Aren't they called . . . brothel creepers?' It was the only time he'd ever spoken to me, and I hoped he'd forgotten it. Anyway, it was hardly important now; not with this ace in my hand.

'Sit down,' he boomed, voice deep and gravelly, as if rehearsing for an underwater Boat Race commentary, his whole frame filling the swivel chair.

'I've had an idea . . .' I said, eyeing the gleaming links of gold watch-chain threaded across his immaculate waistcoat. 'Do you know David Farrer?'

'Who?'

'A director of Seckers . . . David – '

'You mean Secker & Warburg Publishers? Old Martin Secker?'

'Yes. Well, he's asked me to . . . to do this,' and I took it out and handed it over. Then I watched his face.

'Oh,' he said, studying it. 'So he's asked you, has he . . . ?'

'Well. Almost. It's a commiss – '

'Who thought of it? You or him?'

'I did, actually.'

'Huh . . .' He grunted several times as he looked at it, deep in underwater thought, and I watched his face slowly start to change. I watched it soften gradually, boredom turning to interest and then to enthusiasm. He began to glow with pleasure.

'So,' he beamed, looking up, 'walk down the Appian Way, eh?' and I could feel him sharing my pride as he handed the ace back to me. 'What a first-class idea.'

'So I can go? Can I?'

'Certainly.'

'Three months?'

'Excellent. Just what's needed. We're all too limited here, no outside interests. Claustrophobic job, announcing. Too blinkered. Need to broaden our outlooks . . . When are you going?'

That's how I remember it. Though perhaps I should have allowed for those yellow socks and for setting fire to newsreaders' scripts just as the pips went (anything to relieve the boredom) before taking my first deliberate steps out of work, out of a safe job, out of sight and sound, along a very long road – one that became much longer than expected . . . A careless step off the edge of the world.

'Well, I'm back,' I said, three months later.

'Oh,' he answered, looking puzzled – his watch-chain still two perfect curves across his stomach, as if he hadn't moved during my absence – 'I thought you'd left.'

'No . . . I thought you said I could . . .'

'Did I? I don't think I did. Did we write you a letter?'

'No.'

'Ah.' It was soft but definitive. Gently terminal. A sound that expected no answer. A quiet expostulation straight to the solar plexus.

'So you mean . . . I can't . . . '

''Fraid so. Sorry.'

And that is why it wasn't written. The wave-crest had subsided on to a pile of rocks, and I was jobless and penniless with commitments to a home and family. So the Appia was forgotten, and the £50 returned, and as other imperatives took over from the dusty roads of south Italy the notebooks on aqueducts, tomb robbers and olive trees were sent to curl up in a drawer.

Then, not long ago, I went back there to write an article for an Italian magazine.

'Well,' said the journalist I'd last met in 1960, 'where's the book then?'

So I came home and wrote it. I opened the drawer filled with dusty old notes and photographs, began to unravel the thirty-year-old thoughts, tried wiping the mould off memories: Carlo Levi, Mafia murders, amphorae, emperors, brigands, sybarites . . . Was it that long ago, I wondered – Danilo Dolci pleading for the peasants of Sicily who earned £40 a year, Padre Borelli sweeping *scugnizzi* off Neapolitan streets, while plumed Bersaglieri ran up and down outside Buckingham Palace and international gladiators flexed their muscles in the Olympic arenas of Rome, all exactly a hundred years since Cavour had said, '. . . we have at last made Italy . . . now we must show the southerners what liberty can do to their beautiful country!'? And when I'd turned the clock back and completed the cobweb labour into a restless assembly of random, fractured recollections, I sent it all off to where it had started in the first place, to Secker & Warburg, to see what would happen . . .

It was not a journey of scholarship or profound analysis, and the views and errors are mine. More specialised accounts of the Appia Antica can be found in archaeological journals and among various British School papers at Rome, while more thorough insights into the country as a whole appear in John Haycraft's *Italian Labyrinth* and Peter Nichols' *Italia, Italia*.

Mine was another journey.

ONE

Rome

'Do you know the best thing to do in Rome?' he asked.

'No,' I said innocently, desperate for secrets.

'Leave the bloody place.' And off he went.

A most wise suggestion, now I come to think about it: there's little amusement left. The Via Veneto still parades its sun-glassed midden of voyeurs, the Spanish Steps are awash with mindless drop-outs, the lean spider-crab of St Peter's flicks its claws further out each day to suck in more souls, and the finger-warm Pincio whispers all night with the bee-like hum of homosexuals. It has lost originality. Flair and presentation, yes; invention, no. So this time it will be terminal. I've left before, of course – by car, train, bus, tram, aeroplane – but have always come back, just to touch up on some dark eyes or feline body or shaft of sunlight on a silver fountain arcing in the air. It does that with people: it sucks you back like an underwater magnet full of memories then clams its jaws on you. Not this time, though; this time I'm leaving for good.

The old writers knew it best; roll them into one and there's the true picture: 'a most overpowering essence of combined stinks'; 'prostitutes licensed by the Cardinal Vicar'; 'disgraced with filth'; 'dirty dismal pictures of Weeping Magdalens, bloody Ecce Homos, dead Christs and fainting Madonnas'; 'the inside [of St Peter's] would make a nice ballroom'; 'a quarter of the population are priests, a quarter are statues, and a quarter do absolutely nothing'. And even the sanguine Walpole: 'Before a great number of years are elapsed, I question whether it will be worth seeing.' And that was two hundred years ago. They all had the right idea:

He who likes thee does not know thee
He who knows thee does not like thee.

But they keep coming in spite of it: chalk-white girls
from the north still pour on to the termini platforms off
every train fresh as railway-allotment lettuces and launch
themselves giggling into the garlic jaws of romance; hot
little beer-men come to miss a warm heartbeat or two and
make mental grasps at the squeezable shape of those tight
mandolin bums; old maids with guidebooks look earnestly
at statues and churches by day, at waiters and barmen by
night. 'A parcel of staring boobies' was Byron's verdict
when he saw the place full of them. I'd like to have a page
of Hawthorne pasted into every guidebook:

When we have once known Rome, and left her where
she lies, like a long decaying corpse . . . in utter
weariness . . . of her narrow crooked intricate streets
. . . feasting with our own substance the ravenous little
populace of a Roman bed at night . . . sick at heart of
Italian trickery . . . and sick at stomach of sour bread,
sour wine, rancid butter, and bad cookery . . . disgusted
with the pretence of holiness and the reality of
nastiness . . . crushed down in spirit with the
desolation of her ruin, and the hopelessness of her
future – left her, in short, hating her with all our
might and adding our individual curse . . .

He knew what he was talking about; and that was even
before the motor car and those buses Revel said weren't fit
to transport anything but cattle. There are plenty who
wouldn't agree though; Ibsen thought it was 'beautiful,
wonderful, magical', Lady Knight called it 'the finest city in
the world' and Henry James said, 'At last for the first time,
I live,' as soon as he arrived. It's all a matter of opinion.

The English only go abroad for four reasons anyway: to

hate, to complain, to escape from national virtue and look for sin, or to enjoy being homesick. Occasionally there are exceptions who paint or study or write guidebooks, like Mrs Charlotte Eaton, whose book on Rome went into five editions in spite of saying, 'Ghiberto [sic] was a Florentine who flourished in the – I'm sorry I can't remember positively what century', but most are like Smelfungus Smollett, knowing they are being cheated all the time and losing their tempers. Or some just go to get drunk, and stay semiconscious for days like the eighteenth-century aristocrats Lord Middlesex and Sir Francis Dashwood, who were seldom sober the 'whole time they were in Italy'. And sometimes it's that old goblin of sunny lust, as they try to Boswell their way between their legs or, like Thomas Patch, into their bottoms.

Whatever it is they hate it all in the end, and finish by fighting their way through everything – Rome and the heat and the traffic and the mountains of spaghetti and through the whole holiday – and would have done better to have read Hazlitt and stayed at home. He shared Lady Mary Wortley Montagu's view that English travellers were the 'greatest blockheads in nature', and 'Golden Asses', which most of them still are, speaking ill of all other nations and boasting incessantly of their own. And that, announced the Abbé Dupaty in 1785, is what the crowd of English call travelling.

I'm not the only one leaving either; we've all had enough. The poet is off to Paris to finish his translation of Gioacchino Belli,* hoping the boys will be cheaper there; the journalist has written his second novel and got bored with Italian football and H.E.'s secretary; the little leprechaun from Dublin has been leant on by the Swiss Guard about his life of the Pope; and the Australian is safely stowed

* The poet published his translation some years ago, to very favourable reviews. He has since published numerous other works.

away on a ship in Naples because that's how he arrived in the first place. As for Michael, he couldn't get his collection of pubic hair into his suitcase when he had to leave and was last seen emptying envelopes off a bridge into the Tiber whispering, 'Bye-bye, darling,' as each cobweb drifted away.

Nothing has changed after all those years: still a soulless city with Christ's mouthpiece tucked away in one corner, a peacock with borrowed feathers, all confirmed by statisticians. There were 120,000 Romans in 1700, 180,000 a century later, then six hundred thousand in 1900, one and a half million in 1950, and now over three million. So while it preens itself as being some stately Renaissance prince or opulent old emperor, in reality it's a gangling abortion conceived in 1870 by Piedmont, Garibaldi, Mazzini and the Pope, and now turned into a delicious fantasy by foreigners. Just over a century ago their precious Forum was a cattle market and slaughterhouse; every night this year there were a hundred homeless sleeping in the Colosseum.

The wolf is the right emblem for it – a scavenging night beast, cruel and cowardly, that slinks close to the earth. They had one once, in a cage on the Capitol, moth-eaten and miserable, the only thing children ever climbed the steps to see – but now it has gone to the land of animal rights and the cage is full of stray cats.

So, I'm off to the south, to something decent and open and older and still untouched, something rough and pagan and back to good old nature, which Goethe declared was Paradise and Frederick of Hohenstaufen called a Promised Land, and where there was an empire of ancient Greeks, diaphanously dancing Tarentines and languid Sybarites fainting at the thought of work, and where the hollow laugh of Horace still echoes in caves beside the blue sea.

This time I walk out, hissed at by evil, overweight buses that sway like stampeding mastodons as they scatter the opposing traffic and swing their entrails of passengers as if

8

they were corn-ears; they pin me to mud walls mixed with flint and belch black exhaust fumes with puffs of satisfied laughter. This is where they caught St Peter, suffering similar premonitions of a Roman death after seeing his vision; Christ's friendly, oversized footprints are still on a piece of marble by the roadside where He turned him back – scientifically dated as originating from the seventeenth century, but always a place of summer pilgrimage.

This outskirt of Rome wasn't a happy place for believers: Pope Stephen had his head chopped off hereabouts in the middle of celebrating mass (he was just one of twenty-four popes out of the first twenty-eight who met a violent death), and Calixtus caused a riot here for saying fornication and adultery weren't really all that sinful. They've even named these catacombs after him – lugubrious tunnels of ice-cold air filled with withered bodies lying on bunks, and supposedly the first official Christian burial place in Rome – and if the rumour is true that over 350 miles of such tunnels were built under the city to take Christian bodies and there were six million of these, then it works out at ten corpses to every yard.

It would be nice to know more about these early popes with such romantic and floral names as Hyginus, Soter, Zephyrinus, Anteros, Hilarius, Cornelius and even Dionysius, and to know just how they spun their web. They sound too carefree and sunny to have taken on their obsessions with such fervour while Rome was all around them, busily stretching out muscles to rule the world.

Right in front is another victim, St Sebastian, and his Gate, whose name arrived here by no explicable route at all, as it was originally the Porta Appia, and now instead of being full of arrows is covered in rickety scaffolding and having yet another metamorphic face-lift. It would be nice to go up and examine the impostor more closely: a perfect place for kissing Rome goodbye.

'Can I come up,' I shout, 'and have a look?'

'No, you can't, *signore*. We're putting in floodlights,' and they wave and smile. Blast them! I shouldn't have asked. They love the negative: it gives them a sense of power, an enjoyment of godlike superiority, telling you what you can or can't do. They revel in a chance of pompous authority and domination to swell their tiny egos, so they go on waving smugly, singing a capon tenor in their paper hats and dusty shorts as they scurry along the narrow planks like bronzed beetles against the stone, pushing buckets of paint and barrowloads of plaster at each other.

'Why are you putting in floodlights?'

'For the tourists, *signore*. This is a very important monument. 't's where the Via Appia starts – the Appia Antica . . . it's a very old road.'

Not bad, for workmen. The blind senator Appius Claudius devised the scheme precisely 2,300 years ago: a highway from Rome to the south-east corner of Italy, primarily to improve military strategy and hasten the Army's progress along the old tracks already there. He even walked along some of it himself, in bare feet, to test the smoothness of the stones. At last it would be five days' march from Rome to Capua – the luxurious queen of the south – by way of Terracina and Minturno; then it would go east to Benevento; after which the first and bravest would head south into the mountains through Melfi and Venosa till they reached the Greek pleasure garden of Taranto, while the wiser ones like Trajan would go further east to the Adriatic and then move south along the shore to Brindisi.

So off I go along the road of death, the one Addison said was 'melancholy' and 'nothing else but a street of funeral monuments', and Dickens said was 'ruined and overgrown'; and after the last houses I agree entirely. There's one picture-postcard view where it is quiet and lonely and sad with a dignified line of funereal poplars, but it soon turns to mortuary baldness as the trees tire of weeping over the old tombs and tumbled stones that sprawl in misshapen heaps across the earth. A road of thousands of Roman corpses, buried there by a law which forbade interment within the city walls. So mile after mile of cemeteries spread out from the centre like spokes of death.

The tombs are there now, ghostly and defiled, tractor- and tank-torn, wallowing in the ground like old tree trunks, half-drowned in ditches and scratched by thorns, and tumbled into wild hedges, mounds of shapelessness and rubble strewn with grey limbs of dismembered statues inviting useless guesses at someone's extinction. Where did they bury Tiberius' pet crow? Which garbled heap might have held the powdered bones of Cinna? The earth is sworn to silence; and after one majestic sweep of chequered stones the road dies away in exhaustion under a layer of dust and weed. Work it out for yourself, it says, I've been here long enough; and the enormous slabs sink away quietly into the earth, locked together in indestructible defiance as they slide from sight like the scales of some monstrous sea dragon returning to its lair of immortality and myth.

It's gone for ever after the battered tower of Cecilia Metella with walls twenty feet thick. That didn't stop the vandals getting in, though, long after it had been stripped of its white marble; then it was used as a fortress; and later as a toll-gate by the Gaetani family in the thirteenth century. Being friends of Pope Boniface VIII, they had the divine right to demand tribute from any travellers entering the city from the south, but their extortion soon became so outrageous, together with the endless freelance thieves and highwaymen – Cicero said there were always plenty of them along the Appia – that pilgrims walked round it and entered by another route altogether, after which the old Appia was forgotten for a while. Canina was given the job of cleaning it up five hundred years later by Pius IX, and did so very commendably – apart from a few suspect identifications – though no one has taken much interest in it since.

Now that the dragon's back has gone, a narrow pathway

shambles out over moorland, between two wide-spaced hedges and banks of earth, beyond which the flat land bumps away on both sides: a rolling carpet westwards to Ostia that dips into dead ground then floats over grassy dunes towards the hidden sea, or balloons its way inland over bulges of double-chinned fields and paunches of heathland streaked with the sweat of distant grey roads and spiked with telegraph poles and those dark, dry aqueducts that Dickens saw stalking over the plain like giants. Everything's rough and uneven, a veneer of carelessness cloaking the bones of old ruins and dressing the warts. They're even here on the path to touch – wrecks of marble wrapped in brambles, moss-eaten halves of epitaphs and sad slabs of monuments – a shambles of detritus hiding acres of unwanted ghosts. Dust of the dead and debris of empires, Chateaubriand called it.

That's half the trouble – being unwanted. These whispering phantoms are superfluous: there are too many ruins and too much history. What with nearly three-quarters of the world's art and archaeological treasures, the earth is so saturated they can't cope any more – Pompeii, Paestum, Herculaneum, Egnazia, Sybaris, Baia; and then Venice, Pisa and Florence . . . Who wants a few extra tombs, more bones, old stones, another dozen amphorae or geriatric Greek vases, or a handful of dusty coins? It's all too much trouble. They can't even manage what they've got; half of it has been stolen or is falling down. The moment you find an ancient crumb the law says Stop work straight away and tell the authorities – which no one does, knowing just what will happen, so they ignore it and keep it, sell it, hide it, destroy it or throw it away; or else they tell the antiquarian Mafia who, if it's worth it, send in the professionals. I've seen a Roman plumber smash his way through skeletons and jugs and jars with urgent contempt in his determination to get the floorboards down again; and watched ploughs blunt themselves on old sarcophagi; and helped torchlit men slither deep into Etruscan fox-holes.

Is it guilt or triumph, when you find one unwanted iota of the past no one else cares about, and save it from another thousand years of darkness and wasted months of bureaucracy, and help by removing a little more of their rubbish that they won't even miss because their museums, storerooms and outhouses are already overflowing, and the past is so mundane it has become a nuisance? Sink a spade in anywhere in the south and there's a chance you'll hit old Rome: it falls out of hedges after storms, runs down drains, stops roadworks and lies smashed in farm furrows.

Can anyone blame a tomb robber? Would any sane person tell the police his tent peg had opened an unknown sepulchre and left him staring at a pile of gold coins or a figured vase? I doubt it. He would bless his good fortune and help himself, and then steal away quietly to join the august ranks of the robber-lords Elgin, Carnarvon, Burlington (who carried home 878 pieces of luggage), Sir William Hamilton (who did it by the boatload), Lady Holland, who dipped into Herculaneum, Lady Montagu and the Earl of Arundel. And if they weren't good enough company, he could mention Mark Antony and Napoleon and Pope Nicholas V, who removed 2,500 wagonloads of stone from the Colosseum in one year. So stealing the past is nothing new; it is just a little more dangerous today, with more eyes watching, more voices ready to be raised and some very ruthless hidden forces waiting in the wings. And if the Mediterranean lands hold more valuable artefacts than they know what to do with, and if hundreds are abandoned and ignored, and if many disappear into private circulation every year with official nods and winks, why on earth not combine a little more private enterprise with preservation?

It would take as long again to unbury ten centuries of tombs; even in this small distance reaching to the Alban Hills, once luxuriant with private villas and palaces and sumptuous farms, it would need decades to unravel all the millions of fragments. Mussolini had no inclination for it; art has made the Italians soft was his verdict, ordering in the 'motor ploughs' to help fight his *battaglia del grano* and so further decimate the already plundered landscape. Hawthorne would have loved to see it so dishevelled and abandoned yet again: it's 'nice to think that all these idle pains have turned out so utterly abortive', was his comment.

There's an old Vespa tucked up into the hedge ahead, leaning over disconsolately on its stilt, its handlebars turned discreetly away from whatever its owner may be doing somewhere in the lunar landscape. Perhaps it carried two lovers from Rome who are now lying hidden in a fold, wrapped up in afternoon sunlight and mating on a carpet of corpses; or perhaps it's a creeping huntsman waiting for the last lark of the Roman *campagna* to scramble into the heavens and have its twittering silenced.

Otherwise there's emptiness, dimly broken by the hum of traffic a mile away in a different world. 'Nothing bearing the stamp of humanity chequers this wide waste,' said Lady Morgan, hurrying on to misbehave in Naples – which hundreds had done before her, and hundreds still do today, fleeing across this heathland of desolation towards the aphrodisiac fleshpots of Parthenope. This sad plain with its uncharted pimples and pock marks is where Seneca committed suicide and where Milo slew Clodius; and along these buried stones Cicero returned in triumph from banishment, and the funeral procession of the dead Augustus made its way from Nola to the Capitol. By his time the rot had set in, as the greedy farmers had turned the abundant plain from healthy crop rotation into lazy, profitable pastureland, which soon grew so stale and stagnant that the wide fields rotted and the golden farms all perished. Soon the Goths and the Vandals and the Lombards found little worth destroying when they arrived: it had destroyed itself, and has never since returned to use or occupation. Instead of those 'hard stones, planed and polished and cut to form eight angles' marvelled at by Procopius eight hundred years after it had been built, it's now an undulating wasteland disfigured by curious shapes where trees have sprung up haphazardly like self-sown weeds on a battlefield – dark umbrella conifers with windmill arms, or sharp black cypresses sleek and pointed as devils' candles, whispering their epitaphs in the wind as the wilderness of ghosts rolls round them like a sea.

Ahead of me there's a human shape sitting on a grey boulder against the hedge. It's a young girl knitting unconcernedly, and she barely glances up as I draw level, because there's a mountainous dog lying at her feet – several yards of enormous canine sweltering in a jungle of off-white hair, pumping its breath out like slow bellows. Its head is so vast it can barely raise it, its eyes are darker than a Baskerville swamp and its tongue more massive than a slice of gammon.

'*Buona sera,*' I greet her.

'*Salve,*' she answers, still knitting without looking up – all of which is a bit unearthly, that some twentieth-century Chloe should be seated in solitude in a hedgerow in this deserted landscape within ten miles of St Peter's, her shoulders wrapped in an old shawl and wearing a coarse-spun skirt down to shapeless boots, knitting nonchalantly. I unsling my camera carefully.

'Please may I photograph you?'

She nods gently, and gives a soft whistle which focuses the Baskerville's eyes sharply and stills his florid tongue, and I notice suddenly that we are no longer alone but surrounded by menacing men-shapes that have emerged from the soil like dragon's teeth, and slid into view from nowhere: shadows have stepped out of single trees, bodies risen from ditches and sentries bolted upright from the earth. Seven mean silhouettes are standing in a circle of a hundred yards and moving in slowly like Masai warriors before a ritual; so I thank her kindly and move a few paces on – but the path is barred. Ah! What a stupid way to go, you idiot. You should have seen it coming: a pretty girl on her own in the middle of nowhere, obvious a mile off . . . So I light a last cigarette and hold the packet out as trickles of fear icicle towards my leaden stomach, and I watch the wide-brimmed hats and half-hidden faces draw closer, and see how broad-shouldered they are in jerkins of rudely patched cloth and heavy trousers knotted at the knee like leggings then cross-banded down to their boots. They're bigger than town Italians, solid and muscular inside a bulk of mongrel clothes covered in straps and pouches, and their faces are hard and dark, coarse-grained mahogany roughened by every weather. Swinburne took an escort of cavalry; Ramage had his dilapidated umbrella; I've only got a camera and cigarettes . . .

The nearest one considers my offered packet carefully, his eyes dark and watchful, then slides his hand slowly into his pocket without concern, so I withdraw the unavailing arm in resignation and glance at the seated Chloe in a last plea for mercy; but she knits on intently as if nothing were happening, and I turn my eyes back to the leader. His hand is stretched out towards me at full length, and his eyes are bright under bushy eyebrows as he edges closer, and in the gnarled palm of his rugged paw is his offering of a ten-lire piece.

In moments the others follow, beaming their corrugated grins and digging cheap coins out of patchwork linings and lost pockets; above the chuckles comes the satisfied hiss of deep inhalations, and a veil of blue smoke drifts on the evening air and whispers away to heaven as my heartbeats trickle back to sanity.

They're shepherds, recently arrived from the Sabine Hills with over a thousand sheep to spend the whole winter here, nibbling at the crust of dead Rome till April. Then they'll drive them a hundred miles back into the mountains for the summer, and a great wave of wool will surge inland again and block the roads and drown the villages and bleat up dusty lanes, and these dark mountain men will marshal the white ocean and stride before and after it proudly on their way home, while off-white Cerberus pants lolloping and thirstily pink at its heels.

'What do you do all day?' I ask.

'We think, *signore* . . . and watch the sheep . . . and we sing . . . Sometimes we walk into Rome.'

'And where do you sleep?'

'Where we are, *signore*: under trees, or by a wall, or in an old house somewhere . . .'

'And what about . . .?' I glance at the knitting shepherdess.

'Ah! Don't worry, *signore*. You see, she's the *padrona*. Her father owns all the sheep.'

TWO

The Castelli

There is abruptness about the way the land climbs to the Castelli, as if they were sudden warts on skin; and in effect they are, being a bundle of seismic bulges thrown up years ago and grouped around craterous lakes, shabbily unconcerned that this is where the story of Rome is supposed to have started, where fragments of Greek myth came to rest, where Romulus and Remus were born. The people are already country folk and don't care that the Pope retires among them in high summer, or that James III of England and Francis II of the Two Sicilies wept here for lost kingdoms; they're swarthy and remote and as distant from Rome as Calabrians growling at each other in their own dark accents. Half of them have never been to Rome nor ever wish to go, preferring the tight huddle of their narrow-streeted mongrel villages with their sleepy ways to the frenzied rat trap of the capital; so they stick to their scarred and swollen lips of hilltop which have seen more wars than anyone can remember, and only five hundred years ago were little but heaps of rubble.

The feeble track dies for ever in a field at the edge of this bubble of hills where the tarmac road, polished by squealing tyres, starts to wheel away south round the skirts of Ariccia, missing the modest fork that slips away upward over steep grey slabs between leafy walls and then climbs through trees towards the sardine houses that are leaning down the slope or elbowing each other off the edge or clinging desperately to outcrops, congested and cramped like spontaneous battlements.

I used to come here at weekends, summers ago, by motor cycle: a silent American machine that was oversized and

full of New World power, whispering as it went and routing
Vespas as if they were nursery baubles. The local youths
would gather round it like locusts, twenty deep and buzzing
with hunger at its glossy blackness, enormous engine and
silver exhausts; and they would beg to hear it. Then they
would walk away shaking their heads sadly. '*È bella, ma
non si sente*,' they said – It's nice, but it doesn't make a
noise – rejecting it with quiet contempt as something
emasculated and useless. To be significant it had to destroy
the silence, which to Italians is boring and too close to
nature for comfort; and as it lacked the Verdi quality of
pointless uproar they dismissed it as worthless trivia,
because silence makes them uneasy and must be decorated
and embellished and put to use, like a bare wall in need of
graffiti. That is why so many of them stalk off into the
orchards at dawn loaded down with old carbines to search
for fleeting sparrows and tits among the leaves: it's not the
half-inch of meat they need, but the music of the musket.
'*Les coups de fusil flattent les oreilles*,' said Haller.

I've made no appointment this time; it will be something
of a surprise if Franco remembers those weekend invasions
of his *cantina* two summers ago, when we were like
fledgling stormtroopers on holiday. There was Peter the
Pole, who we knew was a Russian spy; Big Mac from
Canada, who studied painting and only knew the word
nudo; a dissolute girl from FAO who lent her flat to needy
couples; the music scholar from Cambridge with watery
eyes who we all thought chopped up little girls; and that
half-godly sage from some Catholic school who wore shorts
and sandals and talked erudite holiness and knew Moravia
and Sophia Loren. Full of wit and daring as we flirted
crudely with Franco's daughter Assunta and spat into the
sawdust, we basked in the cool air of this subterranean
wine tunnel and called for our flagons of Frascati, which
Franco would carry in beaming, five or six jeroboams of
refreshing gold, while dark-eyed Assunta would follow with

our plateful of *supplì*, warm oval cakes of boiled rice stuck together with cheese. As we got more darkly drunken and more distant from the sun we'd risk coarse innuendos and imagine we were making bedroom eyes at her and guffaw at our feeble courage, but she was fifteen and knew more than we did, and anyway the Catholic said he could smell the hair in her armpits.

'Hello,' I say, as he gives a brief flicker of puzzlement and recognition; puddles of wine and stale flagon rings still mottle the long bare tables in the *cantina*'s cavernous shade, but there's no sign of Assunta. 'She's married the barber,' he says. 'She's got a baby,' and there's an empty chill where our infestation has drifted away on the wind, and like flocks of starlings invading spring lawns has gone to scavenge elsewhere. 'Where can I stay the night?' I ask, and he shrugs his unconcern. 'Try Il Paradiso,' and fingers another memory: of a decadent old *palazzo* near the lake where secret lovers from Rome can meet to whisper and walk with guilty stealth among the trees; and where once I touched my own elfin piece of paradise – after springtime walks in Hadrian's Villa and along the magic of Ostia's warm beaches peeped over by the stars – in a huge Tiberian bed where love was tried in two languages and we heard the cicadas applauding beyond the window with urgent little songs, then whirring for encores and applauding again, and an anguished dog howling in jealous agony by the lake. She had just started university and had that only-Italian softness of sensual beauty that can burn the heart to ashes and torture the sight like a wanton flame with the depth of its panting eyes; there were no other sounds in that warm Ariccia night till I heard her heartbeats afterwards as she fell asleep. There was nothing left but a sweet fresh smell in the soft room's darkness – the scent of a sleeping girl.

But not this time: just a small *locanda* tucked up an alley with a little white room at the top of the stairs and a creaking old bedstead and upturned-eyed Marys on the wall.

'You're lucky,' the smiling *padrona* says, 'there's only one room left,' lying without a twitch, so we argue the price in half for three minutes and when it has tumbled from ten thousand lire to five she tells me the season is going well because you can cycle from here to St Peter's in half an hour (which is rubbish), and there are hundreds of tourists begging for rooms, so aren't I lucky – which is more lies, because all the lederhosen lovers and the muscular Teutonic *Wandervogel* I've seen sweating under mammoth rucksacks had tents on top, and are going to get on with it out in the fields where it is free.

My first night out of the airless sweat of Rome and eager to go further; but first a little pause in the morning sun to worship some old gods, and a walk to Nemi along chestnut paths and under giant trees till the lake sparkles below in the hollow like a silver saucer blocking its own crater. It was here it all started, among these sacred tips of Alba Longa, when genealogical confusion was redolent with magic and death, and there were dateless tribes and pre-biblical names; and into this apocalyptic holocaust wandered a son of Aeneas to found a city, and out of it came the wolf-sucking twins to wander north by the river while their Alban cradle was torn at by old tribal kings and blessed by new deities.

And here lived the greatest of them all, worshipped by thousands: to this sparkling lake with its comforting pillows of summer trees stretched from shore to sky came the ubiquitous Diana, transported on an Odyssean journey from Greece in one of her many shapes to be the all-powerful mother and protectress of the waters and woods, of virgins too and mothers in childbirth and all the animals (except the horse which had killed one of her lovers), and so became Diana Nemorensis – Thickly Wooded. Moreover, after her temple had been built at the water's edge, she took a husband – for the Romans, quite reasonably, thought she needed a mate, but being short of unoccupied gods at the time presented her with the best alternative they could find: the strongest, largest and most vicious gladiator available, who became Diana's consort and Rex Nemorensis for the remainder of his lifetime. Whether he was king for a day or longer was up to him, as his crown could only pass to the person who slew him in hand-to-hand combat, thus making his regal position and entitlement to the favours of all his wife's handmaidens a doubtful blessing; for while they enjoyed the strength of his loins another was after his head.

Alas! Such ancient spirits have long since left, though Nemi is still gorgeously wooded and abundant in flowers, with blood-red bursts of honeysuckle, and blue of columbine and the livid greens of buckthorn and myrtle mixed with blossoms of cherry pink; but the elemental magic has crept away and left it to the dreary Madonnas of the Oak and Laurel and Pine, and boring old St Sylvanus is keeping his eye on the grottoes of the nymphs. But something stirs if you listen hard enough and close your eyes; the leaves are laughing softly and Diana's voice is whispering in the wind:

> *Paganisme immortel, es-tu mort?*
> *On le dit.*
> *Mais Pan tout bas s'en moque*
> *Et la Sirène en rit.*

Gone, too, are the imperial barges built by Caligula for his cruises round the lake, his water parties and trips across to see Diana. Because Mussolini got bored with all the stories about a sunken palace, after people kept dredging up exciting bits of ruin, he pumped out half the lake in 1932 and found these two massive boats at the bottom, each nearly eighty yards long; when they'd been restored he had them displayed in a lakeside museum – until the Germans put a match to them twelve years later. And considering they did the same to the library at Naples University I wonder why any of them bother to come back.

It is dreamy sitting here in the sun watching silver ripples, mixing love with hate and myth with reality, and pretending to hear the roar from the amphitheatre where they say the Emperor Domitian fought wild animals single-handed, and sniffing for those leeks that Cicero said were so delicious. One of the fairest spots in all Campania, he called it, luxurious and verdant, and so popular with the Roman nobility that, according to Sallust, the richest men's villas were the size of villages, over a mile in circumference, and Claudius' was so big he could hide a thousand soldiers away under its arches without anyone seeing them.

Has it all gone? Smashed like an English Nonsuch and forgotten within twenty years? Here two thousand have passed; and Goths and Vandals and Franks and Huns have been; and Lombards and Normans and angry popes and all-crushing Swabians and warring Princes of Rome; the French have come, too, and rioters and freedom fighters and Garibaldi's cavalry; and so have Germany's shells and England's tanks and America's bombs. But there's one bit they've all missed, on the edge of Ariccia: the old serpent back again, coiling its way to the curve of the summit in great tiers of stone, where there are two hundred yards of hard brown blocks wedged in a limpid cohesive bond which is ten yards wide and burns ancient yellow in the sun. Here loitered the thieves and beggars on the slow rise to the Pons Aricinus, to whine at the travellers by day or kill them by night, to bully the pilgrims on their way to Diana, to shout at the long-distance Horace and to mutter at Peter and Paul. Addison didn't enjoy it either, as his diligence bumped over the same uneven stones; 'indeed, very disagreeable' was his view.

And then he breasted the summit and saw the start of south Italy in front of him: three hundred square miles of grey-green plain ahead, the blue-shaded Sabine ridge fading to the left, and far on the right the bulbous black shape of Monte Circeo crouched darkly by the sea like a sleeping rat. Beyond that nothing: emptiness and the edge of the world. He saw what I do now, a limitless wilderness stretching to a distant haze then leaping off the brink into the sky, where Rose Macaulay said there were ghostly cities that rolled round Rome like a sea. More than twenty of them, if the stories are correct – Norba, Praeneste, Ninfa, Genazzano, Pometia ... – all sunk into the monstrous quagmire that quickly usurped the ancient fertility of the plain in the days when Tarquin was abroad, when the Volsci, Aurunci, Hernici, Aequi and Latini set upon each other greedily and the ravages of war dammed the fresh Sabine streams that watered it as they flowed on their gentle way to the sea, turning it into a foul-smelling swamp.

They've all tried to put the clock back to those earlier days of wealth and happiness and procreant splendour – Caesar, Augustus, Trajan, Nerva, even the cultivated King of the Goths, Theodoric – anything to stop Horace going on about the stinking mud and the drunken boatmen and the deadly mosquitoes, anything to drain it and get it working again. Then the popes tried: Sixtus IV in 1480 had canals dug, forbade livestock, made arable farming obligatory and called it 'the granary of Latium', but nobody listened to anything he said; so it waited another three hundred years for Pius VI, whose 'incredible ardour' in tackling the problem, said a passing Englishman, 'reflected more lustre on the papacy than the dome of St Peter's'. The actual amount of his lustre was half a million pounds – in 1790 – but as few people listened again it had no great effect on farming, though it certainly improved the main road down to Terracina where the Pope had his favourite summer palace. And it doubtless accounts for the local catchphrase still in use to describe a spendthrift: '*È andato alle Paludi Pontine*' – It's in the Pomptine Marshes. It was one of Mussolini's dreams, too, to reclaim it, there was talk of there being a

Pontinia Mussolonia; he even imported three thousand farm workers from the north to get to work, though as usual . . .

The breeze is fresh as I sit looking at it all, down over the rough bumps of fields below this giant embankment as they tumble over unwanted mounds of ruin, dotted with patches of ploughed earth or rows of vines edged by haphazard clutters of broken wall, to where the pencil line of pigmy road curves out of the valley then cleaves its way like an arrow, gathering speed in its furrow as it flees across the dark marshland with growing urgency. Then it disappears, sucked down into the welter of alluvial green, vanished, like a needle swallowed up in the pile of a hungry carpet.

And no wonder those mechanised ants are hurrying through the menace of that open space, knowing how many secrets its vastness holds and how many corpses, all streaming for home or help or safety, with pinpricks of light flashing on glass as each arrowhead of sun hits a windscreen. 'A scene of horror,' Matthews called it, 'marked for deeds of darkness, robberies and midnight murders', aware that it was one of the most brigand-infested areas of Italy. Joseph Forsyth's coachman didn't once dare to crack his whip or sound his horn during the forty-mile journey from here to Terracina for fear of attracting them. Not so Evelyn though: he was travelling among a party of soldiers so wasn't worried; and even better, there were 'two courtesans in man's apparel' with them who not only rode astride and carried swords, but 'one was marvellous pretty'. He was one of the lucky ones. Evans saw dead men lying by the roadside and hurried on, fearing it might be a trap. Another visitor found a bandit wearing a hat made by Christy, 'the celebrated hatter in Gracechurch Street, London', who had various gold watches, chains and rings, all taken from English travellers.

So nobody is hanging about to claim Pope Pius VII's

reward of a thousand crowns for the head of a bandit chief. It's not on record whether anybody ever did claim it, though I have my doubts, considering how closely the villagers and peasants worked with the brigands – so closely that when the town of Monte Fortino at the foot of the Sabine Hills was given a warning in 1560 to hand over the gang of ruffians it knowingly harboured, the inhabitants refused; it was rased to the ground and salt was sown on the land. Maria Graham had the best idea for dealing with any threat when she was out walking in the mountains: she'd send her Negro servant on ahead of her to frighten people – which it obviously did, as she wasn't once molested in three months. (This lucky fellow was always being encouraged to kiss the children wherever he went: their mothers thought it would protect them from disease and the evil eye.)

Time to go. Addison was right: these stones are somewhat disagreeable to sit on for a long time; so spin a coin – walk or bus? – and I know the answer with a twinge of regret long before it comes down. I couldn't stand it. Seventy kilometres of flat boredom that even Dickens called 'wearily lonesome' going by coach; and that holy Forum Apii where the excited brethren from Rome met Paul, and where Mrs Martin found the accommodation was 'better fitted for pigs than humans'. No thank you. So quickly back to the dear old lady, who is up to her tricks again – because I am a gentleman *per bene* and she has sixteen grandchildren, the price has accelerated during the night. 'How I wish I could help you,' I tell her, 'but the couplings of your family have nothing to do with the price of my room and anyway I am certainly no gentleman.' Nevertheless, we part the best of friends – *'Alla prossima volta'* – and I have even taught her two words of Smollett's English – 'villainously rapacious, villainously rapacious' – which she repeats slowly but happily as I wave fondly to her before heading for the square.

You can hear Italian buses long before you see them. This

one is snorting with exhaustion over by the parapet wall, and if its wheels were legs would be on its knees, for it is old and ill, with tortured skin and gaseous innards giving spasmodic asthmatic hisses, its roof decked with all the southern impedimenta that pass for luggage – home-made crates, splitting suitcases and shapeless cardboard boxes growing spaghetti loops of string and yards of frayed rope – and around it are gathered the passengers-to-be, all bubbling out their excited intimacies as if this were the final journey for all time. Half of Ariccia has come to join in – card games cease in mid-hand, bars empty on to pavements full of advice and comment, unknown relations arrive from the fields, stray dogs cock their legs with relieved excitement – for it is a collective dramatic production where all can be stars and everyone is involved, an experience to be enjoyed by one and all – otherwise how dull life would be. Hence the air is alive with frenzied messages and movement and the flamboyant hubbub of choked embraces and rivers of tears, and the scrimmage of susurrant bodies like friendly worms.

A final wheeze of pain as the door shuts, and a burst of excited laughter when the monster gives a roar of agon-ecstasy and slides forward, bellowing its multiple horn at the first of Ariccia's hairpin bends, with the driver grinning carelessly over his shoulder at all his friends. Somehow he negotiates the road's impossibilities, tipping us all from one axis to the other and uprooting the jovial farmer in the aisle who is insisting on shaking everyone's hand, and there are fleeting glimpses of laden donkeys being squashed into walls and carnival-minded children waving from dried-out gardens.

Then the brute meets the main road and with an eager snort starts a toreador charge towards Terracina, hurtling forward over the singing tarmac and briefly subduing the babble of conversation with its awesome velocity, as it blurs past the trees and fields on either side, and bulges the

Sabine foothills into different shapes of blue and a cluster of new angles. I knew I should have done it properly and walked – like Gregorovius, dabbling through the Pomptine villages in his *Latian Summers* to sense the moods of the old Tarquins – or gone to sit by the ivied walls of Ninfa half-sunk in the swamp, the Pompeii of the Middle Ages, with dark towers and a silver stream and old statues smothered in flowers where 'fairies dance in circles under the moon' . . .

Guilty, Your Honour. It was an accident, just one of those things, I was in a hurry . . . as Oscar Wilde was to reach the abominations of Naples, and as Ruskin was to leave it for being the most disgusting place in Europe, and as Casanova was to get at the ladies; and then there were Milton and Shelley and Beckford and Walter Scott – they all hurried down here, driven on by some private dream, some madness.

This excitement has suddenly released a busful of healthy appetites: the whole place is stinking with the ripping of paper bags and the handing-round of food and the noise of communal devouring – first blood-streaked corpses of cold pizza, then fat *panini* leaking gouts of mozzarella or lip-dripping tomato, then suckable crescents of pip-filled melon, then hearty chews at thick clubs of phallic *salsicce* – all gargled down with mouthfuls of wine and spitty grins of satisfaction in a few ravenous minutes as the racing bus floats along on an effluvia of cheese, garlic and sardines and we all publicly consume each other's private flavours. While outside the tableland is always there, scurrying past in a blur or arcing away slowly in lazy circles to an ever-moving horizon, where fields slide into changing shapes, trees race one another to keep up and humpback dunes squat lower to guard their hidden history. And this is only one of the southern roads I could have taken from Ariccia; the Vie Praenestina, Labicana and Latina too were part of the glittering web that spun south from Rome towards that world elsewhere, that Magna Graecia.

THREE

Terracina

'*Nella bella città di Terracina vi nacque un uomo di sottile
ingenio*' starts the poetic legend – A man of subtle wit was
born in Terracina – after which one expects to hear about a
pope at least or a Renaissance war-lord or even the Emperor
Galba. But no such luck: these particular indigenous talents
belonged to a bandit called Giuseppe Mastrilli, who was
forced into his career of loot and plunder, not by any social
or economic factors, but by the god of love himself; for
while he was an honourable and law-abiding young man,
his *fidanzata* was vilely seduced by a rival, so he dispatched
the villain with no more ado, and then had to flee into the
mountains to avoid the course of justice. In his outcast life
in the hills between Rome and Caserta, he only robbed
when absolutely necessary, and always from the rich to give
to the poor. Obviously a saint of his type, he one day held
up a coach on the highway containing none other than the
Countess of Fondi, the beautiful Giulia Gonzaga, who, with
the proverbial aristocratic predilection for sinners, fell in
love with him. All might have gone well for the amorous
pair had Mastrilli not been tricked into rushing to Terracina
one night, where he had been told the countess lay dying;
whereupon he was seized and arrested and, in due time,
beheaded. Which would normally conclude the tale; but in
this case there is a twist, for his severed head was placed in
an iron grille and hung up at the gate of the town as a grisly
warning to others – until one day the deceiver who had
lured him to his death happened to pass underneath, whereupon the lifeless lips uttered a horrifying scream and the
cage, plus contents, crashed down on to his head.

That is one version anyway. Maria Graham gives another

in which our hero finally dies peacefully in his bed having confessed all and even received absolution. Doubtless there are other variations lurking in octogenarian memories somewhere, if their minds have not yet been blighted by the daily muckwash of Yankee television swamping their senses and doing its best to annihilate all their legends. Such iridescent sparks of folk memory and fragments of oral tradition should be collected before it is too late – before every Italian bandit is called Geronimo.

There are other changes afoot, I notice, now that the bus is safely tethered in a large open square not fifty yards from the sea, steaming peacefully. A slick chrome coach has drawn up behind us, expelling a squadron of storm-trooping *Einsatzgruppen*, pointing their cameras like Sten guns and marching with invasion vigour across the road towards a bar where the waiters are uncertain whether to smile or take cover. Ahead sparkles the deep table of peacock blue, swelling in gently on snakeskin ripples to lap a few rocks with ribbons of white; and along the wide crescent of beach looping north to the angry dome of Monte Circeo is a scattering of *ombrelloni*, fluttering their garish colours over the sand to shield the leisured bodies of the rich. As the shoreline was smoothly yellow and empty when I last came here some years ago, I suspect someone has been reading an old copy of Eustace. 'Few places seem better calculated for bathing and public resort,' he said, as long ago as 1815. There are some concrete outlines of wreckage, too, aspiring someday towards becoming new hotels or apartment blocks, dwarfed by their half-built champion – a grey bunker soaring to ten incomplete storeys and announcing it is going to be the Grand Palace Hotel.

And yet another excrescence and mighty falling is not far away: after all his epic sanitation of the marshes, Pius VI's summer palace is now a school, his courtyard is the children's playground, and they have their lavatories in his private apartments. Such new and awful change suggests that history is merely repeating itself; for the Romans had been as observant as Eustace sometime earlier and had made it one of their favourite seaside resorts, calling it *superbus* and *splendidus* as they sported themselves all along its golden beaches, in the balmy days when it was not Terracina at all but Anxur, one of the greatest and most important ports in the land.

Before they took over it had been the Volscian capital, Monte Anxur, perched on the top of the seven-hundred-foot-high hill that soars above today's town. Then, after the Romans had spread it out along the shoreline and bathed it in decadence, it curled up like a hedgehog at the base of the cliff in medieval disease and dejection for a while, crushed like a tuneless concertina, till Pius VI brought it some breaths of new life in 1800. Now this year's exhalations of fungoid accretions are doing their bit to brighten it up even more with the happy name of Agostino al Mare.

The bus driver says the Old Town is more likely to be my kind of area. 'Somewhere down near the port,' he suggests, fingering the side of his nose to signal the birth of a conspiracy, and mentions an excellent *locandiera* who is sure to look after me – which she does, in low whispers lest anyone should get to hear of her undeclared earnings. What more could one want? – an undisclosed alleyway just wide enough for one, then a spotless square cubicle with an iron bed and sparkling clean sheets inviting in their freshness. What amazing good fortune . . . and when it comes to suppertime, she tells me, I can do no better than visit her cousins down by the waterfront, as they own a restaurant. And that is how I eventually become the owner of two very fine Greek amphorae . . .

There had to be preliminaries of course: mindless enthusiasms about football, and the Queens of Naples being more royally descended than the Queens of England, and didn't Caesar conquer Britain and civilise it, and wasn't Mussolini clever to take over Africa? Ah! those were the days, we agree! The flagons of wine start to flow, and someone remembers the murderous Fra Diavolo, and they all know about Giulia Gonzaga, and just to think that Tiberius used to embark here for his debauches on Capri. Yes, I say, and Stendhal actually sat here at supper talking about opera, and didn't know he was sitting next to Rossini – and back fly heads with not so *bel canto* yells of '*Figaro qui, Figaro qua*', then out comes the Mastrilli saga and the undying power of true love, and the necessity for all good men to break the law . . . which is where the amphorae come in.

'With all these old stories and history, don't you find any bits of remains?'

'Aha!' and eyes sharpen perceptibly, 'you mean *antichità, signore* . . . Why, any amount of it . . . coins, statues, everything . . . Only last week they found a beautiful statue up on the main road where they're building the AGIP station. A white marble youth it was, life-size and not a crack in it . . . Work would have stopped for months if they'd said anything, so they buried it under the concrete forecourt.'

'Pity, I'd have liked to have seen it.'

'Just a week too late, *signore* . . . what a shame. But if you are interested in seeing coins of course . . .'

'Or some votive statues . . .'

'Or a little urn . . .'

'Or some oil lamps . . .' And being born to conspiracy they eye each other in competitive collusion at the rising tide of my curiosity.

'And at Badino there's an old peasant, Antonio, with his figured vases he found in a tomb. Phew! very expensive . . .' nodding at one another in serious agreement about imaginary sums of money, while I allow a moment for silent reflection; a certain ritual must be followed in these situations – unwritten rules obeyed, ideas nurtured, tacit consents given, and expectations first heightened then left to die. Mentally one walks away, then in a moment one of them will say something.

'My brother has some coins at home, *signore*, with Tiberius' head on – he found them last year . . . And Pietro, over there, he has a bronze figure dug up in his garden . . . And Luigi, a week ago a tourist tried to buy two Roman oil lamps from him, but he wouldn't sell them.'

'Oh dear. Are they expensive then?'

'Very, *signore*,' and his voice becomes hushed. 'Some tourists offer twenty thousand lire, but in Rome they cost fifty thousand. And ours are real . . . Even the amphorae we drag up in the harbour: they cost a hundred thousand lire in Rome, *cento mila* . . .'

'And what are they here?'

'That depends on the fisherman, *signore*; maybe sixty thousand or seventy sometimes . . .'

We agree it is worth going to see some – just for interest, you understand. A little walk round the harbour, which is in murky darkness, the air heavy with the sickly smell of fish and passing shadows of men, as we cross the oil-black slabs of stone towards the mole that juts into the inky lapping sea where one or two pale bulbs dangle from old poles, throwing scribbles of luminous pallor on to the water. In the gloom of the warm night air lies a line of sleeping boats, rocking on the cradling swell like infants, blindly silent as we skirt round bollards and coils of rope and heaped nets, drawn on by the warm wink of paraffin lamps flaring on to wet decks, lighting the ghostly murmurs of returned fishermen. He plucks at me anxiously, peering into the uncertain dark for the right face; low words pass and heads shake and I sense the blackness of old boredom; till at the eighth or ninth attempt there's a wet deck gleaming, piled high with mountains of mile-long netting and soggy cork rings heavy with water, and dishevelled skirts of it tumbling down through a hatch into the hold. This time the mutters get darker and darker and the glances

33

more guilty and the reeking sourness of freshly dead fish is worse, then the unwilling lifting of the net fold by fold, as it is sucked away like Salome's veils promising endless palpitations; and there they are in their damp disappointing climax – two long amphorae side by side, so helpless and angry at being born again and mutely defenceless after a two-thousand-year sleep. Sad tears of salt moisture gleam in a hundred crevices like dawn's disappearing stars, jewelling each slender five-foot-long body as it lies there, roughened by shell and coral, its coquettish old elbows thrust engagingly out, then slimming to a pointed base. Urgent mutters grow more hurried in the dark as one veil is thrown discreetly back to hide the vile offence, and a paltry sum is agreed; the boatman is glad to be rid of them.

Such a good night's work calls for celebration and a long, deserving sleep touched with thoughts of tomorrow, when I shall climb Monte Anxur and stand in Volscian challenge at its very tip, scanning the blue Tyrrhenian for purple topsails and listening for the cries of Ulysses being drawn towards the enchanted kingdom; and I shall stare down at the wizened honeycomb of old Terracina and back over the dark marshes towards Rome where John Raymond saw the old Appia 'smooth and shining like a silver highway'; and then I shall look south towards the grey mountains that touch the sky and dare me to enter the Kingdom of Naples . . . It all craves delicious sleep . . .

But I have been duped. This *locanda* is no such thing at all: it is a workmen's dormitory with twenty beds, all occupied, hidden from each other by paper walls, and I am part of a public performance, a guest player in a drowsy orchestra gorging its way through a slumbertime symphony of coughs, sighs, wheezes, snorts and farts, shrivelling me to my chill puritan skin. I must whisper myself into bed on tiptoe and vanish; ignore those flicks of opening buttons, thudding boots on the floor, grating of cloth on skin and percussion-rattle of molten phlegm, and then the grinding glissandos of bed-springs and bugle-flush of drains. It will soon be over, after one more gargle, another grunt . . . No! Conversations have broken out: questions and answers and chance observations are being patted through the walls like tennis players warming up with gentle balls of reminiscences and out-loud thoughts about wives, children, friends, neighbours, motor cycles, Lazio's centre-half, dying away to drowsy murmurs like chuckling birds then swelling again into a pre-dawn chorus. Ten minutes . . . twenty . . . enough. I struck the wall and cried 'No more!' and the whole panel shook and then leant over a little, and with a dignified final pull at its moorings collapsed with awful slowness on to the body in the bed next door.

Travellers seldom stopped long in Terracina. It was the border town, the last outpost of the Papal States where they joined the foreign land of Angevins or Aragonese or Bourbons – depending on whom the popes wanted or didn't want to have as neighbours. So travellers would hurry through, either glad to be out of those backward mountains and eager to see the glittering domes of Rome, or else craving for something more promising and pleasurable and hastening south towards Naples. It has been on the unwanted list of towns for several centuries, and was barely noticed once Ostia and Porto had been built to serve the Roman capital, and the aristocracy had gone off in search of other bathing resorts. Horace didn't have much to say about it, fuming no doubt as he rubbed his sore eyes after crossing the marshes, and his carriers had to haul him three miles up the great white hill and then over the top towards Fondi. If he had waited a few years he could have gone round it – after Trajan had sliced a section of cliff away so travellers could go past along the shore and avoid the mountain altogether. The smooth face of rock carved out by his engineers to a height of thirty-five yards is still there today, more obvious than the rugged stones of hardship vaguely buried in the rocky slope behind.

A few broad backs are still there, popping up incongruously in groves of withered olives, as the town dies away feebly where the ground starts to rise, a jagged and uncompromising surface of rocks and boulders stranded by the washed-away earth. Most of the slabs have been removed to help towards later buildings, such as the cathedral, dismissed by Eustace as a 'dark and dismal pile' and erected on the site of a Roman temple.

I think it wheels up to the left now and loses itself among a hopeless shingle, amid outcrops of toughened grass and a tracework of clefts and gulleys cut out by rivers of rain; in moments the wind starts to bite in from the sea across this brown uphill desert where one or two lonely trees have bowed their backs and surrendered years ago. Ages of useless knee-ache over loose grey stones, bedded clay and chalky boulders up a self-made path, and then a donkey coming down thoughtfully and stiff-legged with a jolly peasant on top – 'Good morning. Going up to Monte Teodorico, then?' – but I am too breathless to answer and only smile; I would have thought it was obvious. Then another hiker; probably his wife, as she's half a mile behind and walking down sturdily with a pitcher on her head: '*Salve*. Going up to Monte Giove?' And now I'm not sure; might there be two mountains, or even more? Herr Baedeker calls it Monte Sant' Angelo and last night I was told it was Monte Anxur. I shall have to go to the municipal library afterwards and find out. But does it really matter anyway? They all know what you mean as soon as you look up and point.

Howling winds tear over the summit like ever-running trolls fleeing from the sea, buffeting the last mad olive trees too stupid to escape and cowering in submission as if transfixed by a gorgon. A man-made line of low dark arches at the very tip slices bravely into it, and some senseless sheep wander in search of grass tufts and moments of shelter; I join them and we huddle together in the crumbling remains of a temple to Venus Obsequens. Or do we? It might have been a monastery, or Theodoric's palace, or a great sanctuary to Giove Anxur: nobody really knows. But at least there's a story . . .

Back in the misty hypogeums of time, when the Volscians felt better after sacrificing humans, their inferior deities were eventually overrun by the more muscular divinities of Rome; and in this particular instance great Jupiter himself decided to show them how to do the job properly. Each year on an appointed day the fairest and most beautiful youth of the town would be chosen to mount a white horse and ride it at full gallop over the edge of the cliff – to plunge over a hundred feet into the sea. By means of this sacrificial gesture the jealous god would know that he had no earthly rival and could therefore grant the people peace and prosperity for another twelve months. No one knows how long this annual celebration continued, though it is recorded that the Christian fathers, far from forbidding it, allowed it to go on so long as the body was recovered afterwards and then burnt and the ashes buried in the temple. It might even have been going on today had not a wandering Christian deacon named Cesario happened to pass by on the great occasion, and paused to watch as Bishop Julius Firminus bent to light the funeral pyre; he then went to have a serious word with him about the unseemly ritual. This so incensed the waiting crowd that the deacon was promptly bundled into a sack and thrown over the cliff himself for interfering – but his screams were so loud on the way down that they caused the roof of the temple to fall in, burying the bishop together with his whole congregation. According to the sixty-fourth volume of *Acta Sanctorum* the only person to escape was the bishop's chaplain, who fled headlong down the mountainside; half-way down, however, he was leapt upon by a snake who 'stung him to the heart', after which 'he promptly fell down dead'. And that, they say, is why the protector and patron saint of Terracina is St Cesario.

There are no crowds here today, just dried-out emptiness buffeted by the tireless wind bending the scabrous backs of three cowardly olive trees, and fanning the golden eye of the sun as it roasts the dark and withered arches which are all that's left of the Ostrogoth palace – for that's what the experts say it is, Theodoric's private residence. Mindless movements of sheep and goats trickle round it, plucking the last tufts of coarse vegetation from between the rocks and stones, while far below silk-white strands float in on a green and cobalt sea towards the toy harbour and the crumbling honeycomb of brown houses squashed shapeless by history, a tangled sprawl marking the one-time end of Italy. Southward the long snout of Sperlonga reaches out like a thirsty alligator, warning travellers that the dark saw-toothed mountains on its back are the walls of the Kingdom of Naples.

Across this phosphorus-tinted sea sped Barbarossa, seeking slaves on the Sultan's orders; the fat corn ships wallowed up from the south to feed Rome; Ulysses sailed in to mate with the enchantress Circe; Lucullus laughed his bloody way with human fodder for his pet sharks on the prison isle of Ponza; creaking triremes sluggishly wandered south to make battle. The dapple-white of summer Ponza is easily visible on a clear day, and so – on occasions – is the cone of Vesuvius, each of them basking murderously in the sun, their centuries of sins forgiven.

Here at the very top sleeps the corpse of the old Appia, a flat and useless ribbon of old bones stretched from nowhere to nowhere through a graveyard of slit trenches from the war, yawning with abandoned boredom or their half-filled, gluttonous mouths choked dry with rubble. Yet again, as I wander on, the chain of old stones bubbles clean from the earth and rambles off downhill in isolation, gathering speed like a giant armadillo as it slinks off through creeping patches of grass then dives abruptly under the walls of a lonely farmhouse. I knock gently for no reason – how nice to meet someone who lives on the Appian Way – and am confronted by a most sturdy matron of the mountains, whose widely folded arms block the doorway completely and who glowers suspiciously. I'm not sure what I said, but she wasn't interested. 'There may have been a road here once, but there isn't now,' she barked, 'this is private,' and she stepped back on to her yellow flagstones and shut the door.

So it's all the way back to sea level and a bread roll and a dip into Bianchini's *Storia di Terracina*. And you can call it what you like, he says: Anxur was the Volscian capital at the summit, Giove had a temple there once, Nettuno was the name of the spring they found when Trajan cut away the cliff, Theodoric built a palace there in around AD 500, and Sant' Angelo is pure invention of the Benedictines, who thought it might be nice to build something there to balance their monastery across on the opposite side of Italy at Gargano.

But more follows. St Francis of Assisi lost his temper in Terracina (perhaps the fish wouldn't listen), and was so angry he dug his staff into the ground in fury, whereupon it promptly rooted and began to sprout branches and bunches of grapes. This Vignola di San Francesco has the power of curing any illness when you touch it. It is said to be near a small church.

My first informant is bending in a churchyard and tending his broccoli plants with zealous affection, and he knows just what I am talking about, but don't I mean an orange tree? There's a splendid one growing wild just down the road. My second remembers it most distinctly: '*Sì, un albero vastissimo,*' he exclaims, throwing out his arms in proof of having seen it, whereupon memory fails him completely and he can't for the life of him recall where it was. And so to the third: 'St Francis' tree, *signore*? Certainly: it's in the hospital gardens, straight down the road . . . *sempre diritto*.'

It is something of a surprise for the idly perambulating patients and solicitous visitors and carefully caring nuns when I arrive among them enquiring after a tree. The novelty alarms them; they back against walls in apprehension, and coagulants of amoebic families disperse quietly in the face of my innocent urgency. Then a breathless doctor appears: 'Ah . . . you want a tree, *signore*? Certainly. Step this way . . . and we rest in a cold office eye to eye like wary wrestlers, till I explain the truth of my mission, which relieves him considerably. We bound up three flights of stairs on to the roof in joint enthusiasm, for the doctor is a Florentine and has recently been gripped by the weird ways of his southern patients who believe in witchcraft and spells and therapeutic sorcery and the hocus-pocus of country *magi*, and he is considering writing a book on their herbal cures and Galenic panaceas and the lampyrine flare of their legends. This is another one he'll have to do some work on, for, as we lean over the parapet and stare down into the brackish green of the disused back garden, there is no sign of any *albero vastissimo* – just five shrivelled olive trees languishing against a wall bedecked with a medley of drying sheets and towels, and grey in the long untended grass the half-buried shapes of two fluted Roman columns, fast asleep.

The search now becomes a matter of honour to him. Such a miraculous example of prophylactic vegetation must be found at all costs; he will see to it immediately. Within minutes the grounds and gardens are being scoured by bewildered nurses turning over boulders; surprised visitors are emptied off sunlit terraces to trace it; pale-faced nuns are accused of knowing where it is; and all the sound-winded hospital humanity is sent to delve in outhouses and under bushes and over walls, while the doctor himself is on the telephone to the Director of the museum:

'Where is the tree of St Francis?' he demands. Then, when the long-awaited answer comes, drops his voice and eyes tragically. *'Non è vero,'* he whispers, replacing the receiver slowly as if it were dynamite, and then turning towards me with mortuary-sad gaze: *'Mi dispiace, signore.* The tree of St Francis no longer exists; it was cut down at the beginning of the seventeenth century.'

FOUR

Fondi

'At Terracina', remarks Joseph Forsyth encouragingly and without mincing words, 'every fifth man you meet is a *sbirro* or an assassin or both.' He was a man of forthright views and opinions, not afraid to speak his mind, and on account of it was thrown into prison in Turin in 1803, where he remained for eleven years, then died soon after his release. In spite of some of the things he said, he loved Italy; it was just certain types of people he couldn't stand: elegant women who spat on the floor and blew their resounding noses into snotted handkerchiefs and clapped gentlemen on the thigh; Genoese assassins who could be hired for fifty lire, and professional perjurers for twelve; Florentine gentlemen who as well as letting out their theatre boxes for the evening would do the same with their wives for the night, 'but Signora secures that perquisite for herself'; and the artist who painted portraits without looking at his work and could make his dog bite a slice of cheese into a correct profile of Voltaire. His pet hate was humbug – meaning bungling officials, upstart aristocrats, worthless works of art and the Vatican. He wasn't fond of Acton either, calling him a barber from Tuscany who at the ripe age of sixty married a girl of barely fourteen: 'she brought Sir John a child during my stay in Naples, whereupon an express went instantly to Caserta. The Queen drove into town in the morning with rich presents, and in the afternoon came the King and made the newborn babe a colonel.' Forsyth's view of the customs official here at the border was relatively mild: he was merely a blockhead and *castrone* – a stupid little eunuch.

No such interferences occur today, and the time has long

passed when travellers had to secure at least six signatures before being allowed to proceed from one kingdom to the next, or, if any was missing, be locked up or sent back. It's a simple case of striding on past the old farmhouse blocking the Appia, then racing on down the hill that tumbles unevenly through gradually thickening trees into the rich parkland plain of Fondi below, honeycombed with bright pinpricks of orange groves among the green, its surface slashed by a silver lake.

An inviting prospect, this first smile of the Parthenopean seductress – teasing with the delicate folds of her skirt, palpitating gently in the sun – hiding among all her vanished customers the legendary city of Amyclae, once central to the plain but then either sucked down into the depths of her lake by seismic convulsion or destroyed by a plague of serpents. Its life and death are a mixture of myth and old fairy tales, though the likeliest reason is disease, considering its closeness to the Pomptine quagmire and the similar way this flatland tapers everlastingly into the sea. Furthermore, barely a century ago it nearly happened again: the sixteen-thousand-strong population of Fondi was reduced to twelve hundred in two months by an outbreak of malaria. They should have listened to the Englishman who passed through a few years earlier and complained bitterly about the 'deformity' of their unglazed windows.

HIC SUNT FINES REGNI NEAPOLIS still announces a greying stone slab leaning by the roadside at the bottom of the hill, where the tarmac highway surges round from Trajan's cliff-face and vanishes through a line of trees towards the distant agglomeration of Fondi; and already the hurtling lorries smack of Neapolitan frivolity and insouciance as they zigzag down the road like high-speed cripples in varying stages of intoxication, with foot-high invocations of GOD PROTECT AND HELP ME blazing in their windscreens. A mischievous spirit of madness tingles in the air, wanton and ungovernable; a soft wind whispers the spontaneous enjoyment of irreverent chaos, the light-hearted laws of *'festa, farina, forca'*. A most pleasing prospect, now I am down on the main road again, heading towards the ridge of white houses in the distance. But not a view shared by Dickens.

'. . . In the name of all that is wretched and beggarly', he announced in his *Pictures from Italy*, take note of Fondi, and then sat back uncomfortably as his coach was besieged by beggars, to watch the obscene rivulets seeping out of houses into the channel of mud, and wondering why the starving people didn't eat their dogs. The inhabitants howled, the children were nearly naked, women scratched themselves, and a madman noticed his reflection in the shining side of the carriage and began chattering at himself and sticking his tongue out. The whole place is 'decayed, and crazy, and rotting away', he declared, and hurried on out, glared at by bad bright eyes that were like 'glistening fragments of its filth and putrefaction'. It's not really that bad today, as I rest at the outskirts and watch the old Appia slice straight through the town and cleave its way down the middle, before I turn aside to an inn. The landlord becomes voluble as soon as I suggest a simple lunch, his interest sharpened by thoughts of money, and then boastful as soon as I seek his views on the story of Fondi. Up swells his bagpipe chest – for was not his very uncle one of its greatest heroes, having been hanged in Naples exactly forty years ago this month for burning his *fidanzata*'s house down?

'Surely arson doesn't carry the death penalty?'

'Aha, *signore* . . .' he winks, and touches the side of his nose in the usual sign of shared southern wisdom, 'she happened to be in it at the time with the rest of her family; he burnt seven of them to death that night. He was a real *figlio di Chiavone* . . .'

'"*Figlio di chiavone*"?' I query, surprised at the frank impropriety of calling his uncle 'son of a fucker' in front of a stranger, but he beams a smile of reassurance:

'Just a nickname, *signore*. Our famous brigand a hundred years ago had a huge appetite for women, when he wasn't fighting those bossy northerners: he sired over six hundred children in three years here in Fondi; some say even a thousand . . .'

Such fascinating details as these are not mentioned by Hilton in his tales of Italian bandits, and he only gives this Olympic copulator the role of an opportunist rascal who had been cashiered from the Bourbon Army and then organised a gang of ruffians to pillage any revolutionary funds for their own purposes. His verdict is that most of Chiavone's three infamous years as a brigand were spent running away – in spite of his calling himself 'General of all the forces of his Majesty, the King of the Two Sicilies' – and only once does Hilton hint at anything unseemly, when 'He was surprised in the house and bed of his mistress', but being a genius at retreat fled in his shirt across the border.

No doubt both versions have an element of truth; how else, one wonders, does a man acquire so prestigious a nickname? Anyway, Hilton is a tediously upright chronicler, and the most he could ever get his squeamish tongue round in matters of bandit debauch with female captives was 'forced marriage'.

Meanwhile mine host has begun to wax lyrical over his hero's feats, and did I know the most beautiful woman in all Italy once lived here? The great Giulia Gonzaga – *'una vera Cleopatra, signore'* – famous all over the Mediterranean for her looks, and even lusted after by the pirate Barbarossa. In his enthusiasm for the subject and for my attention, he has produced a special bottle of wine from his cellar and strokes it lovingly before opening it. *'Rarissimo, signore,'* he whispers. 'I have a few bottles hidden away for special visitors, erudite travellers like yourself. *Il vino Caecubano* . . . taste it, *signore*, it's as smooth and soft as the body of a woman and nearly as warm . . .' I know he'll fleece me, the old blackguard, cunningly poised between half selling it with my meal and half offering it for nothing as a token of my visit and of his hospitality, but it's remarkably good all the same, mellowed by months of dark shade and now richly full-bodied, hovering deliciously on the palate before sliding imperceptibly to the brain, then warming the senses to an easy contemplation of soft shapes and round thoughts and voluptuous images. It must be some distant offspring of Martial's *'Caecuba Fundanis generosa'* that rivalled the legendary Falernian intoxicant two thousand years ago; and I begin to think more wistfully of Chiavone and the daughters he may have left, and perhaps there's a reincarnation of Countess Giulia waiting down the road . . .

But, with the bottle empty and the innkeeper's voice growing fainter by the mouthful, all irreverent dreams are shattered by the sudden invasion of a wedding party, sweeping in with hurricane excitement to overrun the dining-room, thrusting my table into a corner as a hundred chattering guests come tumbling in at all doors and windows, everyone bubbling with nuptial eagerness. Fresh-suited young men hasten hither and thither from one group to the next with dapper enthusiasm and growing urgency, while wry-smiling women blush prettily over their deliberately proud breast-shapes in new flower-patterned dresses, and whisper embarrassed greetings with bright moist eyes, and a pell-mell of Sunday-best children clutching agonised posies of flowers dart and jump everywhere, unheeded in their scramble to find the festivities. How they love this agonised disorder, as awkwardly draped bodies start to bump and thrust, and the open doorways pump in more rivers of guests, surging to join in the tight-fitting Bacchanal already seething with uninhibited self-congratulation. Each shares the excitement equally, and in the swirl of sluice-gate motion the smartest clothes disengage and crumple, spreading awkward untidiness on to each body, multiplying creases on to every surface as men hoist at sinking waist-bands and women grapple at slipping shoulder straps.

As if by magic a starburst of gangways pierces the throng, opening to let trays of liqueurs pass and have glasses drained eagerly. Even my own is filled, just as the newly united pair enter by a main door to beams and *'Bravo'*s and bursts of hand-clapping – he, of course, leading, as she lurks behind shyly in her shining pink dress with a halo of white flowers circling her raven hair. He is uncomfortably confident of it all, twitching his shoulders like a braggart pugilist as he stands there anxiously fingering his carnation. The surge of admirers folds round to suck them in and dissolve his bewilderment to smiles and turn her worried eyes to laughter; and as the children burrow tunnels at hip height to view the attraction, trolleys of food are wheeled in by silent waiters, and attention drains effortlessly from the arm-linked pair to the enticing piles of fruit and cakes, leaving space for the family photographs to be taken and all the arguments to start of who stands where and which sticky child belongs to whom.

'They're *scomunicati*,' whispers the innkeeper in my ear, bending to drain his third liqueur, 'Devil worshippers, pagans, not Christian at all . . . you shouldn't talk to them.' And I notice how cold and silent the waiters are as they hand out cups of coffee. It seems these heretics of Fondi originated in 1378 with the great schism when the first Avignon pope, Clement VII, was elected here; since when it has often been something of a hotbed of dissension, even to the extent of Fondi's own statue of the Madonna della Vergine turning her face to the wall in 1849 on hearing about Pius IX's theory of the Immaculate Conception. Perhaps she knew something he didn't, or had heard about the young Chiavone; for it is reported she only turned round again when the Pope arrived in person to make her a gift of his pontifical robes.

There were disagreements earlier, too, when the Roman

general Vitruvio Vacca led his four thousand rebellious legionaries from here against Rome – for which he was executed. His memory is still honoured, however: the old Appia as it cleaves the town is named after him. There's even the Contrada Scomunica, as if to prove their soft spot for deviation; this particular alleyway leads to the quarter called Giudea, where one of the early immigrants is remembered for successfully blackmailing the bishop into baptising him by threatening to reveal his dream of seeing the reverend gentleman entering a brothel.

Then there's Via Orazio and Virgilio and Tasso, all passing travellers, and Thomas Aquinas who paused to teach, and after Empress Livia comes the incomparable Giulia Gonzaga – to whom they owe no thanks at all, as it was on her account the town was rased to the ground by Barbarossa in 1534, having been sent by King Suliman of Turkey to capture her for his harem. Her escape was so narrow, history relates, that the enraged pirate slaughtered all the men and took captive all the women and children, which left an Italian traveller passing through shortly afterwards only able to count 150 families still living there, surrounded by *rane, rospi e serpi* – frogs, toads and snakes.

All that is forgotten now and she is still the household goddess, having gone on to marry a marshal in Charles V's army, Vittorio Colonna, from whom the present lords of this manor are directly descended, and in whose honour the Colonna flag still flies from the castle tower whenever the family comes south to enjoy a day's shooting in the mountains. A short time ago, when the late prince died in Rome, over five hundred faithful inhabitants made the journey north to mourn at his funeral.

This feels like another country altogether: people smile, children wave, there are bright calls of '*Ciao*' and '*Buon giorno*', and even the dogs have a sprightly tread, relaxed and self-assured – or is it the effect of Caecuban wine? The cobbles in the narrow streets bubble from the ground with jollity, banners of Joseph-coat washing strung from sill to sill flap friendly gestures, and the fragments of upside-down-sideways Latin in the walls spell out simple messages – GLORI . . . MAXIM . . . HIC SUNT . . . IMPERA . . . DUX . . . EBAT . . . – locked firmly into the groundwork of vertigo buildings soaring up to reach the sun. Holes in their walls burst through huge double doorways where carriages once entered, and where now there are quiet courtyard Edens of palm trees swaying in the shade, balustered stairways and stone lions spitting water. Each slender cardine leads to yet another sunlit square, spread with butterfly wings of pink weigelia, invading blue bundles of wisteria and powder-puff balls of spirea; one is dark with a line of eyeless porticos where old dames, chirping on the knife-edge of shade and sun, sit by their push-carts piled high with rainbow splashes of ripe fruit.

What precisely is different? And whence comes this breeze of happiness and mischievous exhilaration, the vital exuberance that made the child at the fountain laugh as I photographed her and then dare me to do it again and again? The surly brats of Terracina would probably have picked up stones. God knows what the answer is – unless there's some vapour in the air, gas from a bubbling cauldron underground being laughed up by friendly guardians of Hades and acting like a soporific. Or it may be those fickle winds of the past that have randomly blown their confetti of blessings and curses all over the land, aimless and unconcerned, some lighting on miserly hilltops or rotting plains or dark valleys, and others, like jewels, among the mountains or into sparkling lakes or along playful sandy shores. I am walking towards a limitless coalescence of all things different, an illusion scorched by an oven of sun, a geographical expression, a concatenation of patternless people seeking congress, the quintessence of arcane hope-lessness, boiled dry for a thousand years . . .

*

I need coffee before moving on. No sign of Giulia; just dulcet air and everyone taking their time. I must make Itri by tonight, and that means mountains – not big ones, just a few outcrops to practise on before the real business starts. The road goes out flat through the fields, where there's a bursting harvest of oranges on either side, with men balanced on ladders among the bloated trees, grabbing armfuls of mammary sagging fruit into barrel-sized baskets, then pouring them like yellow geysers into panting lorries. Each orchard lines up to the horizon as if it were a parading army waiting for relief; and the lorries crawl away in a sandstorm of dust to empty their camel-humps of gold into Fondi.

Looking back as the pathway turns to stone, the roofs are a dwindling quilt of uneven browns, sewn into a patchwork which leaks out streaks of white wall where everything is topped by lonely towers. The sandy track ahead starts to rise uphill, laid out in a strip of wizened parchment among dried-out scrub. This is an entry to the Aurunci mountains, a desolate green-grey wasteland of murky and unloved ridges that rolls on in sterile hardness all the way to Gaeta and the plain of Naples, a dehydrated old corpse whose crust was once freshly soft with trees. Sad ravens flop across the empty air ahead, swept sideways by the wind and floating like the Devil's petals, and head-down finches streak like frightened lightning between bushes. Then a fat Bourbon milestone announces that on this spot the last blood was shed between north and south in a skirmish just after the Battle of Volturno – a noble exaggeration, as the partisan war went on for at least another decade, while the unhappy Francis sent money and means down from Rome and renegade bands of mercenaries made mayhem and everybody suffered. The last blood in that sad affair has yet to be shed.

One last look round at the tempting bowl of Fondi far below before crossing the ridge – its dark green palette splashed with sparkling oranges, its beetle-dust of eager lorries, its mirror-ripples on the lake, its toy-town houses half-hidden – where Ariosto sang in the Colonna Palace, where a roast chicken came to life in the middle of a banquet, where a giant bluebottle sat on the madonna's nose to warn them about approaching malaria ... No wonder poems and novels have been written about it – and an opera.

Then a cowbell mutters a bored metallic plonk somewhere ahead over a dip, and I watch for movement on the greyly serrated flanks of land, and whip away drowsily insistent flies thirsty for sweat, as a tree trunk stirs somewhere in front into a dark-cloaked shepherd boy rising like a goblin gustful of leaves and staring from under his old cloth cap, dumb till I'm past him.

'*Salve,*' he calls. 'Are you going to the shrine of the madonna?' I let him walk up to me, tumbling over clattering stones with deep welcoming eyes.

'No, I'm going to Itri,' at which his face beams like a muddy ray of sun, because that's where he lives and where he'll wander back to before sunset, pushing his slow straggle of beasts.

'Have you seen our madonna?'

'No . . .'

'Where are you from then?'

'England.'

And again comes the sun-ray smile but touched with dreaminess: 'It must be beautiful. I've seen pictures . . . And of Princess Margaret . . .' and his opal eyes fill with stars. 'But our madonna's beautiful too.'

I let him tell me about her. How long, long ago monks from Formia had saved their sacred effigy from Turkish pirates by hiding it away in the mountains and then hadn't been able to find it again, because – you see – the wild animals had moved it away for extra protection. But two years ago, one of the other shepherd boys, who wasn't any use in the village because he was deaf and dumb, lost one of his cows up here in the mountains, and when he found it at last – *signore* – it was kneeling at the roots of a fallen tree; and there was the lost madonna lying in the earth . . .

'And that's not all,' he whispers in bright-eyed urgency. 'The boy ran all the way back to Itri to tell the villagers, and when he got there he found he could talk again – like you and me . . . *Non era un vero miracolo!*'

Of course it was a miracle – like the hundreds and thousands of others that have been invented to divert their empty minds, sap their energies and send them on Mary-chases all over the mountains. Barely a month goes past without another amoeba-split of this whirlwind goddess of Italy, and she's seen up a tree or in a cave or delivering another sensation. 'The hearts of children and fools are easily taken,' said Joseph Hall as long ago as 1617, and even Garibaldi had no time for the perpetrators of such idiot lunacy – pestilent scum of humanity and ministers of falsehood was what he called them.

But I won't tell this to the wide-eyed shepherd, nor remind him of the commandment about graven images; I must let him dream out his sun-scorched fantasies day by day as dryads peep out of the bushy grass at his idle hours, and Syrinx sings to him from the leaves, and his own bearded goats start to dance on their upright feet for him in his sleep.

He stands on a rock to wave as we part company, his dark shape smudged against the sky like a cowled sentry; then one more dip of land and the air blinks white and empty. Further on beyond a humpbacked spur the squat tartan squares of Appia heave themselves out of the earth again, and wander away as if hopelessly lost in their inexorable march towards limbo, shrugging time off their bowed shoulders as a petty irrelevance. Scales of a nightmare escalator, they march unperturbed into infinity, crushing the scrub aside with the same unfeeling ease as when they soaked up the blood and cries of the Spartacan traitors who hung there crucified.

I follow as the land beside flattens out on to a green lip of hillside broken by Polyphemus lumps of rock, and dips into scorched saddlebacks of muscular scrub rolling endlessly away towards a bulwark of granite-grey escarpment in the distance beyond which is the sea. And splashed on it is one fragmented bird-drop – what's left of a crumpled stone hut, still half-white but exploded in uselessness. The milky sun takes on a blushing tint of dim gold as it sinks down for its evening dip in the waves, and the contours darken to edgeless bottle green, and slide gently into each other like the snaking limbs of lovers, making every shape shapeless, and the skyline float darkly as if it were some genesis of thunderclouds.

Half-darkness creeps in with an evening shudder bringing thoughts of Forsyth's every fifth man, because this silent wilderness was part of the sovereign territory of Fra Diavolo – a bloodthirsty Bourbon freebooter worse than any Chiavone, who so delighted King Ferdinand with his patriotic savagery during the Republican uprising that he was given an annual salary of three thousand ducats plus a locket of the Queen's hair, and was then made Duke of Cassano. God knows what really happened in the slaughterhouse lives of the hundreds of brigands who roamed south Italy under the Bourbons – and after them: Pagano, Cirillo, Scotti, Basso, Don Ciro the priest, Crocco, Ninco Nanco, Borges the Spaniard and Caruso. Any attempt to follow their stories would be to enter what Harold Acton calls 'a world of picaresque fiction' – a charnel-house of legend and heroic invention gloated over by starry-eyed vultures. All we know is that Fra Diavolo was a young peasant from Itri called Michele Pezza, who may or may not at one stage of his short existence have been a monk, for the uniform he chose and which struck terror into thousands was a hooded cassock in which he was liable to arrive at dead of night in any village or hamlet where it was rumoured there were French-supporters. Perhaps it was his appearance during these demonic visitations that gave rise to his unearthly name; perhaps it was the simple southern belief that priests and the Devil have a common quality – invincibility.

And invincible he was – for a time. Once a common country thief with a Bourbon price on his head, he wisely diverted his criminal tendencies into the King's service, and rapidly outstripped his rivals in notoriety and excesses of cruelty; the number of blood-chilling massacres he performed grew so vast that his overlord Cardinal Ruffo felt impelled to complain to the King about them. Admonish him but don't displease him, was His Majesty's response, elevating him to the rank of general and then hurrying him away on clandestine missions between Rome and Benevento and Sicily to raise funds and armies of partisans, and to stop him burning French-supporters alive while their families danced round the flames, or emptying whole suspect villages out of their beds and over the nearest cliff into the sea. Eventually he was captured near Salerno, taken in for routine questioning in the guise of a beggar, but recognised by one of the French soldiers and – in spite of various recommendations for mercy – was hanged wearing the full uniform of a brigadier-general in the Bourbon Army. It was Joseph Buonaparte's personal decision – for not being in uniform when captured.

As darkness creeps lower like the closing of a raven's wing, the beacon lights of Itri give firefly glints, and tease with will-o'-the-whisp dances through the cumbent shadows ahead, flickering with the uncertainty of medieval tapers. I want to run the last leaden mile and burst from this swallowing blackness where unseen animals tap on stones and there's a whirr of night wings; but it's an hour before I'm in the cold village lamplight, gathering a wide-eyed wake of curious children and lean curs bawling an astonished chorus – just out of stone-shot – all of them washing me on down the alley to the doors of the only *taverna*.

Thirty miles! What was it Gibbon said? A Roman soldier marched twenty miles in six hours in full uniform . . . and then had enough energy to make camp. I sigh despondently at the lavatory cistern upstairs and it sighs back at me for a long time, older and more exhausted than I am (both of us in the dark so it probably went on the floor, but it doesn't matter as there wasn't a seat anyway). Along the passage there's a room with an iron bedstead and a wooden wash-stand – acme of a night's happiness – and down below there's a stone-flagged floor and an uneasy table and an open doorway full of scrutinising children's faces as I drown the day in a steaming bowl of lamb soup, then bury its memory under a mountain of spaghetti.

FIVE

Sessa

It is a morning of copious exuberant sun, a tempting time for unwary decisions. I shall desert the Appia and seek a diversion inland towards the cloud-covered mountains and the unknown, bracing myself for the great overland trek. Bread, water and cheese are required, with which my overnight lady is most obliging. '*Mazza ti*,' she says. 'Walk all the way to Brindisi? *Madonna! Sei scemo* [Mother of God, you're mad]. Go to Naples and catch a train,' amazed at my obvious lack of intelligence and adding cheerfully, 'Anyway, they're Arabs, thieves and layabouts. They aren't Italians like us, they're foreigners.' I have been warned.

My route will do little except anger the purists by cutting off the Cicero-studded corner of Formia and Minturno – which is something I shan't regret, having always considered him a talented but obnoxious chatterbox. Fancy boasting about not knowing how many villas you have or how much furniture or exactly how many books and statues, and not even knowing where they are, but forever talking about them and telling everyone how rich you are. It's not surprising he was banished, what with that and his mellifluously persuasive circumlocutions, his quibbles of casuistry and his nimbleness of pragmatism, which meant he could argue any problem from either side just like Dr Johnson and make circumstances alter cases. It didn't help him in the end though; when the volatility of Roman politics ultimately demanded that the old chameleon choose his colour and stick to it, he chose the wrong one. None the less he has left a host of monumental memorabilia, scattered liberally between Minturno and Rome, in the form of broken walls and arches and bits of terrace and lumps of foundations, which the locals will adamantly insist with the reverence of acolytes are the remains of some of Cicero's villas.

I am also cutting off an Appian dog-leg, as after the old road had passed Minturno it turned inland at Mondragone for a few miles, then suddenly bent southwards to Lavernium on the River Volturno, where there was an important crossroads. Here the Appia Antica turned inland again towards Capua, while the Via Domitiana carried on south towards Naples; and here near this crossroads Horace fell in with more travelling companions for the journey to Brindisi: Plotius, Varius and Virgil.

God knows why Edward Hutton called Sessa Aurunca 'green and golden'. It is unutterably miserable, as dark and evil as a Jacobean tragedy, haunted by a race of brooding, sullen men with faces like Faustian death masks. The mist swirls off the mountain like a preying beast, the grey walls drip with tears and the road is a-slush with sorrow. And it rains everlastingly. It has done so from the moment I arrived, dripping from the trees in relentless sighs of dark green anguish, dribbling off the roofs, pouring from gutters and gurgling along the pavement bearing lumps of captive mud. The sheets on my bed are wringing with malevolent and demonic damp, and the whole place is locked in by a dungeon wall of gloomy mountains as black as a tribe of angry Othellos.

I have found the only affordable inn and am far from welcome, met by a sullen, lumpish girl who knows the place is completely empty but still has to fetch the *padrona*, who is even more of a prison commandant and snatches my passport like a vulture grabbing flesh. She's a wizened old spider coated in shapeless black, with evil eyes waiting for death and an edging of aged fur on her top lip as Stygian as her clothes. 'How many nights?' this witch of Sessa asks, then creeps off down the passage before me, shuffling like a wounded beetle till she opens a door into a monkish cell then shuts me in on to a floor of brown lino with a skeletal bedstead and a naked bulb.

Beyond the cobweb window grey rivulets of rain merge with mist, and the endless outpourings of cracked gutters spout disordered fountains on to walls and ledges, while down in the swollen yard a tethered dingo stands drowning and shuddering in statuesque misery with his paws under water. Why on earth did I abandon that sunny riviera of Formia just twenty miles away – with its tingling beaches and dancing waves and shouting children, its ballet corps of brown-muscled volleyballing men endlessly prancing, its curving girls whispering unmentionable messages with their tenacious thighs and tighter buttocks – for this soggy graveyard dripping with requiem gloom and smelling of death?

It's the same outside in the road: they all glower with downcast eyes, either brooding on past guilt or awaiting some tragedy to come, paddling along soaked pavements, over craterous puddles and through gutters gurgling in spate, and sprayed at by hissing car tyres. Then from a dripping patch of road a sigh sounds and a weird inky pantomime erupts like poison oozing from a boil, as down the sodden thoroughfare weaves a score of nightmare figures in black, hooded like rabid monks, with egg-white eyes gleaming through slits as they dance, moan and chant – an infestation of hellish maggots writhing on to the pavements among the soaked umbrellas. The wings of their cloaks billow like wounded vampires, and they all wave hissing yellow tapers. Someone must be dead. Then the chorus gives way to two plumed black horses shaking their angry bridles and heaving the shafts of an even blacker bier, crunching on slow wheels and encasing a coffin behind storm-swept glass and buried in broken tumbled flowers, all followed by a mourning family phalanx draped in veils of jet or heads bowed in half-drowned misery. As the death's head of corybants flops on through the puddles dirging its graveyard litany, there's a mild flutter of women's hands crossing themselves, or the impassive stare of silent men not lifting their caps.

Death is common around Sessa; it's a boring and contemptible event and appears to affect nobody except the unfortunate victim. Mussolini was so aghast at the aptitude of these mountain villagers for killing each other that he transplanted entire populations to the north in the hope of reducing the tendency, but it didn't: it merely changed the location and exacerbated and prolonged old grievances. It is still a common custom in this arena of mountains for a proud father, on the birth of a new-born son, to press a loaded pistol against his tiny hand, as a sign of his masculinity – an expectation that he will grow up proud and aggressive and stand no nonsense. Like the young farm worker a month ago who was driving home on his scooter from the fields when he was overtaken by another boy from a different village, so he shot him; or the young man who was teased by his elder brother about his girlfriend: the elder brother went the same way. It is all very matter-of-fact, and governed by protocol: there are certain things you don't do, otherwise you may find your barn on fire or your sheep poisoned or your wife mutilated. All proven by the statistic that in the mountains around Sessa there are nearly twice as many murders each year per head of population as there are in the whole of Sicily.

One wonders where such callous hatred comes from, what Ramage called 'a ferocity of character which perpetuates family feuds from generation to generation and regards revenge as a right and duty'; and what Sandys had seen two hundred years earlier in the remoter parts of Italy: 'No night doth pass without murder,' he wrote. No doubt both of them had read about the Montagus and the Capulets.

One ponders romantically on whether its origins might lie in the merciless courts of Renaissance princes, or in the blood-lust of ancient Rome, or in the warrior cult of the tribal kingdoms before that; or perhaps it's the curse of the Cumaean Sybil lingering over those Euboean invaders from Greece, who fell on the land in overwhelming hordes three thousand years ago. It could, of course, be simpler: just overweening and tempestuous pride, an egotism of such irrational ferocity that the mind is completely blinded to everything except *figura*. One Victorian traveller tells of seeing a weeping mother clasp her child's hands together and make him repeat a solemn oath to take revenge on a murderer's nearest relatives; she then pronounced a curse on the child if he failed to do it. Such events have the fearsome and godless simplicity of Greek tragedy. So perhaps King Ferdinand was right after all, to think that all they wanted was a little sensation to illuminate their boring lives – if flour and a *festa* aren't enough, he declared, just give them an execution.

I walk across the road to a bar full of listless youths gathered round juke-boxes, their faces all showing the same bitterness and jaundiced disaffection with life as they slouch and jostle together fractiously in the endless dance of the *disoccupati*. They squeal like irascible pigs at a half-full trough, ostentatiously inhaling from long tubes of king-size Pall Mall that hang slackly from their lips as symbols of their position in the contraband market. It comes up by the lorryload from Naples according to local demand: American cigarettes, Swiss watches, Scotch whisky, German cameras – the law is of little significance in Sessa – and other loads too: the occasional jeep engine or new refrigerator or box of Army uniforms so you can choose your own style – Panzer trousers or khaki tunics or smooth American overcoats. There's very little you can't get in Sessa on a rainy day.

Happily these barbs of disillusion and cynicism haven't yet entered the hearts of the very young – or so it appears. It has nearly stopped raining, and a crowd of them gambol like freshly loosed puppies as they follow me up to the cathedral, where they display a spectacular lack of interest in things Romanesque or religious, and urge me to enter. The priest and the sacristan being away, they say, they will be happy to show me the Roman pillars and anything else I fancy. The result is regrettably an irreverent carnival such as must have been practised by the young Lords of Misrule during their reigns of juvenile sacrilege. Within seconds the Roman pillars have exhausted their interest, and half of the robust crew is swarming up the sanctuary steps to enact a series of ungodly rites with candles, while two more bounce snoring on the bishop's throne, one climbs up the choir stalls, another brays enough amorous advice from the pulpit to make Ovid blush, and there are heavy snorts and lewd movements from the confessionals. Amid the guttering flames barely lighting the solemn and high-fluted darkness there is minuscule bedlam, which only ends when one of them tugs a stray bell-rope; as a boom of disapproval floats out over the town they cringe with guilt and melt silently away through the vast doors on tiptoe, like shrunken and cowardly mice.

Only briefly contrite, they then accompany me to the amphitheatre, which they assure me is even less remarkable than the cathedral; with which I am forced to agree when we all stand at last on a raised bank of mud at the town's perimeter, and gaze down into an open bowl of land that might well be an old bomb crater or disused quarry and now resembles a rubbish dump. '*Teatro romano*,' they announce proudly and await my reaction, but there is none; I am counting the old car bodies, and watching the shambling pink of pigs wallowing belly-deep in mud around old olive trees and leaning enthusiastically against the paintwork to scratch their rinds on the sharp corners, giving ecstatic whirls of their electric tails.

Yet another noiseless evaporation follows as a figure appears from among the debris and begins scrambling up the embankment in our direction, gasping that all photo-graphy is forbidden. It is evidently the *custode*, anxious to inform me that I am standing on top of the outer walls of *il teatro romano di Sessa Aurunca*, and the solid floor is still preserved there in perfect condition, six metres under the earth in the centre of the basin.

'We dug it up last year, *professore*, a huge excavation. Experts from all over the world came – German, French, English ... You see the ministry never send me any weed-killer – not for two years – I have to clean it out every week and show tourists ...' There's an embarrassed silence as together we survey the overgrown refuse sinking deeper into the quagmire year by year; then he gains his second wind and develops new authority: 'It was a Roman *municipium* ... visited by Ovid and Virgil; the birthplace of Lucilius, father of comic poetry; great battles were fought here against Hannibal and Pyrrhus; it was captured by Spartacus ...' Then he falls into a medieval silence and only emerges again with the bombing of Monte Cassino and the battle of Garigliano, and the cruel *tedeschi* and brave *alleati*, and the beautiful cemetery down at Minturno.

He demands I see his *ufficio*; he thinks he has a pamphlet somewhere, '*una guida del teatro*', but we abandon the search in seconds, having ploughed our way over the mud and into a cavernous portico on the crater's rim, a Roman arch leading into subterranean tunnels where the floor is littered with farmyard droppings and old jerrycans and piles of ex-Army blankets. But he hasn't finished yet, the old scoundrel, and begins shaking his fist as we climb back up the bank: '*Sono imbecilli, traditori*,' he shouts. 'They are defacing history. They throw their rubbish here every day – I try to stop them, but the pile grows every week. What can I do, *professore*? The government does nothing to help me ...'

I'd better leave him to his rags and tins and old mat-
tresses, and his maze of old cars and collection of pigs; so I
bid him a gentle goodbye and watch his shoulders droop
pathetically. And as he turns away a sodden groundsheet in
the wasteland raises itself on the wind in a friendly bubble
of brown, as if welcoming him back.

I have found Da Nicola's. Every town must have its
central eating place, where the real business is concluded,
the bargains are struck and 'arrangements' are made; and so
it is even here, through this unassuming doorway into a
narrow neon-lit *cantina* dining-room; and I am hoping the
fare will be palatable. Nicola himself is in charge, plump
and smiling and watching over his discerning Auruncan
clients with friendly attention, squeezing gently between
the tables with a diffident readiness to hear their secrets.
The Maresciallo is there; the priest who buried this morning's body; the satisfied lawyer; the Sindaco himself; the
local doctor; and two uniformed *guardie di finanza*, after
hanging their pistols on the coat rack. It has the air of a
quiet and satisfied dining club, full of whispers, knowing
nods and the discreet dabbing of mouths with linen napkins. This evening's speciality is *abbacchio arrosto alla
Caprese* – tender morsels of lamb dressed with *peperone*,
parsley and thyme and bubbling in a creamed wine sauce –
though one or two have obviously put their orders in earlier,
for the lawyer is busy with *frittura di mare* and the Sindaco,
having dealt with his *fettuccine alle vongole*, is now enjoying *vitellino alla Marsala*. As the diligent mopping-up starts
and sponges of broken bread are swept round the nearly
naked plates, Nicola sidles up to each table in turn and sits
like an expectant *confidant*, to glean some of the latest
wisdom and impart his own.

When at last it is my turn, he is a little perplexed and so
am I. What on earth shall I tell him – folklore, Brindisi,
Roman roads, dialects, ancient history, American deserters,
architecture? So I pluck a name out of memory's dustbin –

Vito Nardiello. 'Ah,' and he nods wisely, 'the Wolf of Irpina; he's further south, *signore*, with a big price on his head, half a million lire . . . But they won't catch him, he was one of Tito's officers in Yugoslavia with the partisans.' We go on to skirt round such delicate matters as Lucky Luciano's return to Naples, Salvatore Giuliano's murder in Sicily and the confused issue of *omertà*, his non-committal and evasive platitudes punctuated by shrugs of innocence, till he drops his voice and leans forward: 'If you want to find brigands today, *signore*, go and look in Parliament . . . that's where they all are now, in the government and the Vatican . . . the real ones are in Rome, not here.'

It always ends the same way. Ask anyone where the trouble is and they say it's *il governo*, where the Members of Parliament are all either Mafia-ridden, Pope-ridden, Mason-ridden or just money- and sex-ridden, all grinding down the powerless and defenceless population for personal profit. He starts to whisper about the Mayor of Naples with his shipping line, contraband arrangements, property developments and a luxury apartment in Switzerland, then sighs hopelessly: 'It's always been the same, *signore*, always . . . before Garibaldi, under Mussolini, even now . . . *Siamo troppo individualisti*; in order to live in Italy it has to be every man for himself. You see, we're not a nation at all really, just an odd collection of people put here by God: he just threw the leftovers down in south Italy when he'd done all the rest. That's us; that's why he gave us the Pope later – to try to make up for it.'

A pessimistic indictment of one's own nation, when you come to think of it: existence drowned in defeat before it starts. 'A sad country' President de Brosses called it with exactitude, a comment seconded by most sensitive observers acute enough to brush aside all the vain superficiality – Lampedusa, Levi, Dolci, Manzoni, Barzini – each of them seeing the fundamental bitterness and melancholy underneath the awfulness of the suffering and humiliation which are almost national characteristics. Even the Neapolitan song, that emblem of everlasting *joie de vivre*, is no more than a poignant lament on life's endless cruelties, its strings of misery and defeat.

We talk again later, when the room is emptier and the wine has produced its miracle of contented expansion. Sessa has become a little rosier at this hour and considerably warmer, and I'm in no hurry to return to the evil inn; moreover, I've heard there are gypsies camped near the town, and there may be a fair, as it's a popular meeting place for itinerant nomads. The mention of such a possibility seems to bring back memories, and his eyes lose their focus: 'Yes, we get groups of them every year – either in spring or the end of summer – they don't bother us really, just a bit of begging now and then. The leaders are very strict: last year a woman was caught with a stolen chicken; the chief took her in front of the cathedral, stripped her to the waist, and gave her ten lashes with a whip. She never murmured.' He pours us both a little more wine and chuckles: 'The problem is that some of them are very beautiful, *signore – veramente bellissime, anche caldissime, piene di cuore* [incredibly beautiful, hot-blooded, full of passion] ... Sometimes it causes problems,' pausing briefly to enjoy the nostalgia. 'I was robbed by one of them when I was young: I had a little café then and this girl came in offering to tell my fortune. She was like an eastern princess – the most beautiful thing I'd ever seen, with raven hair and dark opal eyes and soft coffee-coloured skin – and she made me sit close to her, our thighs touching under the table ... I was in heaven, *signore*. And just imagine that to reveal the final secrets about my future she asked me to touch her heart, to put a hand inside her blouse on to her bare breast ...' He sighs deeply and wistfully, caught up in his wicked dreams. 'Afterwards, of course, my wallet had gone and all the day's takings.'

Women haven't changed much, we decide, and nor for

that matter have men; the same thing happened in the
Garden of Eden, and Swinburne reports similar gypsy exhibitions during his tour of the Two Sicilies in the 1770s – a
group of them would indulge in 'grossly indecent' acts to
attract the crowds while others went round the empty
shops and houses helping themselves to the contents. We
both roar with laughter, for by this time there's nothing left
in the wine flask, and we know that men are complete
idiots – but can't help it.

A most beautiful morning. The sun strikes copper flames
off the trees, and at last Sessa is golden and fresh, as if
yesterday's inundation had never happened. An unrecognis-
ably handsome dog is patrolling his patch of earth beneath
my window, investigating green grass-tufts with ears
pricked in quizzical re-recognition; even the spider woman
presents a lopsided grin. I shall seek out these haunts of
didicois, like Borrow, and be their friend and admire their
painted carts and tambourine-whirling Saturnalias, and I
shall take Russell Flint pictures of dusky maidens . . . an
exotic fantasy which rapidly dissolves into acres of ugly
earth pock-marked with yesterday's puddles and the diseased scattering of sagging bivouacs, all coated in gusty
whirls of straw and a Bosch nightmare of scavenging children like hungry Lilliputians. So this is romantic gypsy-
dom? Matters get worse as the ragged mites cluster round
like iron filings drawn towards a magnet, followed by a few
inquisitive goats, to see if I have money or a crust. 'Where
do you come from?' is the total of my morning's contribu-
tion, for just as the query dies on my lips the nearest tent
explodes into a fully grown gypsy genie squashed in a gorilla
crouch, with anthropoidal arms and Piltdown face and chest
as sooty as a flue-brush, and all I am aware of is baleful eyes
and animal growls and a discus swing being taken in my
direction . . .

It is unfortunate that the next bus out of Sessa doesn't

leave till evening. In the interim I shall practise solitude and investigate something inanimate, such as Rocca Monfina, which is the highest of all the mountain domes roundabout, rising resolute and overpowering behind the town, and as crimped with massive oak trees as a Hadendowi's hairdo. It's reached by an old track, meandering desolately out of town then roughening and rising rapidly through bushes that spread into dark walls of oak and chestnut reaching up to impenetrable infinity, while the mottled brown patchwork of Sessa's roofs sinks down to a scrambled blur. Branches touch in soft drawing-room whispers to break the silence, twigs patter down in dry raindrops, and leaves sigh in long parachute falls, then a jay screams a warning and swoops away pink into darker trees. The forest closes in, massive tree trunks tightening their prison grip as they slide round like muscular ballet dancers waving me on, showing only flecks of unreachable sky high above the path and their quivering arms. Suddenly a goblin figure darts round a bend ahead and we each leap in terror as he hurries past, dancing over the ruts: a priest, swirling his black robes and letting his white ankles peep like guilty rabbit skuts in their eagerness to be gone. What ecclesiastical mystery can possibly lie ahead, I ask myself, in this endlessly uphill jungle – a dying woodcutter perhaps, or some distant mountain shrine receiving its annual visitation and blessing? I never did find out.

High up among the heavens with the roof-tops long gone from view, I look down over swelling fields of tree-tops rolling over the hills like a turbulent sea, as the earth of the path softens to grass and in a little while disperses itself altogether into a maze of tree-lined aisles strewn with deep carpets of leaves. Cushion-shapes of rich green fern swell from damp tree roots, and dark clusters of bushes crouch in the wings like caves to the underworld. First there's one path, then another and another, as the trees move to close in and the patter of dropping twigs and acorns rattles to a crescendo, half drowning each eerie footstep of kicking leaves. Somewhere there must be a summit to these endless mountain ridges and a sky that can pierce this matted roof with enough light to let the silent birds sing.

It comes in the end. Three hours of climbing, and the silver streak of the Garigliano gleams in the distant north, and somewhere southward flows the muddy Volturno – both visible from one point, were I on the correct crest of this furrowed summit; but that last effort escapes me. Instead I turn and run.

I bound with increasing speed down this tangled hill of trees and undergrowth, leaping over mounds and gulleys, jumping past ditches and dead branches, sliding on earth and dead leaves, tearing through the smothering clutch of branches and the whiplash of offended saplings. Closing ranks behind they give chase, their sounds and shadows growing ever taller as I flee, gulping for air in panic and exhilaration at out-running the army of furies. Through ripping thorns and stumbling bushes and minefields of rotten stumps I jump and hop and flounder, scared by my own noise following behind, as gradients vary from precipitous to gradual, and daylight through the thinning tree-tops stays miles and hours away.

Suddenly I burst into sunny air and a clearing of waist-high grass, then a plantation of carefully tended saplings standing in pristine order, and beyond them a sloping field and the edges of friendly tree-tops half hiding the distant muddle of Sessa's roofs, clustered like a flotsam of pebbles. A bent figure chopping wood in a corner straightens without surprise: 'The Ponte Ronica is that way,' he points, and resumes his chopping, having assumed I need a road, so I climb a fence and push through a thicket of tall silver-barked saplings then stumble down a bank on to a pathway leading towards Sessa. An old earth track, rutted by cart-wheels for half a mile, gradually flattens to dry mud and stones of coarse immovable hardness, faintly cut into huge emerging squares of man-made smoothness, and drifts on through the verges of grass in an implacable line of ancient determination as far as my eye can see. A perfect Roman road again, come from nowhere and leading nowhere, useless and long-forgotten, bordering a deep ravine filled with tangled trees that merge further up into an arc of thick foliage spanning from bank to bank and dripping with curtains of ivy that seem shapeless, until you get nearer and see the legs under the trailing skirts: massive pillars of immaculate brick soaring up from the gully and fanning out into huge arches of bridge. There are twenty-four of them, leaping in graceful Palladian futility across this jungle chasm that today holds nothing save the last trickles of the River Travato, seeping far below like an open drain.

On approaching, it is less romantic, irreverently carbuncled by the temporary homes of miscellaneous squatters who have reduced its splendour to a miasma of corrugated tin, tea chests and rusty scaffolding, clinging round its ankles and swarming up its arches like the sad accretion of departed house-martins. The inevitable pig shuffles delightedly on the muddy bank, and the old bricks weep with hacmorrhoids of brcczc-block, lcaking ccmcnt and raggcd sacks – the idyllic fantasy of Piranesi being devoured by the savagery of Brueghel.

I pause between horror and sympathy, followed by overpowering guilt. What right have I to criticise? The old bridge has the age and wisdom not to care that garbled television antennae crawl up its ivy, as long as someone makes use of it; it has its memories of legions tramping to the relief of Capua, of togaed travellers from Venafrium hurrying to reach the coast, of holiday crowds surging to the games at Teano or the temple at Treglia. Is it worth the effort to be angry here, when there are vagrants sleeping every night under arches in Rome? As Cicero would say, the circumstances now are different ... And then, sweet anaesthesia in the rumble of a cart as the woodcutter rattles by with his load of sawn logs, waving as he passes, his shout drowned by the creak and bump of wheels on ghostly stones that jolt him towards the distance. I watch his contented straight-line disappearance shrinking to half size then toy size then nothing; but still the shrill echo persists of faint wheels on stone, held on the air like the ghostly passing of a chariot . . .

Then back to Nicola, who has agreed to give me an early supper so I can catch the evening bus out of Sessa. I don't think he's sorry I'm leaving. Do I know about the Madonna of the Cheese? he asks, putting a plate of it in front of me. Did I visit the sanctuary up on the mountains? 'No,' I smile weakly. I'm developing an allergy to madonnas: the whole land is festooned with them; every corner of Sessa has one standing in a niche like a coyly draped stalagmite; every hill has one, every road, every family, there's even one sweating greasily in Nicola's kitchen. This is Mariolatry gone mad. And now it's cheese! Is nothing sacred? He takes my glassy stare for acquiescence: 'You see, a shepherd found a statue of the Madonna half-buried up the mountain, and when he pulled it out of the ground there was a rush of water. It was a spring, and when the shepherds take their sheep there to drink they find the ewes are suddenly full of milk – overflowing with it. So there are monks there now who collect it and make it into cheese – the one you're eating. The place is called Santuario delle Lattanti . . .'

Dear Multiplying Mary, please stop before I go any further – nothing personal; it's the deception I can't stand, the omnipresence of hocus-pocus, guilt and cunning. Big Mother is watching you. That holy face is everywhere with its soft accusing eyes – in bars, bedrooms, shops and buses; up mountains, trees and rivers – and such a multitalented idol, too: laughing, weeping, walking, dancing, lactating, head-shaking, finger-wagging, bleeding, speaking, stone-throwing and flying. You are a potent and irrepressible union of pagan earth mother with holy scripture, and of lust with sublimation. Not much further down the road, at Maschito, you appear as Madonna of the Seven Veils – as Maschito is so-named because it originated with an all-male population it obviously needed some prodigious intervention. I shall have to see what you do when I get there. If people knew which pagan deity you have replaced there'd be a riot. But for the moment, please stop.

I board the bus, and wave a tired hand at Nicola; but he has turned and gone already, as if drawing a dark curtain of friendlessness between me and Sessa, a town of no farewells. It feels a lot safer when the bus has left it behind and hissed down to the clean-air comfort of sea level, and the shaggy eyebrows of the roof-tops have ducked down below their parapet of hills to mutter their evening curses while we race away across the wide plain of Capua, flecked by a watery sun.

SIX

Capua *1*

Just to make life difficult, there are two Capuas, the Old
and the New, and they are three miles apart. Old Capua, as
its name implies, is ancient; not just older than Rome but
in its heyday bigger, more splendid, richer, far more
debauched and altogether infinitely more enjoyable; in fact
so pleasurable that Livy described it as the most opulent
city in Italy, and Cicero called it one of the three most
fabulous places in the world (the others being Corinth and
Carthage). Such was its magnificence and attendant delights
that Hannibal, having wintered his troops there, couldn't
persuade them to mount a spring offensive against Rome:
they were too exhausted, and in the end could only just
manage to drag themselves back to Africa. Then calamity
struck in AD 850, when the Saracens overran it, ending its
epicurean existence for ever; though the few who survived
made off three miles to the north-west, to the old Roman
outpost of Casalinum, where they began to build New
Capua.

Had Old Capua died completely the issue would have
been resolved, but it didn't: it grew again, more rapidly than
New Capua, with the result that two Capuas stood side by
side eyeing each other suspiciously, one with the history,
the Roman remains and the whispered reputation of a
glorious past spiced with unmentionable infamies, the
other appointed as regional capital with the power, the
administration and the museum and, of course, Frederick
of Hohenstaufen's Triumphal Arch. And to make matters
worse, not only was Old Capua soon far bigger than New
Capua, but the Camorra moved into Old Capua and made
it their headquarters.

Another problem is, why should anywhere be called Capua? Presumably, one supposes, it derives from Latin *caput* – head – which, as it was undisputed queen of the south, would be a most reasonable assumption. It would, however, be a wrong one. It was an Oscan city first of all, named Kapys – Hawk – in honour of a chieftain's favourite falcon, so legend has it, that made a significant dive to earth hereabouts and so founded a city. Later it was taken over by the Etruscans and then, eventually, by the Romans; so one day its three thousand years of history will be taken seriously and it will be gently opened up, and wondrous remains will be found of old civilisations we've hardly heard of . . . one day . . .

Directed by the driver again – these men know everything – I have found an inn in Old Capua: nothing of great consequence but a little better than the one Matthews found at the beginning of the last century. 'Both the town and the inn look dirty and miserable,' he wrote. 'I am too much fatigued to say more at present.' He was certainly right about the town: the evening gloom shrouding its hybrid buildings has forced the façades into disjointed charcoal grimaces of discomfort and apologetic guilt, and there are cars that creep furtively about their business with hooded headlights.

The inn is little better, its entrance chilled by the light of neon tubes and the passage blocked by stout Victorian furnishings, and the disenchanted innkeeper would rather attend to old customers in the bar than bother with passing guests. Once established, I sup a gruel of *pasta-fagioli* in his stark dining-room, a sanctuary of half-life where all the other tables are taken up by muttering card players or engrossed figures bent over dominoes, hardly moving as they eke the evening out towards infinity as though it were some nightly ritual before death. The dormant tableau is mused over by a spare-time waiter sunk against the bar in vacant inertia, and a dusty juke-box blinks weak and coloured tears in a corner, pale with lack of love.

It is then that I hear it: creeping sea-waves of non-Italian Italian, rough pebbles of alien sounds grating in sandpaper whispers – Slavic, Croatian, Polak, Serb, Bulgar and rasping edges of *krishni . . . var . . . dosvey . . . sheramik* – with eyes always down in fierce concentration, no one gesturing or spitting on the floor. I've stumbled into a warren of displaced persons, muttering old men from Omsk and Minsk and Riga, roughening their tired tongues over aces of spades and knight's pawn two, flotsam from a dead war hunched together in friendly combat like creaking ballet dancers. Occasionally one rises quietly and walks to the counter with slow dignity – Might I please have an ashtray? – then bows as he takes it, the silent wash of weary resignation floating over the others in their abandoned cul-de-sac of time. For a short way out of Capua is the last camp of offal left by the war, and they walk in two miles each evening to see some embers of real life, draped in long overcoats that reach the ground and capped by squat Muscovite trilbies last seen on Al Capone. As if mesmerised into detail and tidiness, they drop no ash, throw no cigarette ends, leave no glasses or napkins on the table, but take everything back to the bar or to the bin with immaculate concern.

But there is anger there, too. A tubby child of eight or nine has come in to buy sweets, followed by his new puppy which is a joyous brown ball gambolling at his exciting feet and delicious shoe-laces; so he kicks it away – yelping. A tall overcoat rises silently from a table and walks over without a sound, an arm swings viciously, followed by a pistol-crack and an outraged scream of surprise . . . a dancing child exits left holding its yelling head.

How I envy such wasted courage, and remember lacking it as I sat in a Roman restaurant once, watching a carter belabour his horse outside, leaving it to my female guest to run out and give him the same treatment with her fists and handbag. 'You can't change the world,' I told her. 'You're an English weasel,' she said, and left.

Later at the end of a game I speak to one of them: a pug-nosed, leathery-faced Latvian with a shining cranium and marble-bright eyes set deep in cobweb skin, dreaming of flat Baltic landscapes; and over a drink he talks of university days, of a two-year walk from Riga to Dubrovnik, of Russian rapists and German tracker dogs and endless nights slept in the snow. He remembers, too, the night he found academic friends in Prague who hid him for a day, and how they had a pet dachshund, and then gave him a celebration dinner down in the cellar where the Germans wouldn't hear: 'A most delicious meaty stew, the best I'd ever tasted.' But when he left in the morning the dachshund wasn't there . . .

It's all in monotone as if it doesn't matter any more, not worth a comma in history, as pointless as Belsen or Hiroshima, and told in slow and rugged English mixed with spasms of Italian and German fighting to unscramble the babel turmoil inside his mind. Another bastard of semantics struggling for air, just like that earlier one a thousand years ago when the Italian language was born here in Capua, and the peasants had to swear an oath on renting land from the Abbey of Monte Cassino: '*Sao ko kelle terre . . .*' – I know that this land . . . Nor is its battle over yet, for last week there were three Sicilians on trial in Capua who needed an interpreter in order to give evidence.

The real Old Capua, '*fertilis et gloriosa*', has long since disappeared; so have its togaed playboys and millionaires, its easy money and pleasure, together with the scent of its roses and poppies brought daily from Paestum, and its gracious streets full of beautiful youths with 'braided hair and brightly rouged cheeks'. It had three hundred thousand inhabitants then; today there are only fifty thousand, and while many of its ancient sites have been identified none has been excavated. It would be worse than trying to raise the *Titanic*.

The amphitheatre, built over a temple to Mithras, sits skeletal at the northern end – supposedly the arena where mortal combat originated for the amusement of the Oscans, and later appropriated by Rome as a holiday spectacular, a peace keeper and vote catcher at election times. It was also the revolutionary cradle of Spartacus, that early example of a successful left-wing insurgent and guerilla leader, who nearly changed the course of history, and might well have done so but for the petty bickerings of his commanders at the moment of glory. Leading an army seventy-thousand-strong and with numerous victories behind him – after which he sometimes made captured Roman officers fight each other to death in true gladiatorial fashion, just to see how it felt – Spartacus wanted finally to take his triumphant forces north into Gaul and to freedom, while his mutinous commanders wanted to scuttle back to the warmth of Calabria – which is eventually what happened, with disastrous results. A house divided against itself must surely fall, decided the Roman general Crassus; and having cornered what was now a factious rabble in the Sila mountains of Calabria, he wiped the entire rebellion out, those unfortunate enough to be taken prisoner being crucified along the Appian Way between Capua and Rome as a warning to others.

As for the rest of the old city, Pratilli and Maciariello have assiduously located some fifty of the major sites including the baths, gymnasium, Temple of Mars and Temple of Venus, detailed research which has helped no one so much as the tomb robbers, who have been doing such a lucrative trade for years as a result that the Mafia is now taking an interest in ancient history.

It is a simple procedure really, provided you use reasonable caution – one that you either take on yourself, if you have the time and patience, or one that you delegate to a friendly farmer, which is the method Sir William Hamilton used, believing that his servants should live for him. It is important in this case to choose the right friends and then be on hand when the find is made – usually after a storm when some cumbersome piece of farm machinery sinks to its axles in a muddy cavity that turns out to be the entrance to an underground chamber. If you don't act quickly others will: the whispers will travel like jungle drums, and that same night mysterious strangers will arrive from town and, when paltry sums have slipped from hand to hand by moonlight, the nimblest of them will slide into the hole feet-first, and excruciating sounds of subterranean mayhem will follow. Not long afterwards yet another unrecorded treasure from antiquity will be marketed discreetly in the private salons of Rome, New York or Geneva, and will eventually come to a final and gracious rest in a millionaire's cabinet; while the sweaty farmer goes on ploughing his dusty furrows. Alternatively, you can take on the entire procedure single-handed, by finding your own site and then digging it up yourself; which method is only to be recommended if your research has been extremely thorough and if you've ensured you won't be discovered – as the authorities have a nasty habit of locking you up, or envious snoopers of becoming violent. Having used both methods with reasonable success I would advise the former for the staid and retiring, and the latter only for the adventurous and foolhardy.

In the mean time there is no shortage of material, and the Capuan *tombaroli* are doing very well. They may be seen at intervals, driving north in their battered cars with curiously wrapped shapes on the back seats; while the bureaucrats left behind fidget at their desks and pray silently that no one will come in to tell them they've just found some more old remains.

The Director of Capua Museum is such a person. Young and enthusiastic, with his desk buried under a snowstorm of paper, he is affably excited to be bearded by a nosy visitor, but the very thought of more excavations terrifies him. 'We already have more than we know what to do with,' he sighs, dragging earnestly at his cigarette and pushing papers aside in the search for an ashtray. When at last it emerges my eyes fix on it: a delicate circular bowl of black earthenware with two slender handles and tapering elegantly to a narrow base. He notices my stare as he taps off his ash: 'Etruscan, third-century ... we have so many we should give them away as Christmas presents to make space for something better – except nobody would want them. That's the problem round here, if we find one we find hundreds. Come, I'll show you what I mean. Have you heard of Mater Matuta? ...'

He unlocks a door across the passage outside into a long gallery, lined with shadowy figures which adjust themselves, as he opens the shutters, into mummified shapes of grotesquely pregnant women rolling in squat obesity and swollen with mammary corpulence, puffed up into misshapen doughnuts and hugging infants to their mammoth breasts. It's a herd of obstetric bogy-women – giantesses of fecundity fatly spread from wall to wall.

'You see how many?' and he sweeps his arms, 'and more in the cellars and some in Naples and plenty more underground.'

'What are they?'

'Who knows exactly?' with a shrug. 'Pre-Christian fertility symbols probably ... *ex votos* perhaps, thank offerings to Mother Earth for producing food and babies. Early deities are always female. They're about 800 BC.'

'Are they from here?'

'Yes. Dug up on the outskirts at La Petrara about a hundred years ago. They knew about it earlier, but had sealed it up again as being too obscene: a peasant had fallen into the underground cave apparently, and come out screaming about she-devils feeding their babies; so the priests had a look and filled it in. That was in 1845, and of course some were stolen straight away – two are in Rome, two in America, one in Germany and several in private houses. We know now it was an Oscan temple and have seen the decorations and inscriptions.'

'Are they holding babies?'

'Yes – five, ten, twenty . . . and a pomegranate in one hand for fertility, and a dove in the other for fidelity and prosperity.'

It is a Pompeian maternity ward gassed into immobility, with petrified pupae of baby-shapes glued to the rough-hewn breasts of square-shouldered earth mothers squatting on barrel haunches, some primitive celebration which the Romans adapted into the Matralia of 11 June, when proud young mothers met together to bless each other's babies; and which the holy fathers adapted still further into the worship of Mary and the infant Jesus.

'*Capua fertilissima* . . .' he smiles as we withdraw. 'We also have a collection of the male equivalent, but not on show to the public – it would embarrass an elephant. There were as many temples here to Priapus as there were to Venus; if you've read Martial's epigrams you'll understand . . . We think most of them refer to Capuans . . .'

We reach his office again, where he searches for the visitors' book, anxious to record another signature.

'Mostly Germans, I'm afraid,' he says. 'We have the only known statue of their Emperor Frederick who once ruled the whole of south Italy. Capua was one of his capitals; that's all they want to see, nothing old or beautiful. They're only interested if it's German.'

'Don't Italians come?'

'Pah! Italians in museums!' and his eyebrows shoot up in amazement. 'The past bores them; the only names they know are Julius Caesar and the Colosseum; all they think of is football and cars and sex and sometimes politics. At least the Germans have a sense of pride and history and know what they want.'

I sign the book for him and he shows me out into the

porticoed courtyard, beaming as he shakes my hand, then his eyes twinkle and he bends towards my ear: 'Go and visit the church of San Prisco,' he whispers. 'It was once a temple of Priapus. There are some interesting remains there; and women still lift their skirts up sometimes and rub themselves against the altar.'

Such stirring revelations will have to wait, for the shade in this cool columned courtyard is as sweet as ether, and I can sit on a marble bench, under trees of white trumpet lilies, and bask in day-dreaming splendour among Ali Baba urns trailing waterfall webs of escaping geraniums, and watch an old gardener working at half speed as he sprinkles some light refreshment on to a dried-out lawn.

So this is the town Frederick of Hohenstaufen fell in love with and called Capua Fidelis. There is a comforting touch of warm constancy in these stone arches, and in the deep silence that reaches out into the squares of cobalt sky; the gentle air has the caressing innocence of an opiate. What an amazing person he was, this twelfth-century colossus, the *stupor mundi*, born of royal blood into Sicilian bedlam, and fighting his way through the treacherous coils of medieval anarchy to take over the German empire and unite it with three-quarters of Italy – and, when not at war, had time to write books, design castles, collect works of art, study mathematics, compose music and rabidly hate all popes, to name but a few of his accomplishments. 'The first of the Renaissance princes' are the wise words of Georgina Masson, though regrettably when the tempest of all that magnificence began to burst a hundred years later it was in the part of Italy he hated most and had never conquered, while the seeds of beauty he had so carefully sown in the south were uprooted and destroyed by the Angevins.

Poor Frederick, driven by two interconnected ambitions: to unite Italy with Germany, and to curb the power of the Church; but before he could achieve his territorial goal he had to overcome the religious problem, and this developed into a lifetime's confrontation with two powerful popes, Gregory IX and Innocent IV, involving war, Machiavellian politics and verbal acrimony – for which he was twice excommunicated. 'A tyranny wallowing in riches' was one of his first anti-clerical outbursts when things went against him, saying priests were 'drunken with terrestrial delights and they fattened themselves with alms', to which the Church replied that he was 'a friend of the Infidel', 'a beast from the sea' and 'the head of a brood of vipers'. Nothing daunted by this and the excommunication that followed, Frederick accused Gregory of hypocrisy, corruption, nepotism and lies, adding for good measure that Moses, Mohammed and Jesus were the three greatest impostors in history, a virgin birth was a biological impossibility, and God wouldn't have chosen Palestine to be the Promised Land if He'd seen Sicily first. Such blasphemous utterances were too much for the Pope, who now began to get personal: You're a heretic, he proclaimed, you are Anti-Christ, you have a bath every day, you're a fornicator and adulterer. It's not just your four wives (at different times), it's your *puellas lascivias*, your caravan of eastern concubines and dancing girls that follows you everywhere. You're excommunicated . . . again. Fine, shrugged the Emperor, hardly pleased that Gregory had just decreed that contraception merited the death sentence. Meanwhile, as you seem to be having problems with Jerusalem, perhaps I'd better lead a crusade and recapture it for you. Which he proceeded to do, at the same time uniting most of Italy, founding the University of Naples and improving the Medical School at Salerno, building numerous castles, collecting Greek and Roman statuary, drawing up legal and administrative systems for south Italy, studying the stars and the human digestive system, writing a scholarly book on falconry – *De Arte Venandi* – solving complex mathematical problems, speaking Italian, Arabic and German, breeding thoroughbred horses, writing poetry, singing songs, collecting his harem of beautiful women and siring numerous children . . .

In spite of such genius he failed in his great ambition, finally outwitted by the Pope and rebellious princes; what might have been a political and cultural revolution crumbled to dust and was then swept from the face of Italy by the vengeful Innocent IV who, on Frederick's death, demanded that the whole Hohenstaufen brood be exterminated and every sign of it destroyed, a job the next pope, Clement IV, gave to Charles of Anjou – offering him half of Italy as a prize. He accepted this task willingly enough, and promptly spent the next twenty years hounding the last of the Hohenstaufens to extinction.

So perished one of the first great seekers after knowledge, lovers of beauty and patrons of the arts; and so died the first flowers of south Italian greatness; and so came the Angevins to rule over the Kingdom of the Two Sicilies and to turn it into a wilderness of desolation.

A burst of opening doors breaks my reverie, and out flops the director on his way home to lunch.

'*Salve*. Still here?'

'I was thinking about Frederick.'

'You must visit the Capuan Gate,' he laughs, 'and then read your Dante. And this evening please come to dinner,' and he sails away into the sun, coat hooked on to a thumb over his shoulder, and bowed to reverently by the gardener.

So I obey him and go to the Capuan Gate, but it is no longer there: it was pulled down by the Spaniards three hundred years after it was built, and our only knowledge of it is from contemporary sketches recently unearthed in a Viennese museum, and from André of Hungary's description of it as a deliberate copy of a Roman triumphal arch, costing the Emperor twenty thousand ounces of pure gold to have built. So, like the silver-bound presentation copy of *De Arte Venandi*, the majestic gateway into his favourite city has gone for ever, together with almost every other vestige of beauty and greatness he gave to his favourite land.

Time needs but little encouragement to be as barbarous and unthinking as we are; and this is a land where Time is both inconsequential and king, and moves hand-in-hand with the invincible sun. I can feel the hot breath of his careless greed as I stand, hugged by warm air that sucks up tired moth-wings of dust on the road and weighs me down sticky with crucible heat, watching everything scorched to hazy yellow or melting into eye-blinking white; and I can almost see his fiery jaws as he brings the noonday pendulum of New Capua ticking to a final stop. When all is scalded to immobility except a distended dog on a pavement, pumping its tummy like maddened bellows and walked on by thirsty flies, it's time to slip past him through a cool curtain of *cantina* darkness into the stale musk of wooded wine, where some of it may dampen the sandpaper tightness in my throat. But he's still with me after a flaskful, giving an over-the-shoulder grin, ghoulish and charcoal-black, gluttonous scavenger of all Frederick's litter of greatness, obliterator of his places of solitude, even of Castel del Monte – the queen of castles, over towards the Adriatic – to which he carried his trophies of Greek and Roman antiquities, and which was still fabulously rich with variegated marble in the seventeenth century (according to Dánieli) and had a balconied courtyard. But when Lear saw it in 1850 it was a desiccated ruin used by Apulian bandits and occasionally stormed by Bourbon troops. And who should have saved it from further wreckage but a German? – Gregorovius, pleading it be made into a national monument, which it became in 1875, followed by a flurry of scholarly Teutonic monographs: Schubriz, Haseloff, Ebhardt . . .

Another flaskful, landlord, to smooth this gravel-throat of dust . . .

So, who is grinning most then? Time or that toothless

old popephobe Frederick – a bleached pattern of bones
sought after and loved by an army of blond *Herrenvolk* who
loathed the south at the time but have worshipped it since
as a sun-blessed paradise, and stormed it in lust or paced it
in minute examination: Mommsen, Beloch, Rodenwaldt,
Winckelmann, Von Duhren . . . But he gurgles at them now,
eyeless and maggot-shrunk, glad that they've come too late.
You should have been here earlier when it was a land of
castles and green paradise, and when I was recording the
habits of the cuckoo . . .

Never drink at midday under the sun on an empty
stomach.

'All bloody homosexuals.'

   'Oh yes? . . .'

'Hutton called Frederick a nigger in a top hat.'

'Hamilton wasn't – '

'He wasn't anything.'

'But the Volturno was navigable then . . .'

'Didn't Hamilton go to Isernia?'

'Oscar met Van Gloeden in Sicily . . .'

'An Arab said Frederick wouldn't have got a bid in a slave
market . . .'

'Lear was . . . so was Gissing . . . and Corvo . . . and
Douglas . . .'

   'Douglas was a shit.'

'Don't be so bloody xenophobic. So was Winckelmann
. . . and Michelangelo . . .'

'Don't talk about Douglas . . . I knew him.'

'So did I . . . and Orioli . . . and Cerio . . .'

'I met Gracie Fields . . .'

That was my voice, stopping the conversation and giving
the director a chance to pour out more drinks, so we can all
settle back again, pink and silent with full glasses and china
thimbles of coffee, hearing his wife washing up in the
distance, me and two other guests who've come from

Naples – an aged book dealer shrunken bird-like into a clumsy suit, with long fingers, a shock of snowy hair and brightly alert eyes peeping from crumpled skin, and a pre-war artist from Germany settled on the Ganymede coast, both wasting and thick-set in a wheelchair with a rug spread over useless lower limbs and huge strength bursting in his shoulders and a burning torrent of opinions on everything. He devoured religion for his first course: 'The Pope is a wonderful man, it's just a shame he believes all that rubbish; and what kind of religion is it anyway that lets naked Jews dig their own graves but won't even allow a woman with bare arms into a church?' and then came the Jews: 'They're racists, worse than the Nazis. Why don't they recognise Jesus? He was a Jew . . .'; and for the second course it was politics: 'Italians don't have elections, they have contests in lying and cheating. They enjoy a hero's fall more than his victories . . .'; and now over coffee it was sex: 'Italy has always been the bisexual brothel of Europe'; and finally sex in the south:

'Capri was a bugger's Olympic stadium.'

'And Taormina.'

'It's all the Pope's fault . . . deifying women . . .'

'It's the Arab blood in Sicily. Look at the Moroccans in the war . . .'

'Woman's like an egg – she's better when she's beaten . . .'

'What about the Germans then? And the Americans?'

'And the English; Norman Douglas – Kingdom of the Two Cecilies . . .?'

'He was a shit.'

'*Un uomo molto simpatico, anche eruditissimo.*'

'Smut, cocks and bad manners – pervert who jumped bail.'

'. . . Lizards, pumice-stone, beavers, Herodotus, Darwin, Capri, mythology, Greek, Russian, German, Latin . . . you couldn't do it.'

'Wouldn't want to . . . museum and library stuff, nothing original.'

'Forty books, hundreds of articles . . .'

'Derivative, unreadable, self-opinionated . . . never went near a church except to meet a little boy . . .'

I'm out of this shrapnel; it's the German and the bookseller hammering and tonging each other with crazy half-smiles on their faces as they rattle out memories and bygone incidents with dodges and thrusts, the wheelchair getting more and more dogmatic as he bulldozes questions aside like a fly-swatting tank.

'It's all cribbed or lies or fantasies, a confidence trick – that rubbish about Milton; always pinching other people's ideas . . . And his behaviour was ghastly too, like a spoilt child who wanted attention: swearing, shouting obscenities, throwing food on the floor . . .'

'Giving money to orphans and charity . . . the whole island at his funeral?'

'Sucking up to aristos or pimpy waiters . . . it was their sons he was after; and all those fat Calabrian mothers with lots of pretty children. He was a typical Puritan who wallowed in filth.'

'And Cellini . . . Giulio Romano . . . Tchaikovsky . . . Marlowe . . . do their private lives diminish their art or genius?' and the bookseller reaches slowly up to touch a row of spines in the shelf beside him.

'Yes . . . if their lives touch ours.'

'His first editions, all inscribed: *Siren Land, Street Games, Capri, Limericks, Herpetology of Baden, Plea for Better Manners* . . . What will you leave for posterity? . . .'

'No bloody manners at all . . . I've seen people walk out of a room as soon as he came in. Some people wouldn't have him in their houses.'

'Wouldn't life be a little boring without intelligent eccentrics, educated individualists with original views? . . . Like you?' And as the defused German snorts and looks peeved and prepares to rumble on again, I make a clandestine creep for the bookcase.

'Look how he treated his wife: self-centred and arrogant, never admitting failure or defeat ... Exaggeration too: all his little boys had cocks like candlesticks – bloody liar!'

And out it slips: a sand-coloured binding like sacking, with a red title and erudite smut on every page:

> There was a young man of Cape Horn
> Who wished he had never been born;
> And he wouldn't have been
> If his father had seen
> That the bloody French letter was torn

and did I know that the Merovingians used deerskin condoms, and Gibbon called them 'detestable precautions'? No, I didn't, so on we go:

> There was a young lady of Kew
> Who said, as the curate withdrew,
> 'I prefer the dear vicar
> He's longer and thicker;
> Besides, he comes quicker than you'

which, according to the notes, shows how ignorant she was and suggests she'd do better to stick to the curate ... But I am feeling guilty and creep back again – and now Lawrence is in the middle of the minefield:

'Another unreadable man ... turgid and repetitious and not even grammatical. Diarrhoea of the soul – only he didn't have one. I remember ...'

'Books translated into thirty languages?'

'Pah! Working-class pornographer. I remember him in Florence boasting about putting sex in his books just to become famous – a fake – said the public were stupid.'

'But still a best-seller,' and again the finger goes up to touch more spines, '. . . all his first editions, too.'

'Sulked if he wasn't the centre of attention, fawned all over us at Florence Station and said he had no money; so Douglas lent him some and bought him a box of chocolates. And do you know what the miserable little bugger did? He opened the box to count them in case we'd taken some – evil bastard . . .'

My eyes are straining at the bookshelves to make out names – Ruskin, Rolfe, Crowley, Light, Eustace, Ross, Swinburne, Strutt, Hamilton – while the bombardment goes on dimly through the warm mist of Strega . . . I must remember that brown binding: 110 copies privately printed in 1928.

'How long will it take me to walk those three miles to Old Capua?'

My last sight of them is lined up watching television, arguments forgotten. The flickering face of a young man is telling them how he's going to spend the millions he's just won on a lottery. 'My mother first,' he sighs milkily, 'then all the poor orphans in Naples who won't have anything at Christmas . . .' and the German fighting to get a handkerchief out of his pocket, tears streaming down his face . . .

SEVEN

Capua 2

Old Capua is slothful. Nobody hurries, and even the buses are relaxed and piano as they lumber through dust. It has an air of not caring, almost smug and self-satisfied, casually disdainful like the slow movement of a Mozart piano concerto – lost in realms of the ethereal. God knows why. It's far from appealing to look at: all staccato and cacophonous, the dark shambles of nineteenth-century houses with a carbuncle collection of later additions. But I am in no hurry to leave; it has snared me with its atmosphere of levity and its air of faint aphrodisia and unspoken promises.

'It's Diana's fault,' said the director yesterday. 'She was the big goddess here and obviously quite a girl; she had a huge temple. And then there were four to Venus and at least three to the dirty old man. Quite a sensual and pleasure-loving people, the Capuans; and of course old Silenus kept blowing his breezes in from Naples. Go for a walk up Monte Tifata, that great hill over there; you'll see everything . . . and smell the air.'

So today I go for the walk obediently (it takes all the hours of daylight and a little more), through the village of San Prisco – a pause to visit the church – then across sprawling and useless land peppered with hard-baked, tumbling houses and dry, grey walls flecked with wild shoots of henbane laced amid the dust, till I come to the neat chocolate-box picture of St Angelo in Formis, which is a white oasis at the foot of the mountain. No one knows why it should be called Tifata – it could be after *tifo*, *Tifeo*, *tifone* or *tufo* – but its name isn't important because there it is straight ahead, rising gorgeously into the sky like a green dome awash with luxuriant vegetation, and disappearing towards a distant summit darkened by a microscopic flutter of eyelash trees.

The climbing starts, hopelessly crooked along a path that saunters round the base then zigzags back a few yards above itself, and then does it again – so by walking a mile I have only risen some seventy feet. This must be the *pazienza* pathway, where time and tomorrow don't matter, so I break the routine and start to scramble upwards more vertically, puffing in no time, feet slipping on the uneven ground as I grab at tufts and ridges to haul myself up. Four more paths crossed, then five, and the warm wind is licking my face to soften the sting of the sun, and I can look down on the sprawling tiled roofs of Capua locked together in their chequered squares, all shades of brown as if swimming into each other like sodden biscuits.

Eventually the slope gets kinder and the west wind helps me forward over each gentle ridge towards the next, but always climbing and always growing more silent, till the faraway noises of the town vanish completely and there are no more paths to cross, just open grassland fanned by breezes into waves of changing light that dance and ripple and chase each other over the mountain. High up ahead against the sky is the silhouette of torn trees that cower from storms, and among them the jagged teeth of long-abandoned buildings. Larks twitter their shrill cry as the wind wafts them upward out of sight, and they race and dip ahead of me on vibrant wings beating against invisible fingers of air; while the slopes of grassland rise and fall round me like a mantle on a corpse, sliding into space and darkness off one limb or swelling up on another.

Finally I reach the summit, long and craggy, where coarse grass clings round a witch's scalp of broken rocks, and the huddled bodies of trees cringe from the wind, and webs of wild brambles smother the smashed stumps of ancient towers, and above it all a scattering of ravens wheels and floats in a mournful airborne dance. 'There's treasure buried up there,' said the director last night, 'but no one ever finds it . . . and a hermit used to live there too – perhaps he's dead now.' But nothing stirs along the ridge among the scrub, the pointed stones and the amputated walls except the everlasting wind; so I sit behind a rock to escape it and devour a squashed *panino*.

To the west and far away gleam moving sunspots which sparkle on the waves as they lap their way laughing to the shore at Castel Volturno; and disappearing southward into a distant haze is the infinite stretch of warm and luxurious plain that so bewitched the old world. Small wonder Rome envied such prosperity and decadence, and the Hohenstaufen emperor made Capua his capital, drawing up plans for buildings 'with his own hands'; what a 'place of solace' this would have been, perched high on these flanks of green mountains which drift dreamily down in the sun towards the winding Volturno, all wafted by the beguiling breezes from Parthenope. Casa Giove – House of God – is what the locals call this peak, still awestruck in their infinite primitivism, though Frederick, with his views that direct descendants from the Prophet Mahommed were more credible than arbitrarily elected generals of Christ, would have felt less charitable. No doubt he rode out to hunt here, accompanied by a magnificent display of lords and courtiers on horseback, dog handlers with lean wolfhounds and speedy whippets, and liveried pages to launch hawks from their gauntleted hands, then watch them rise and hover or streak over the slopes after hare and young deer. A far cry from vexatious state affairs, scheming princes and rebellious corners of kingdom; peacefully away from the noisy sprawl of his queen of cities, spilling its patchwork of houses across the river; free at last from the stench of his menagerie of wild animals that invariably accompanied the court – elephants, lions, cheetahs, leopards; but thinking perhaps of his eastern beauties waiting for nightfall. For the warmth of this wind is voluptuously provoking, and even sweat gives the restless body a sensual tremor of well-oiled luxury. *Gloriosa . . . fertilis . . . licentiosa . . . opulentissimaque . . .*

Nor was it just Frederick and the Romans. The Oscans had enjoyed it too, and staged salacious dramas in a theatre near the base of the mountain at Atella, revelling their way through healthy obscenities and lubricious games that were later elaborated by the body-loving Greeks, then turned by the Romans into something more personal: scabrous and scatological comments on the behaviour of famous personalities, so recklessly shameless that they had to be banned – by Tiberius of all people. The Atellans asked to be given his body when he died, so that they could incinerate it in their theatre; a pleasure they were denied. Thus perished the staging of early erotic entertainment and goatish caricature, a stale crumb of it remaining in Pulcinello, the direct descendant of Macco the Oscan clown, but tame by comparison and nowadays only coyly indelicate.

Poor New Capua; a victim of its own success just like Old Capua, and just like Sybaris and Taranto and Paestum and Naples, and even Rome, Venice, Constantinople and Jerusalem. They all suffered or perished through jealousy and vindictiveness.

It was 24 July 1501 that New Capua was sacked; and even now, on that date each year, the church bells toll their lamentation for the five thousand inhabitants massacred by papal forces. Caesar Borgia, son of the Pope, smitten by the beauty of the King of Naples' daughter Carlotta, requested her hand in marriage, but, as the Aragonese were in the midst of angry quarrels with the Vatican anyway, found himself refused. A truce was declared; and for the payment of a fine of forty thousand gold ducats the papal Borgias would forgive the Aragonese and the Capuans everything and be at peace again – an offer the Capuans accepted gladly, and in celebration arranged a banquet of feasting and good cheer for both parties to last all the night; which it nearly did, until at a signal Caesar Borgia's soldiers drew their swords and began to slaughter every Capuan in sight. 'The blood of the slain ran in great streams along the streets,' reports a contemporary observer, gruesomely detailing how the Borgia mercenaries tore away teeth, nails, eyes and genitals before dispatching people, while Caesar himself had the forty most beautiful maidens in the city taken to his private quarters for some late-night entertainment.

Notwithstanding such a papal-inspired attack, the defence produced a high incidence of miracles that night. A stone virgin covered its eyes in horror; nuns leapt into rivers and wells and swam for days; an army of angels outside San Benedetto hurled rocks at the invaders; and the sanctuary steps in Sant' Eligio turned into a defiantly moving escalator, thus saving the gold statue of the madonna from being stolen.

'*I lieti onor tornano in tristi lutti*' – Joyful celebrations turn to miserable grief – says Dante, already wise to the politics of envy and man's urge to meddle in other people's affairs, tendencies that both Capuas have seen often enough, from the days when the dictator Sulla defeated the consul Norbanus to those lawless shambolic weeks a century ago when a fading Bourbon rabble struggled uselessly against the new rabble of Garibaldi. This hilltop has watched the whole plain repeatedly stain itself with the sweat of exhaustion and the tears of strife – a tennis ball of goldenly opulent land smacked to and fro by arguers and rivals and outsiders, torn up by land-grabbing lords and princes and crushed by a medley of unwanted creeds and ideologies.

And as it goes on today, under the guise of politics and law and economics and the search for peace, small wonder they're bored and cynical, and their only true God is self-interest.

*

Down again at last from the rubble of memory's forgotten chaos, and back to that clean and bright oasis of the great usurper – the Basilica of St Angelo in Formis. Immaculate in virgin white and surrounded by decorous palms, it sits snug and comfortable at the foot of the gentle slopes. I have been here for ever, it lies, emphatic and crisp, exuding complacency and divine righteousness, its glow of eternal sovereignty protecting it like a halo. It is so divine and righteous that the little priest forbids me to take any photographs – 'It's all there on the postcards,' he says.

We are standing, of course, on the bones and ashes of yet another Diana – Tifatina this time – and the long-obliterated remains of one of Italy's most important and luxurious sanctuaries, once flocked to by enthusiastic thousands, where the temple doors were reputedly of gold and silver, the columns of alabaster, the floors inlaid with emeralds and sapphires and the altars encrusted with diamonds, rubies and pearls. It was a sacred estate that stretched for miles round Monte Tifata, with its acres of dense forests – where there were arenas and theatres and purifying baths as well as palaces for the twelve lords of the temple, houses for priestesses and attendants, and endless accommodation for pilgrims and visitors. This, they maintained, was where the high priestess Iphigenia had fled to from Tauris, bearing the sacred statue concealed in a bundle of wood – and what better welcome for one who had supervised the occasional human sacrifice than to arrange a feast of them? So primitive tribal romance in the Mediterranean mind was ripened further by the sun and new legends and evolved into rituals of death, enjoyed by the thousands who came to witness them and enrich the goddess' coffers.

Then St Peter passed by on his way to Rome, accompanied by a friend called Priscus, to whom – so ecclesiastical history states – the apostle delegated the task of Christianising this bloodthirsty pagan goddess, which he must have done with some success, for around AD 44 he

94

became the first Bishop of Capua; but twenty years later the Capuans obviously found his message unexciting by comparison and threw him to the lions in the amphitheatre. The Diana Tifatina, however, had been exorcised for ever and had drifted away on her own sacrificial smoke towards the ceiling of the world, to join her friends the Cyclops and the Laestrygones and Minotaurs, and to ride her Pegasus down the sky and sing with the Sirens . . . Until, after the dark millennium of credulity's metamorphosis, a small Byzantine chapel emerged here in the eleventh century, decorated with paintings of weeping martyrs and etiolated saints, joyless images of a far sadder mythology.

There's a high bank behind St Angelo in Formis, and there I sit in the late-afternoon sun, gazing at its comfortable hindquarters; and then he emerges from a little house I'd hardly seen, carrying a bottle and two glasses.

'Did you find any treasure then?' and he sits down self-invited and pours the wine, unaware of my private thoughts – but then they're not private people. I shake my head and take the brimming glass from his old fingers to sip it gently. 'No, I didn't think you would. You need a plan; it's no good without one. But there's treasure up there, lots of it . . .' and his eyes grow dreamy, as if remembering some lost love of his youth. I sip again – cold and freshly bitter on a dry throat – but wishing for solitude, while he rumbles on quietly under his broad-rimmed beret which shadows the angles of his bony face with its piecrust of weathered skin and noble nose like a falcon's beak.

'I found some once; years ago when I was a boy . . .' and he pours both of us more wine. 'I remember this stranger coming, and taking four or five of us boys up the mountain to look; he had a piece of paper with him and made us pace out distances and measurements, and then we had to dig.'

A pause to savour an imagined nostalgia and to clutch at cobweb embellishments and to dream of an escaped Nirvana; and we sip more wine . . . 'We found a big stone and had to turn it over, and there it was. A huge jar full of gold coins,' and he expands his arms to embrace a colossus, then sighs away his long decades of dreamy anguish. 'And he took it out of the ground and walked off down the mountain, and we never saw him again . . .'

His voice has no bitterness, just soft resignation, as if long accustomed to failure or the unkind dealings of fate; and, as if to acknowledge his betrothal to defeat, he splashes out more glassfuls of wine. Here in his tales lie a few moments of vanished happiness, and we cool our greedy throats in unison to acknowledge our private humiliations. It's always been like that: a life of lost chances, a land of If only, an existence full of infinite possibilities, raked over by this oven of sun that cauterises hope.

A lizard darts at that very moment, spiderishly dancing on the baked earth by my feet then sucked into an unseen hole, which I finger for something to do, and dislodge a shard. I clean it slowly – useless crumb of an insoluble past – as he watches expressionless . . .

'*Tanta roba, tanta roba*' – So much stuff – creasing his cracked-leather face to a smile, 'my father found it everywhere ploughing up these fields,' and he looks round at the slopes high up behind us where breaths of air are combing the soft grass. 'We'd throw the old pots away, or break them up if they were big ones. We found a great slab of stone on a tomb one day, too heavy to move, so we smashed it up with a hammer.'

I don't need to know any more, but on he goes feeding my misery with his soup of old memories: 'It's everywhere, *signore*. Just two years ago some of the road fell in over there,' and he points out in front of us, 'and it was the roof of a temple that had caved in: everything was hollow underneath like a great cathedral, and so huge and dark you couldn't see down to the floor, just columns standing up in the darkness and the heads of statues and flashes of colour on the walls . . . *una cosa bellissima*. But we filled it in because we wanted the road mended quickly.' He drains his glass and pours us more, emptying the bottle. 'There's a temple underneath the Basilica of St Angelo too; no one's allowed to see it. They say it's "*pericoloso*" so they can keep people out; but I went down there years ago, into vaults and caverns with marble pillars and walls lined with jewels and solid gold . . .'

His dreams are his and mine are mine: of a little Sybaris crusted over by two thousand feeble years and baked into oblivion under my feet, where the bronzed and golden youth of Hellas passed lifetimes ago; and these then-wooded slopes were bowers of bird-song and dappled, twitch-eared deer and powder-white billing doves; and sun-ripe nereides coursed with unjointed limbs as if burnt on to the round bellies of Greek vases, or poised on lean pigtailed tiptoe with supplicant arms aloft (did you ever see a fat lady in Greek art? Unlikely) – all savaged by sun and secrecy and the crushed dust of inertia.

I have to leave him, and stumble down into the pitted roadway, turning to thank him. *'Buona fortuna,'* he calls, crouched on the bank like a loose-limbed old spider, eyes shaded under his cap, and with a little gesture we wave each other out of our separate lives.

Down the hill against the basilica there's a plaque on the wall: HERE ON I OCTOBER 1860 A HANDFUL OF VOLUNTEERS UNDER GIUSEPPE GARIBALDI DEFEATED A VAST BOURBON ARMY . . . A somewhat romanticised touch of hyperbole to describe the series of chaotic encounters and skirmishes that pass under the name of the Battle of Volturno. Garibaldi had at least ten thousand troops, albeit rather scattered (his general Bicio alone had over five thousand), while the Bourbons had probably twice as many – but lost their advantage through mismanagement, misjudgement and fatal hesitation over too extended an area between here and Caserta. The reference is probably to one of Garibaldi's own incidents, supposedly near this spot, when his coachman was killed and he and his band of followers were forced into hand-to-hand fighting with some Neapolitan soldiers who – according to Bandi and Ciampoli – soon fled. The rest of the day is history: the Unionists won, though whether through the efforts and genius of Garibaldi – *'Ses yeux dévorent l'ennemi, ils le consument . . . comme l'archange Michel piétant . . . sur le démon'* – or through the ineptitude of the Bourbon generals – 'more as a missed attempt than a lost battle' explained one of them afterwards – will always be debatable.

As usual it is the footnotes to it all that are the most diverting: English sailors from *HMS Hannibal* fighting on Garibaldi's side 'just for the fun'; not one single Neapolitan (according to Elliott) showing the remotest interest in the raging battle nearby; the meat for the wounded in hospital being taken home by the cooks to give their families; the donations being pocketed by the staff . . .

One has heard it all before somewhere. Were it not for the bloodshed and loss of life, there could not have been a more splendidly useless pantomime to celebrate the dying stages of Bourbonism and the hideous birth-pangs of a new Italy, rising to new heights of horror when the uninformed Garibaldi took it upon himself to govern Naples personally, causing riots and anarchy and more suffering, and then additional storms of protest when the French 'blackguard' Alexandre Dumas was put in charge of the excavations at Pompeii.

Here then was performed the unwanted and useless union of Italy, a weird genius' masterpiece of incompetence, the futile paper integration of the unrelated, the unsuited and the unmanageable.

EIGHT

Montesarchio

The Alban Gate, according to Pratilli, marks the road leading eastward; one takes it warily, for these are the first steps off the edge of the known world. The low bar of grey mountains far ahead adds a worrying chill, and its frown is an invitation to be afraid like Hannibal and to stay in Capua. All that is visible at first are the foothills, stretching their muddy outlines forward into the early light, then unfolding their curved backs in mild supplication, with fringes of villages marooned on distant spurs; shapeless patterns of plots, trees, casual orchards and ribbons of plough emerge, thrown randomly together, all swept at intervals by a wave of invisible sheep bells. Somewhere strewn under the old earth is Roman Caiata, and just north is the Palace of Caserta, Vanvitelli's unfinished symphony, stretching among the woods and hillsides as a royal retreat and hunting-box away from the hubbub of Naples, a slab of Bourbon pretentiousness to outshine Versailles where Sir William and Emma sometimes took their ease and where in 1945 the Germans surrendered Italy. Embedded among this serpentine growth of hills are twisted valleys competing for the honour of being the Caudine Forks; no one knows the exact site, though every peasant will provide a location with unerring certainty. As the sun reaches higher the line of mountains ahead turns blue-black against the sky, touched by uncertain haloes of cloud, waiting like a barrier to be challenged and breaking the horizon with jagged, iron-hard peaks.

As soon as possible I stumble off the road into a small valley running beside it, and amble along a verdant track lapped by swathes of luxurious grass, all edged by thickets of slim, silver-barked trees. Soon it curves away along a sylvan avenue, still vaguely heading eastwards, and having carelessly shrugged off the road it follows its own counsel and burrows resolutely towards Benevento. Then it spreads into a broad, tree-lined gorge with sides sweeping upward into dips of dead ground with hidden summits beyond; the peace is sudden and alarming, and the silence becomes heavy, save for the ghosts that whisper behind and before of 6,831 marching men.

For that, says Gibbon, was the size of a legion, accompanied by nearly as many attendant auxiliaries, and proudly led by a hand-picked cohort of 1,105 fully trained regular soldiers, one of them bearing aloft the imperial eagle. They marched to the sound of flutes, and doubtless to the din of their own breastplates, bucklers and greaves, each man carrying a spear or javelin and a sword as well as a spade or pickaxe for making camp and some cooking pots and personal provisions. This weight 'would oppress the delicacy of the modern soldier', he remarks gently, leaving us to imagine the marching conditions in the climates of Egypt or Greece or northern Gaul, adding that they were then expected to advance at a regular step 'in about six hours, near twenty miles'. Their training and discipline was such, he adds, that they were more frightened of their officers than they were of the enemy, and then unwittingly he helps solve the mystery of the Caudine Forks, by calculating that twenty thousand Roman soldiers could camp within a perfect square of sides seven hundred yards long.

But there's nothing here any more: just my own moments of cowardice and hesitation after the honeyed air of Capua, as I pause before grappling with the sour shadows of those distant mountains. I sit to rest beside the footpath – immediately applauded by an unruly playschool of cicadas excitedly rattling their diaphragms – as I watch the sun streaking its lines of silver dust through the leaves of the eucalyptus trees. Behind me, half hidden in the grass and matted with thorns and bushes, are stumps of an old building long left to decay, and ahead the valley is broken into haphazard patterns of carefully nurtured agricultural plots, just like a grandiose and teeming allotment, a confused carpet of anything that grows – corn, tomatoes, beans, vines . . . – all marked off in uneven rectangles.

And then an alien sound: the slow creaking of exhausted cart-wheels breaks through the warm dust, closer and closer, till round a corner inch two white oxen heaving a wooden cart blistered by years of sun and now piled high with faggots. They trudge past wearily, heads down and eyes dark with flies, ears twitching in futile protest; astride the load of sticks perches a grinning brown-faced farm boy, waving a greeting as he lets them find their own way home. His shrill voice sings out through the air, '*Cocceio, Villa Cocceio*,' and he waves again till they all trundle out of sight into a dip.

So this is where Maecenas went to play at tennis, a little way beyond Capua, while Horace doubtless sat in the shade, watching and toying with irreverent dreams. Nothing remains, save more bright ghosts in the imagination, and haunting echoes of their patrician laughter, still audible in the soft, breezy chuckles of the silver-green leaves tickling each other against the sky. Everything sinks into lazy peace; 'a sylvan theatre carpeted by deep verdure' said Eustace, where memory 'amuses the eye'. Then he fell in with a reverend gentleman who recounted the story of the Caudine Forks with such ferocity that he was obviously descended from 'the Samnites'; he even called them '*nostri Sanniti*'.

Midday, and unwilling to move further I doze in the sun, lulled into pantheistic dreams, and watch with one eye for the nymphs of this pagan place to peep from the trees and dance a light-veiled Bacchanal; perhaps they'll lure me with gentle laughter to shed my crust of clothes and join them in some wicked journey to the woods . . . The spires of the tree-tops tremble as if the Queen of the Night were fanning them on with her hot breath . . .

There's sudden movement: a fledgling scorpion darts from buried roots on to a point of rock beside me, and stands on guard with stiff tail arched in suspense, pulsing his black body in the heat. He has sprung from nowhere, disturbed by the crumbs of my *panino* or the flakes of cheese, and he tiptoes over the rock in indignant authority, billowing his little sail and shining with displeasure. Inches lower in the stubbly roots, dark spiders are coiled on springs and watch suspiciously from the grey hearts of matted webs. Cocceio . . . still a common enough name in Capua; Dr Antonio Cocceio was a friend of Isaac Newton who wrote a treatise on the tapeworm, and a preface to *Paradise Lost*. He also translated novels into Latin.

Later I walk on towards Montesarchio, spread in grey corrugations up a slope and on to a hilltop, and shadowed behind by the oppressive might of Monte Taburno. All the valley is vegetation-rich, overladen with vines, heavy with ripening harvests and splashed with cornucopias of blue and crimson flowers – everything filled with gorging insects. There are no birds, but the cicadas rattle on in their insistent frenzy as I pass, and poised on a spur to the left are the dusty white houses of Bonea, crumbling in the sun as if ready to tumble into the valley. Then at last the road rises towards Montesarchio, a long path edged by rocks till the rough houses draw closer. Beyond them stand the pinnacles of two castles, hunched like dark vultures skulking on the same branch. Gingerly the habitation starts, as hens peck warily in the dust by tumbled walls, and the grass path turns to uneven stone, and tousled-haired children run from the shadows bare under their smocks. Further on there are open doorways ringed with crazed plaster, where bent women crouch in the shade knitting quietly with lowered heads or noiselessly moving their walnut fingers over hand-held looms.

I climb on in the heat towards the castles, silent eyes following, hearing the beaded curtaining stir softly to right and left, till I reach the untidy plateau of dusty earth where a single deserted tower perches baking in the sun on the edge of a precipice. The door is open, and stone stairs spiral up in the half-dark past numbered metal doors, and over Number 9 hangs a faded plaque: HERE CARLO POERIO LAY IN CHAINS, DREAMING OF THE DESTINY OF A SUFFERING ITALY. A little too sensational perhaps, although his forced contemplations in Montesarchio did last for five years – all part of his punishment for being a leading liberal agitator against Ferdinand towards the close of the Bourbon dynasty, which earned him a sentence of twenty-five years in chains. In fact he was a persistent offender, and this was his fourth term in prison for subversion. However, he was also a friend of Mr Gladstone, who became his champion, and spent so much time being outraged by Neapolitan poverty – rather than by Dickensian London – that he had to be put firmly in his place by Prince Schwarzenberg for political interference. Such are the tortuous machinations of history; Nelson had championed the Bourbons against the French, Gladstone considered them an abomination. One wonders what Carlo Poerio would think now of his Italian dream were he to return. Would his restless spirit want to beat on, or would it prefer to be borne back ceaselessly into the past?

My arrival has been noticed, and an ill-shaven man is hurrying towards me, full of confident authority, along the ridge. It must be the *guardiano*, for he is obviously on important business: his stride is urgent and his braces are bared like raised hackles. What do I want? he demands. I'm just looking, I tell him. Do I have a ticket? No. Where is my car? I'm afraid I don't have one; I walked. This confuses him and he rubs his chin to fill the pause, then hunches his shoulders and peers down the hill suspiciously . . . Where have I come from? England. Ah, England? London? A rich country. No wonder England won the war; Italy is too poor to win wars ... He pauses again, a little regretfully this time, and taps the side of his trousers as if feeling for something in the pockets. Do I happen to have a cigarette? ...

He is a very minor official, somewhere below the first rung of authority's ladder, but with dangerous potential nevertheless and to be placated. Earlier travellers met the species round every corner – cantankerous investigators of passports, luggage, financial status, bills of health, entry and exit certificates, travel passes – and either lost their tempers with them, like Smollett, or bribed them to go away. The key to it all is, of course, their love of power: allow them this small satisfaction and you're safe; Barzini saw it and so did Carlo Levi stranded at Eboli, and even the great southerner Lampedusa knew how the greed for power obsessed them, and how at ground level it multiplied into a thousand petty tyrannies. That and the endless striving for effect.

It is wisest therefore to give in gracefully and to allow a few moments of prima-donna satisfaction, rather than to take up arms against a national characteristic; so I find the cigarettes and see his lungs swell in inhalations of gratitude, and I accept his offer of a guided tour of the castle.

It's a few yards away at the other end of the rough summit, this single tower, obviously an outpost of observation, so we walk towards it – a gaunt, derelict building with cracks in the walls, one end bastardised into a farm and another part of it, he says, closed off as a convent. This is probably a lie; it is more likely an excuse for not wishing to exhaust himself by showing me everything, plus the hope that I will respect him more for his additional position as guard and manager to a holy sisterhood. He goes in a doorway, kicking straw aside and chasing hens, then the next room is for pigs, and in another there are goats, and along the stone passage a donkey is fettered – none of which disturbs him, for the first showpiece is just round the corner. He calls it his 'museum' – in reality an emporium of miscellaneous fragments from the fields roundabout which he considers related to archaeology or history, and which he collects from the farmers under threat of reporting them for tomb-robbing. The dirty shelves are heaped with them, filling the old vegetable pantry where some illiterate scullion once skinned hares or tore the tops off vegetables, and which is now his 'laboratorio archeologico'. He fondles the items at random – pot-handles, urn bases, halves of lamps, clay weights – reverently murmuring, 'Bello, antico,' as he picks out a piece of glass or a fraction of figured bowl from the indescribable mess to convince me of its rarity. On a top shelf high above the thousand useless fragments are some old bottles and four steel helmets almost invisible under dust – two iron-grey and two khaki.

As I survey the scattering of debris he begs to retire for a moment, then minutes later re-emerges in his proper guardiano uniform, an amazing spectacle taken straight from some Gilbert and Sullivan nightmare: a bright blue tunic, gold sleeves laced with crimson braid, spotted with white buttons, some of it tucked into his faded black trousers held in position by an old leather belt and a dangling revolver holster. He has donned it all in my honour, and for the tour of the castle. I listen for fanfares but instead have to negotiate more miasmas of liquidly complaining straw and the wrath of fleeing chickens till we eventually emerge at a flight of stairs and hear our own footsteps echoing upward on the empty stone. All is vast and desolate: cavernous rooms connect with cavernous rooms, cold and peeling with grey pock-marked walls and sad coats of arms glowering uselessly over fireplaces; vaulted ceilings with faded paint stretching up to pathetically bulbous finials; the floors slabbed with cold grey stone; and all the windows cracked or glassless. It echoes on in endless hopelessness.

Then for a moment we balance together on a rotting balcony and stare at the ragged quilt of roof-tops below, and beyond them the uneven switchback of hills and valleys disappearing back towards Capua. He mutters something about faded greatness, his voice rich with satisfaction that the aristocracy – and therefore vicious inequality – no longer exists, and then tells me that Montesarchio was once Mons Arcis, and before that Mons Herculis, and long before that was called Guaria, but it disappeared in a huge flood like Atlantis, which must be true because they've found the remains of prehistoric monsters.* But he is rambling on again, about international conventions of archaeologists held here every year, and how he tells them the real story of Montesarchio and why the Samnites buried their dead with the feet pointing to the east, and is about to share this potent secret with me when he finds he has quite forgotten his cigarettes. Could I possibly oblige? He thinks he must have left them in the museum among all those Roman remains ... and perhaps I would like to accept a little memento later in exchange – a ring perhaps or some old coins or a small votive statue – and now of course I must join him for a drink ...

The old fool is a perfect artist, a most consummate performer; and in no time I am paraded like a prize lion by its ringmaster as we cross the dusty expanse towards a distant bar sign; and from somewhere he has even produced a gold-topped cane to salute his admirers. Adroitly he pauses to greet one, just long enough to ensure I reach the counter ahead of him, then he pats his pockets again ruefully and soon inhales in deep gratitude and bemoans the frantic pace of our strenuous lives ... 'Just to think, dear professor, I must stay up half the night labelling all those remains ready

---

* Swinburne had a similar opinion, curiously enough, and guessed that the whole valley below had once been the crater of a large volcano which had later turned into a huge lake.

for sending to Benevento Museum, 644 pieces to be done by the morning, and each one priceless.' His eyes start to water with emotion ... Which was nicest do you think – that lamp or the little head or the Roman earrings? Perhaps in England they'd appreciate a souvenir from Montesarchio – these coins possibly? And a purse appears, dragged from the inner linings of his tunic, spilling its contents along the bar – denarii, ases, serstii and drachmae – pinpricks of history, rolling towards unwanted infinity.

Later I move away down the hill again, past the staggered and peeling houses full of silent women, and along tilted streets broken only by movements of half-hearted animals. The castle is tumbling and the town is wretched, said Keppel Craven as long ago as 1820, just as Carlo Poerio's hopeless idealism was gathering strength. A quiet spur of land reaches out beyond some buildings like a lip, and as the sun starts to weaken I sit and look out over the valley towards Monte Taburno sinking into an evening crouch, clutching her brood of young hills round her. The gaunt summit scowls over everything, guarding its deep secrets, twenty-five centuries old, of Appian travellers trudging east or south towards Magna Graecia, or muttering armies camped round glowing fires, or those scheming Samnite shepherds telling the Roman legions of the best short cut through the valley towards the relief of Lucera. It was all over very quickly: a carefully planned misdirection of thirty thousand soldiers into a cul-de-sac, then the entrance blocked, and finally the emergence of a vast Samnite army on the heights above, surveying their easy prey. It should have been a massacre; but the more gracious southern tribesmen were used to a certain measure of reasonable coexistence with their neighbours and just gloated over them for two days, so tightly packed they could barely move; then sent the generals crawling back to Capua and Rome with humiliating messages and offers of peace. They should have known better. The infant Roman Republic had already decided that progress required more ruthless and bloody tactics than olive branches; the hand of friendship was refused, and swift to avenge their shame they redoubled their efforts to eliminate this nucleus of turbulent southerners by politic alliances with the surrounding Lucani, Vestini and Frentani. Remorselessly the Samnite territories were encircled and the people slaughtered, and within twenty years of the mortifying incident at the Caudine Forks the Romans had crushed them and were spreading their power over Italy like spilt ink.

And no one knows precisely where this simple trap was sprung or which valley it was that encased a whole Roman army. It has seized the imagination ever since Livy's account, and has been earnestly plotted by Cluverius, Romanelli, Gandy and a hundred others. Their results are inconclusive, their guesses hampered by the shift of earthquakes and by erosion and the quixotically errant beds of streams; thus the event has disappeared for ever into the mythology of the mountains, where it still rests, mysterious and unopposed, a dark footnote to history known only to the stones.

Evening comes slowly, as pinpoints of light start to waver through the autumn haze like sleepy glow-worms opening a weary eye; and one or two threads of smoke seep quietly upwards from chimneys; and the pallor of the sky slips towards hungry darkness, where over towards Benevento the last arrowheads of light fade against the far-off wall of hard-backed hills. An early star glimmers in soft surprise and tries to withdraw again for taking the night stage too soon; the tuneless sound of sheep bells mutters its way closer, till a trotting herd of bed-bound beasts rumbles over the ridge and heads happily for home, all shaking their heads wisely and swinging their swollen udders in excitement as they ripple along the paths like a passing wave. Outlined behind comes the biblical shape of a stooping shepherd, with stringed trousers and a staff digging at the soil, and he mutters a greeting as the light slides inexorably to darkness, while his rambling herd disappears through gaps in walls or into open doorways, to be sucked warmly into the womb of Montesarchio for the night.

Tomorrow will see the last few miles to Benevento, and then the long journey south into a land crushed by an unkind history. I shiver and look back, searching for the warm Tyrrhenian, but it has long gone – sunk far beyond Capua – and the purple topsails of the laden corn ships are now only a dream. Leagues ahead lies the lazy Adriatic and the Trajan route to Brindisi down the coast; but mine is another road, a rough one south to the Ionian, where gentle seas lap at the old Hellenic shore, and the faded opulence of Taras, Sybaris and Metapontum groans like a partly unearthed skeleton, and where the waves still manage to smile and sparkle as they patiently try to comfort this 'crumbling piece of land between two seas'.

NINE

Benevento 1

There should be the remains of three Roman bridges along the road between Montesarchio and Benevento. According to Swinburne, confidently trotting this way in 1779 and protected by a cavalry escort to lessen the threat of brigands, they were 'built of immense blocks of stone' and the road was 'very fine'. Thirty-five years later Eustace saw only two Roman bridges, but five years after that, in 1820, Keppel Craven counted three again. It will be interesting to see what remains today.

The sun wastes no time with a seductive welcome, but soon starts to punish with a merciless heat; 'the true ruler of the south', said the author of *The Leopard*. The hills have slipped behind, and with that abrupt change of landscape that only happens near the Mediterranean, the fecund valley teeming with generative power has flattened out into baked open fields and a plain of dry upturned earth. Harsh in the cleanness of morning light, the land ahead wavers in variegated shades of scorched browns and fading dehydrated greens, and in the windless air sweat trails off my eyelids. In the wide distance, one skeletal tree shimmers through the heat; when I reach it there is an old man stretching upward for the last half-dead leaves to give his donkey, and behind them an old stonework grotto guarding a small cave of tempting water. '*Bevi, bevi,*' he says with rustic generosity, but I pause a moment, having just seen the dart of a tiny fish deep down – and doubtless there are other aquatic invaders crawling over those cool stones. To hell with it! Not far away a thirsty Swinburne had to hold the tadpoles back with a knife to prevent the 'little frogs' from slipping down his throat. It's magically cool, running its rivers of ice into my chest; now I've endured the initiation the old man sits me by him on the lip of grey rock and unwraps rolls of cloth packets he has taken from the bags straddled over the rump of his donkey. LUGEBANT HIC DIBUTIS IN VIVARIIS NYMPHAE ... 1679 reads a faded inscription above us as he brings out a long stick of bread, red weals of uncooked ham and a dozen tomatoes, then his own bottle of pale yellow wine, while I contribute my poor packet of crumbled biscuits from Montesarchio. 'How are things in England?' It's always the same question, prompted by that childish dream that any place in the world other than this must be some sort of heaven. But as soon as I start to talk about factories and London and Welsh coalfields and the steep pine forests of Scotland, his eyes glaze and he stares round us at the brown expanse of earth: '*La terra è la madre di tutto,*' he says quietly.

Our chewing over, he leads me along a gully between ridges of land till just ahead gleams a ribbon of river water, sluggish against the far bank, and beyond it the distant roofs of Benevento merge against the curving shoulders of land in the outlined form of a crouching animal. 'You can cross further up,' he tells me, 'where it's shallow but faster'; he leads me patiently along the bank to the ford. From the rush of rippling water the enormous severed trunks of a Roman bridge rear in massive and sad futility, but he barely notices them, bending to wash himself in the shallows. They were used by the soldiers in the war, he says, '*per precisare i canoni*', then waves as I start to wade across, cooled instantly by the swirling water as it laps urgently up my thighs and bends me against the current. As I reach the other bank he shouts a final message – lost in sounds of rushing water – and now the protesting squelch of the Calore is groaning liquidly inside my boots.

Just to the west of Benevento the river completes a loop of 360 degrees, which I discover too late; I now have to cross it again, whereas I needn't have crossed it at all.

Presumably there was a second Roman bridge somewhere over the other half of the loop, though the third one remains a mystery. This time the river is more amicable, the water gentler, pierced by dark rocks, the banks wide and covered in trees and bushes arcing across in protection; then as it slides towards the town I hear the excited cries of children.

I find them a mile ahead, swimming and splashing in the shallows, urged into extra excesses of jollity by my approach, cavorting like pink and brown seal pups and flailing their uninhibited limbs in chubby susurations of *putti* nakedness, racing each other off the bank into the shaded pools in wild water-dances, veiled by delicate fans of spray. Beyond them and nearer the town some older, more serious boys are fishing intently, with unwieldy lengths of cane that dangle thin lines into the water, baited with the remains of wingless and pop-eyed bluebottles. I wait to see what luckless fish it is inhabiting these depths that possesses such a minute brain and enormous appetite, but little moves except a pile of permanently grounded, limping, leg-waving flies beside the nearest boy – all of which, he tells me, he collected in the kitchen this morning. A few yards on by a pool of deep water I hear an insistent but irregular 'plop', as if nuts or storm drops were falling from the trees, but the sky is clear and open overhead, while the phantom sound continues with invisible crispness and not a single ripple. I watch perplexed till I see the answer. Armies of tiny green frogs are squatting among the stones then leaping with Olympic accuracy and kingfisher speed into the water, and so fine is their trajectory that they slice it like a knife-blade; nothing moves; just a 'ping' of crystal to break the silence.

I climb up banks and hillocks towards a stone bridge and am suddenly in teatime Benevento, straight from a sylvan stream into a mêlée of din, breathing the dry dust of cars and hearing the agonised song of hot tyres on roads, surrounded by paper-hatted workmen sitting in pools of sun on the pavement. It's a cauldron of exuberance where everything in life must be made to sparkle, says Barzini, and so it does. Here on the bridge everything happens at once, and it all floats in the heat against the pale brown stone of buildings.

Benevento is flat and sun-baked, caught in a low circle of hills, and being a gateway to the south has been heavily fought for and deeply scarred, and never once fully mended. No single building seems brother or cousin to the next, no street seems straight or related to its neighbour, no shapes or angles or skylines are consistent. It has suffered two thousand years of resourceful barnacle additions and reconstruction as and when it took anybody's fancy, since the days it was called Maleventum – on account of that contagion of the south, malaria. The Roman, the Norman, the Angevin tumble together and interlace in garish patterns; proud marble slabs of empire are patched into everyday house walls; and gracious Renaissance balconies are cemented solid.

I wander into the first square among untidy lines of long-nosed blue buses – hissing and grunting and jostling like dust-caked farm animals at a stall – all bearing competitive names: Zeppieri, Marozzi, Segai, Perotti, Zamparella, Cam. Now and then one of them roars away in a cloud of smoke, pushing the crowds back with its fustian bow-wave of sound. Exotic destinations hang on shabby labels – Avellino, Salerno, Campobasso, Foggia, Potenza, Sant' Agata, Bari . . . Is there anywhere one can't go to from Benevento? And it has always been the same, for at least six roads led out from here in the days of imperial Rome: the Appia to east and west, the Latina northwards to Rome, the Egnazia to the coast via Equus Tuticus, the Trajana to Canosa, and yet another to Avellino. It was the hub of the wheel that pushed the legions south into Africa and east beyond Palestine, and later was the Lombard capital of south Italy, later still the site of the treacherous battle that ended the Hohenstaufen rule and extinguished its 'nest of vipers'. More recently, it was damaged by Allied bombs in the war, including at least one direct hit on the thirteenth-century cathedral, almost destroying the famous bronze doors made up of seventy-two lavishly decorated panels of stories from the Old and New Testaments. Local gossip has it that the damage needn't have been nearly so bad if the bishop hadn't allowed the powerful brewing family of Alberti to hide thousands of gallons of their vicious yellow Strega liqueur in the cathedral vaults – which in the event proved so highly flammable that the resultant inferno took days to put out.

A helpful crowd gathers the moment I ask about a hotel, and with nods and winks suggests that I can get considerably more than bed and breakfast for four pounds a night at the brand-new Jolly, as Count Marzotto has arranged for two young ladies to be in permanent residence as part of the inducement to northerners to venture south. The count is apparently opening a string of similar establishments at strategic points throughout Calabria and Basilicata prior to the planned arrival of the motorways. I must remember that for another time. Eventually I fade away into the back streets, followed by jovial innuendos as to whether I qualify as *una persona potente* or not, till I come across a more humble, string-beaded door which announces it is a taverna. The rest is simplicity itself; for of all improbabilities Gildo, the owner, once lived in Glasgow for fifteen years and, as soon as he has seen my *documenti* and is sure I'm not German, starts to scratch into his Glaswegian memory for long-forgotten sounds – 'Och aye', 'Well noo', 'I dinna ken' – which tumble out proudly, rich with strange distortions of music-hall Italian, while his round wife beams with uncomprehending delight, and a trio of graceful young faces peers out from behind a curtain to watch in wide-eyed astonishment at such an outrageous means of communication. These are his daughters, sylph children radiant and miraculous with tantalising coal-black eyes, softer than Landseer animals, marooned in this desolate town of dust and war damage and exuding that untouchable warmth and welcome of soft angora. Even Ramage might have lingered here, caught only once by bewitching glances and having to hurry on; as for Stendhal, one hates to think what he might have done in a country he declared was only fit for making delicious love in . . .

Upstairs there is a clean room and a trickle of running water from a tap, and the grime of miles gurgles away down a friendly drain. Supper soon follows in a small tableclothed dining-room that slowly fills with comfortably expansive and habitual locals who want to drink or talk or play cards. Conversation stops each time Gildo comes over to speak to me, all alert to the alien sounds, while the *signora* eavesdrops with unashamed pride and the three girls eye me, first with extraterrestrial apprehension and then with feline jealousy in their blushing eagerness to serve me first. Maria is twenty perhaps, slender and dark-haired, assessing the customers with distant and knowing smiles and already feigning a wise and firm-breasted adulthood. 'With what exuberance they fill the grasp,' said the Grand Tourist in his diary, amazed by their seeming urge for procreation. Lydia is fifteen, with quick bright eyes that are easily troubled, nimble and soft-faced and full of smooth movements as she crosses the room, her expression increasingly aware of matters beyond innocence. And Rosa, the laughing girl-child of twelve with the twist of the kitten still in her tiny hips, full of that much-maligned poet's 'passionate purity', and the unwanton freshness that is always eager to please.

I ask Gildo about thrushes and he scratches his head, but as soon as I mention Horace the whole room livens into an unrehearsed Verdi chorus: *'Orazio, Orazio,'* as if he passed through only last week, and they laugh about the Taverna di Orazio next to Trajan's Arch in the square and say thrushes only come to Benevento in winter. Conversation sweeps like a gale across a loch, from the making of haggis to the sweet, nutty biscuits of Benevento, from the fortunes of Glasgow Rangers to the American Army deserters still hiding in the mountains, from the tartan kilts he has carefully wrapped in a drawer upstairs for the girls and which they never wear to the dance of the Benevento witches on Saturday nights. Imperceptibly the girls join hands with a quiet smile and bend their knees as if about to start a Greek *sirtaki*, then move their hips in cautious rhythm: '*Sotto l'acqua e sotto 'l vento,*' they chant, '*sotto le noci di Benevento . . .*' fading the words away nervously under their breaths lest the Devil himself should suddenly appear, horned and cloven-hoofed, to spirit them away over the roof-tops; and I see the timid gleam of fear in Rosa's eyes as she glances up at her sisters for reassurance.

'There's a *festa* tonight,' says Gildo. 'Go up and see it with the girls. It's St Bartholomew, one of the twelve; his bones are in the cathedral. Anyway,' he laughs, 'they were, before the *bombardamento*. It's a bit like the Edinburgh Tattoo . . . brmm, brmm . . .' and he flaps his elbows to play imaginary bagpipes and looks excruciating. Tonight there'll be a band from Bari – they won a national competition last year – and there'll be fireworks and a procession and roundabouts for children, and there'll be a big bonfire and dancing. He tries to remember how to toss the caber and runs half-way across the room clutching his bowels, and everyone laughs. The room fills with imaginative suggestions: clowns on stilts, Negroes who breathe fire, gas-filled balloons, a television crew from RAI, perhaps a lion from the zoo at Foggia, and certainly the latest Ferrari on a transporter. Maria spurns it all with superior dignity, but Lydia's eyes shine, and Rosa jumps up and down with excitement, and they beg me to go. A few moments are

allowed for cleaning up before I am escorted into the road
and towards the orange glow of the town centre, the air
already awash with sounds of competing loudspeakers, the
growing hubbub of throaty excitement, ululating
crescendos of shouts mixed with surges of music.

It's a joyous *manifestazione* to relieve the dismal monotony of earthly life, a most brilliant way of raising the spirits
from impenetrable gloom and each day's ugliness and suffering, and of making the heart beat faster for a few trivial
hours. The gossamer crust of Nazareth floats over the vital
merriment of all things pagan, and some profane and laughing deity lies under this sacred topsoil, deeper than any St
Bartholomew, watching its old pandemonium being stifled
into dull sobriety – for nowhere are the old gods so close to
the surface as they are in south Italy, and nowhere have
fanatics spilt such rivers of blood for what should or should
not be believed; and nowhere have despotic lords clamped
their iron censorship so often over primal ebullience, only
to find it bubbling out through the cracks like the irrepressible effervescence of the Phlegrean Fields. Ramage knew it:
'It is in these remote parts of Italy that the customs of their
Pagan ancestors have been preserved in their greatest
purity,' he said. And Emerson had his opinions too: 'There
is no true majesty in all this millinery and imbecility.'

We move through a line of swaying women, chanting and
bearing candles, and into the path of slow-moving cars
trumpeting megaphone messages between blasts of music –
'*Cittadini . . . Beneventani . . . operai . . .*' – as silver rockets
splash the sky with tumbling stars, and boys blow hooters
and whistles at pleased, head-tossing girls, and older youths
bawl exorbitant greetings from across the road. A single
Vespa, smothered in five well-balanced bodies, strains to
complete its epileptic wriggle through the press of spectators by bleating its anguished horn; and a scattered
regiment of roundabouts all jangle into dizzy life, hurling

excited children on long journeys of coloured circles, their ecstatic cries drowning Modugno's yells of 'Volare, volare . . .' Less lucky babies trip along the cobbles, bewildered at knee height, shining in pin-fresh clothes as they cling to the hands of giant parents. Then more sky-flying explosions of fireworks, and a friendly bear on a chain sitting on a rostrum and turning his brown face with agile bulkiness to catch apples and buns thrown by a half-teasing circle of watchers. A trio of earnestly muttering priests passes in uniform, eyes down or nodding curtly at anonymous pas-sers-by; then the road is blocked by a half-dressed band-stand, gloriously caught in dishabille but already an ant-hill of arriving musicians splendid in crimson uniforms and all bending to greet old friends, popping from seat to seat in trial, or delivering quick virtuosi solos. We stop to watch, Rosa holding my hand in excitement, our nostrils filling with the sweet scent of boiling toffee, as two absorbed *carabinieri*, both revolver-hipped, pause beside us. Then at least half the agitating band bursts suddenly into life, silencing its immediate neighbours and ignoring a dozen or so skew-capped members still tumbling over chairs to reach their instruments: martial airs from *Cavalleria Rusticana* gather momentum and charge at the crowd like disorgan-ised cavalry. The whole world smiles, for at last all is noise and happiness – St Bartholomew is enjoying another massacre.

Lydia tugs my arm, urging me away across the square to where she has caught the strains of other music. We pass lighted stalls of vegetables and tents full of old clothes, barrows loaded with sweets and all shapes of cheese, open-backed trucks with noisy vendors whipping up balls of candy floss and selling plastic virgins and slabs of *tortorella* as well as photographs of Marilyn Monroe – all watched by a hundred hypnotised eyes deliberating the festive temp-tations and the voluble demonstrations of soap powder.

Grey television screens flicker somewhere among the rau-
cous cries, and there's an urgent throb of rock and roll
coming from behind a tent; a group of teenagers stands by a
lorry bathed in flashing lights and huge pictures of James
Dean and Elvis Presley, and the air is alive with nasal
American screams and pumping guitars. The girls' eyes
shine with magic at this dreamland vision of the New
World with such a tantalising culture to stir the blood, and
Rosa's hand squeezes mine as she looks up. Do you really
belong to that spell-binding land of miracles so far away?
her eyes ask. Do you really?

Benevento is falling down. Or it gives that impression – as
if all its efforts to stand were no longer worthwhile, and it
would be happier to collapse from exhaustion and be mummified under suffocating dust. Nothing is finished, just a
hundred projects started, threads of spiderwork scaffolding
still perched on the rubble of war, open cracks and gaps in
buildings still tilting from forgotten earthquakes, and the
seeming devastation of Pyrrhus' elephants when they were
routed here and turned on their leaders, and then Rome
changed the ill-wind name of Maleventum to the fresher
breezes of Beneventum.

At the eastern end squats the massive Arch of Trajan
which they call the Porta Aurea, square and dominant,
wrinkled by a hundred detailed carvings to show the emperors' triumphant passage through history, and said to be the
finest Roman arch in Christendom. It's the golden gate to
the riches of the east, and monstrously lords it over the
prettified exteriors of eighteenth-century palaces nearby.
Early prints show it shrouded in branches with mud-bricked
hovels built against it – just part of the wall, a simple hole
into the town; today it's a convenient surface for siesta-
time football, where shirtless workmen skid and leap
among eager youths, banging the rebounding leather con-
stantly against the worn faces of gods and chariot parades

of victory. A mile away at the new, northern end is the arrogant sweep of Mussolini's Viale dei Principi, wide enough for the victory parades that never happened, reaching from the railway station to the centre of the town and ominously uncluttered – a desolate avenue of tree-lined pavements and hopeful bars where sun-glassed voyeurs sit at tables in the shade for hours on end to watch the girls getting off the trains.

Somewhere at the centre was Roman Benevento, built in a convenient pocket between the Calore and Sabato Rivers, where Nero often came and Septimus Severus, and where Hadrian and Caracalla had a theatre built to seat twenty thousand spectators. Some of it is still there – enriched by the usual tracery of scaffolding, blossoming a bed of dry weeds in the centre, a few houses leaning on it for support – and, preoccupied among the weeds, a small boy kicking at pebbles. There's an underground passage, he tells me, that goes from here all the way to Rome. He knows where the entrance is, but has never dared go in because people say it's full of wild animals left behind by the Romans when they used to kill Christians. My curiosity intrigues him: I am something out of the ordinary and a receptive audience, so he follows me towards the cathedral, along thin slices of alleys never touched by the sun which take labyrinthine twists under medieval arches till we reach daylight again, where groups of men are wearily dismantling last night's *festa*, and a few others are trailing up the cathedral's steps to study an official announcement. It is in forceful coal-black letters from the Bishopric of Benevento, and gives notice that the socio-political problems of Italy cannot be considered separately from religion, and as all Marxist ideologies are openly anti-Christian no one should collaborate with them or even with the socialists. The audience is singularly unimpressed and mutters a few blasphemous indecencies before turning away with wry smiles and a fresh touch of cynicism to add to what exists

already. The stifler of intellectual liberty, Revel called the Italian church, the destroyer of 'scientific curiosity, love of beauty [and] extreme interest in ideas', making his book a worthy addition to the Vatican index of prohibited reading.*
But then Addison should be there too, and Forsyth, and Maria Graham, and Samuel Rogers, and Smollett, and their own Danilo Dolci and Cardinal Contarini, and Garibaldi, and Il Duce himself – they all said much the same thing and even worse; even Barzini called St Peter's 'God's own holy playhouse'. And as for Pius II . . .

How easily one forgets as one reaches for the great unknown: 'Nel mezzo del cammin di nostra vita' – at the half-way house of life. One forgets how demurely the holy fathers tolerated Fascism and Nazism, who now hold forth angrily about anything that is vaguely unacceptable while their golden coffers flow with extorted millions and their faithful crawl in the streets dying of hunger in rabbitly increasing numbers. One forgets too the blatant nepotism, and the thousands of mass murders committed in the name of Christ. Even here at Benevento a vile and rapacious end was put to the Hohenstaufen empire by a beleaguered Pope Clement IV, who promised Charles of Anjou the whole of south Italy if he would only defeat Frederick's son, Manfred, and then exterminate the entire family. 'Allès e dit moi à le Sultam de Nocere,' was the message sent by Charles to the new emperor before the battle, 'hoggi metterai lui en enfers, o il mettar moi em paradis' – Go, and tell the Sultan of Nocera from me that today I will send him to hell, or he will send me to Paradise – and he then did exactly as the Pope had asked, by defeating him at Benevento, throwing his wife into prison, then publicly beheading his fourteen-year-old brother in Naples, and finally incarcerating his son in the dungeons of Castel dell' Ovo for fifty-two years until

* This is the *Index Librorum Prohibitorum*, which went out of use in 1966.

he died. So ended that particular Teutonic challenge to the papacy, after which the pontiff told Charles to burn 'the putrid carcass of that most poisonous man' and to scatter his ashes to the wind, though no one knows if it actually happened. A more charitable version has it that his naked body was left here by the Ponte Leproso and then gradually buried under a pile of stones thrown at it by the victorious French soldiers as they passed. Benevento's own story is that one of the inhabitants carried his body through the streets on his donkey crying, 'Who wants Manfred?' but received no answer.

That was in 1266, when King Henry of England was offered the same inducement but regretted he was otherwise engaged – since when the Vatican has not been over-zealous in its care of its southern flock, tending to regard that particular pasture as something akin to a distant and worthless estate it had the misfortune to inherit, but a useful land mass to bargain with on occasions. Such machinations of papal politics are of little concern to Gildo; in the face of any such manipulations he is quietly and phlegmatically wise enough to lower his head behind the comfortable rampart of an old proberb: 'Quando cantano troppi galli, non fa mai giorno' – which can be roughly translated as When too many cocks crow, dawn never comes. For Maria, however, it is altogether different: she belongs to a younger, less quiescent breed, and her eyes blaze in fury at the thought of the threat of blackmail on the cathedral door; she says that since she was asked at confession whom she voted for in the last elections she has sworn never to go to mass again. She knows too of a bank clerk who hesitated to cash a large cheque for a visiting priest without some formal proof of identify, the result of his caution being that two days later he was out of a job. The whole dining-room starts to mutter sympathetically with the vehemence of an awakening volcano and everyone talks at once, louder than anyone else, each with his or her own story of clerical misbehaviour; then the eruption disintegrates rapidly into Rabelaisian bawdy or eulogies of self-congratulation for having such temperaments that render them secularly, sacredly and sexually ungovernable.

I fear things are getting out of hand when extremes of coarse and vainglorious uproar are reached, and there are dextrous verbal leaps from males being *caldissimi* to the merits and demerits of using contraceptives whatever the Pope may say ('What decent woman wants meat covered in pastry?'). Then on to today's Fascists wearing their black shirts down to their ankles, and how many children have already been sired by the young priest at Ariano. But perhaps I am over-anxious: Maria is laughing and blushing prettily at the earthy badinage, Lydia is listening with careful disdain and rippling her young nose like a rabbit investigating a doubtful lettuce, while Rosa is busy clearing plates and seems oblivious to everything. Or is she? She brings me a bowl of fruit and most definitely winks. I fear I may be becoming decorously over-sensitive, for is there not a proverb in these parts that '*Una serva Calabrese più ama far un figlio che un bucato*' – A southern girl would rather make a baby than do the washing? And didn't Levi see it as he walked round the village for days as a prisoner, the women eyeing his trousers with X-ray glances, measuring the size of his virility? So perhaps our virtue is still our greatest affectation after all.

TEN

Benevento 2

I explore the eastern outskirts afterwards, risking the furnace of the sun as it scalds the panting streets, where prostrate bodies lie in angles of shade with heads covered in old newspapers, all fast asleep. Not far beyond his arch, Trajan's dusty road pushes out towards the sea through dry unforgiving hills which were once wooded and pastured, and where giant trees used to cast their protective shadows against the calcifying heat, where streams ran down the valleys and joyful birds swooped and sang in the waving branches. Once a paradise fit for epic poets, plunder, greed and wanton vandalism have turned it into a bulging desert of desolation, where skeletal limbs of dead earth curve corpse-like into the distance. Down an unused path obscured by dry brambles, lumps of old Rome sulk among a scattering of wild bushes, passively draped in a careless négligé of branches to which nature has added her own sad joke from time to time by bringing floods, famines and earthquakes.

A hammer is beating not far away, and round a corner I find a *capo*, sitting in the shade of a rock supping his bottle of wine which he holds out to me as I pass: '*Vuol' favorire?*' He's the overseer of a house being built by four workmen, each of them recently married, and when it is complete there will be four rooms – one for each family – with a communal tap and a lavatory in a passage outside. The possibility of congestion doesn't cross his mind: what on earth would they do with two rooms? he wonders; and anyway, apart from not being able to afford such luxury, they are happiest when herded together in a small space – it makes for safety, and for complicity and fellow feeling. A most accurate observation, one that has been commented on by many a perplexed traveller on finding the Italians' active dislike of space an impenetrable mystery – forgetting that in a land boiling with anger, isolation means vulnerability, and the real purpose of forming a compacted group is protection and a bulwark against outside interference and disorder. In Italy, those who stand alone are lost.

Fortunately, we northerners have largely dispensed with such primitive prerequisites; we guard our privacy jealously and seldom suffer the tumult of three generations confined in a small rectangular space pooling experiences from dawn till dusk, and then sharing in each other's night-life. Opportunities for Puritan ethics hardly exist when the only chance of solitude is to draw a string of blankets or curtains across part of the room, thereby allowing a sick child to sleep, a new baby to be born, or a grey and skeletal grandmother to expire without fuss. One room is the quintessential element of their existence, the epicentre of life and death; all the peripheries can go on out of doors.

The *capo* is effusive: wine has loosened his tongue and he has simple solutions for everything. The afternoon sun has also heated his imagination, for when I mention a Roman poet who may have stopped to have a meal here some two thousand years ago, he is certain he knows the exact spot, though he rather thinks the poet may also have been a giant. 'It so happens that there's a big cave further along the path,' he explains, 'where they've found lots of human bones buried, together with the remains of an enormous cauldron; and that's because a giant used to live there who offered hospitality to passing travellers, and then killed them and cooked them so that they were nice and ready for the next arrivals.' He knows the spot, but unfortunately can't take me, because it is still completely haunted; and as fast as anyone tries to excavate the cave he is sure to find, when he returns next day, that some mysterious beings have filled the holes in during the night.

I should have known! This is the edge of goblin country: the land of *anthropophagi*, chanting mermaids, levitating saints, powerful magicians and supernatural visionaries – the very hotbed of all psychomantic wizardry from the *Odyssey* to Padre Pio. 'A cauldron of demonology' was what Douglas called it, loving its archaic paganism. One of Benevento's great anthropomorphic events began with the arrival of the Lombards, in the seventh century, who brought their own curious northern gods like Wodin, full of all the exciting paraphernalia that infant Christianity lacked. Their rituals involved sacrifice and dancing round a reverential tree – the walnut – all at dead of night, and they found a perfect one two miles outside Benevento where they began practising their devotions. Such outlandish rites did not please the local bishop, St Barbato: the horned goat they killed and then hung from the branches was obviously the Devil; the flesh they cut from it and devoured was an obscene lycanthropic communion; the long-cloaked Lombards themselves were demonic women; and their tribal dance was nothing but the prelude to an orgy. Such poisonous heresies could not go unchecked, so the bishop took it upon himself to march out of the town one day with an axe and chop the tree down, with the inevitable result that after more than a thousand years the Witches of Benevento have assumed a considerably more prestigious position in the memory and the annals of local drama than the bishop and his particular philosophy. Even the Alberti family have named the local liqueur after them – which might help account for that devilish inferno after the bomb had hit the cathedral.

The whole business of sorcery and necromancy is a serious issue to these worthy folk, and always has been. Swinburne's coach driver knew of people who had heard the sound of the witches flying through the air at night; and Vieusseux in 1824 came across an old woman lying half-dead on a pavement in Naples because she had flown too near a church spire on her way to the annual coven at Benevento, so losing all her supernatural powers. And Levi knew of werewolves at Eboli; he found peasants wearing the triangular abracadabra inscriptions, and came across love potions that were mixed with menstrual blood. It must be Mother Earth again: the simple need to relate a mystery to something that is known, to symbolise the intangible by the concrete, and with their natural inventiveness to garnish the insubstantial till its origins are nearly lost under the embroidery.

The site of that ominous tree is a harmless enough place today, at Piano della Capella, about two miles from Benevento and marked by a small chapel built on the spot to exorcise the heathen idolatry and superimpose the one and only true God. For religions, like dogs, try to cover each other's leavings in order to obliterate them and publicise their own. So an unused chapel adorns the spot where the crumbs of the Welsh druids and Greek Cybele and Roman Diana once all coalesced into a cabalistic ritual.

Lydia and Rosa are horrified when I tell them at suppertime where I've been, and they both step back in fear lest I should be contaminated. They assure me the chapel is haunted, and tell me about the hunchback in the town who was once young and beautiful but needed to show his *fidanzata* how brave he was; so he elected to spend a night there on his own. When he woke up in the morning he had a huge hump on his back. Cautiously, wide-eyed Rosa moves closer:

'Don't you put a broomstick and a comb outside your house at night in England?' then looks worried when I shake my head. 'You must . . . the witch won't come in if she sees a broomstick; she'll stop to count the twigs, and then she'll fly away on it.'

'Oh . . . and what about the comb?'

'That's for doing her hair with, to make herself look beautiful so no one knows she's a witch. Then she likes to count the teeth, and it takes so long usually that the sun comes up and she has to fly away . . .'

Her father comes in and shoos them both to the kitchen, and as I am the only person eating early he sits down to air his knowledge of the witches, which is altogether more masculine and cynical. Martinello, for example, the demon-king who served two thousand Benevento maidens in a single night; the left breast of a real witch which gives blood instead of milk; the celebratory dances that must only be performed by naked virgins; the miraculous oint-ments that have to be smeared on a woman's body in the dark – the myth has grown into a plethora of splendid indecencies and he delivers them all with a suitable mixture of reverence and coarse appreciation. Then for his final tale he draws his chair closer . . .

Not long ago there was a Benevento man who married one of the witches and kept pleading with her to be allowed to go to a meeting; so she eventually let him, and on the appointed night they undressed and covered each other in oil. Then at midnight, a big black goat with long horns tapped at the window, and they flew off together on its back to the meeting place under the tree where hundreds of other witches had already gathered with nothing on, all singing and laughing and dancing and . . . all around a fat golden serpent standing up proudly in the middle. But when the feasting started he wasn't happy because the food seemed tasteless, so he asked for some salt; but there was so much noise that nobody heard him and he had to shout; then when it eventually came he said, 'Thank God for that,' and suddenly everything disappeared in a flash, and he found himself sitting in the middle of a field with nothing on and his *cazzo* shrivelled to the size of a raisin . . . A lively imbroglio of *malleus maleficarum* and convoluted thauma-turgical nonsense, enmeshing the cuckold's horns with lycanthropy and salt on the Devil's tail, riding the night sky on Pegasus and everyone enjoying some healthy hours of debauchery . . .

After supper the girls plead that I accompany them on a *passeggiata* again. They are already prepared for the ritual public parade, to the square and back again several times, which is a necessity each summer evening. They are in fresh, clean dresses with crisp-cut folds and pleats and pale spotless surfaces, and their supple brown arms reach neatly out of puffed sleeves. They wait for me, poised and narrow-waisted as if teasing with two competing triangles of body, and Lydia and Rosa have white laundered socks – beaten to purity on the stone by a proud loving mother – and in the raven black of their shining hair blue and red bows flutter like feeding butterflies.

We walk slowly up through one of the squares, soon joining others in the loose-limbed promenade, and eyeing the dismembered corpse of last night's *festa*. 'We call this Piazza dei Disoccupati,' says Maria, lowering her voice. 'The men hang round here all day instead of working. They're just lazy: there are plenty of jobs but they won't take them; they think they ought to be *grandi signori* in Rome or in America, driving fast cars without lifting a finger. They won't even go to Germany because they make them work too hard. They're disgusting.' Ruefully I remember what someone had shouted at lunchtime during all the chauvinistic trumpeting: '*Tanti figli, tanta providenza,*' an echo of Mussolini's sad dictum that families with empty cradles were not worthy of empire and the war effort needed more babies, so start the fight in the bedroom; all now a pathetic memory. I ask her if she'd like to go back to Scotland where she was born, but she shakes her head: 'No. I want to stay here in Benevento. I don't ever want to leave Italy.'

We walk on slowly; coolness has crept down like soothing ointment on the tortured streets, and wisps of girls are gliding past in coloured snowflakes of dresses, tossing manes of flowing hair; while at half the speed trudge pram-pushing couples, proud but bending, with pristine and soft-eyed blinking infants earnestly sucking elaborate dummies. Vespas throttle by with confident purrs and slow delibera-tion, their riders eyeing legs and faces, the loose swing of skirts on hidden hips and invisibly suggestive bottoms where folds of clean dresses cling jealously. Maria is unmoved, but Lydia's eyes shine as they look ahead, her back braced upright against the harsh undressing gaze of whispering boys as they pass.

There's an air of sadness as we walk: they know I am leaving tomorrow, and their father has bet I will never walk to Mirabella Eclano in one day. He wants me to go on one of the long-nosed blue buses; then the girls could come with me and return home on the same bus afterwards. They're mystified by my idea of walking all the way to Brindisi, and think it's pointless, as it would be much simpler to go by train. Lydia knows something about the Battle of Cannae but has never heard of Sybaris; and Rosa is sure the south is full of Africans and must be terrible. We turn at the bridge and start sauntering back, and I know I shall miss their warmth and friendly welcome – Gildo with his jewel-case of Scottish phrases, the coltish energy and half-innocent looks of Rosa still caught up in dolls and the blossoming thrill of her first-communion dress, those liquid depths of mystery in Lydia's eyes as we matched faces at mealtimes. She has made me promise to send her a postcard of Buckingham Palace when I get back to London. And I shall miss the patient, languid stare of Maria, standing in the kitchen doorway at mealtimes and noting each man who enters, but whose dark appraising eyes stay softly mute.

One thing remains to be done before leaving. Gildo has arranged for it to happen before sunrise, and only Maria knows. I am going to be ill and seek help from the *strega*. I have seen her in the streets already, and watched the others stand aside: a most conspicuous figure wrapped in a billowing black shawl from neck to ankles, tall, hawk-like and bony-featured, as angular and voracious as a bird of prey, striding along with strings of swept-back grey hair and fire smouldering in her eyes. She is the *inciarmatore* of Benevento.

In the whispering dark of morning Maria hurries me down narrow alleys, glancing over her shoulders in case of pursuing Furies, till we push at a heavy medieval door in a wall of stone, and creak up a flight of narrow wooden stairs. There are no black cats to spit or toads to croak – just a door into an ink-black room draped with curtains, where a wavering candle flickers a yellow light; as Maria creeps away again down the stairs a grey shape rustles and rises from a bed in the corner, its shadowy head against the ceiling, and the eerie sound of a flapping cloak being wrapped round old bones. The drum of my heartbeats bobs like a sodden cork on the soft noise of her invisible preparations, and with breathy whispers a chill hand leads me to a chair. I have a migraine I say, as cold fingertips touch my neck and slide up over my face in a flutter of moth-wings lost against my eyes and forehead. She's a grey shape in the candle-light now, the folds of her gown wafting as she moves; and I hear the mutter of her lips somewhere above me as she wanders her icy fingers in delicately chilling streaks across my face. One minute passes, then two, my breath touching her grey gown, then she moves away suddenly to bring a shallow basin and hold it over my head, swirling the contents slowly. I listen for the incantation, but her fingers are teasing at my eyes again and round my neck, and there are mutterings in her throat; then she pauses to dip a finger into a jar and hold it over the basin, and I hear nine slow falling drips as she starts:

> *Uno, due, tre*
> *Quattro, cinque, sei,*

Sette, otto, nove . . .
San Nicola
Mal' testa fuori *

The basin sluices as she swirls it above my head in slow circles, then a damp finger touches my brow, and draws a small cold cross on the skin before doing the same over her breast, and she lowers the basin so I can see it in the candle-light. It's half-full of water, but swimming on the surface are the nine gleaming spots of oil she dropped from her finger, sliding like beauty marks across a cheek, and as I watch them they all burst and disappear. They vanish like exploding rockets, and the exorcism is over; the water spins on empty and pure, voided of evil spirits.

I am free. I walk down the stairs and out into the dawn's freshness, where early-moving people are fumbling their way to work, and I step from an old world of heathen priestesses and dark necromancy into the grey of a new day's reality. But nothing has really changed: the thin skin of Christian superstition has decorated it with its own tribal reasoning and given holy rulings to all that may be heresy or miracle.

I need the real substance of existence, the comforting hiss of Gildo's espresso machine with its bright, bulbous, twentieth-century chrome, and that thimbleful of rich coffee squeezed through its packed and resisting filter — slow brown drops of sanity.

There are formal goodbyes over breakfast, five pairs of hands to shake and a crowded doorway as I leave; but by eight o'clock I have pushed out into the flat land beyond the town to the south, and am following the tiny stream of San Nicola as it bends through green-brown fields that throw

* One, two, three, Four, five, six, Seven, eight, nine . . . St Nicholas Headache away

up occasional bursts of emerald lushness. Long wealds of deserted and joyless country stretch ahead against the sky, and the folds in the land swell and dip like the endless limbs of dead elephants. As the morning heat starts to tremble and dance above the ridges, the wide Calore bends back again under Monte Roccheta, and there are more jagged stumps of dead Roman bridge with bubblestrings of silver water sweeping past them where the balked current arcs back in curves of anger. Deep down, fronds of weeds sway like lazy ghosts, and a dark pack of fish-shapes sits on the sandy bottom all sipping at their own shadows. I've lost the Appia now, and plod on towards Aeclanum by watching the sun and the next ridge and the next, and each time I look up the sea-swell of the brown horizon has changed its pattern. Perched on faraway slopes are small single buildings with chalk-white walls and ochre tiles − or half-buildings sometimes, roofless and broken and silent of life, all bleached cruelly to the bone. Sweat drips, and the hot distance is meaningless; it's impossible to say how near or how far they are.

By early afternoon Gildo's bottle of wine is empty and his soft-crusted *panini* have long gone. Miles of endless uphill paths stretch ahead, and far behind me Benevento is hidden behind swelling flanks of hills. Why didn't I take the blue-nosed bus? What madness to accept this pointless torture in place of the speedy clatter and mobile eccentricities of good-natured local transport. Did the crusaders do this, I wonder, driven by zealous fanaticism? And all those other hosts of muscular overland pirates who came here, pausing at intervals for restful bursts of rape and pillage, the Alarics and Rogers and Roberts and Pedros? Imagination sees them: serpent tendrils threading the landscape, thick with the chant of dark voices and the crazed shouts of prancing knights with their baggage trains and servants. The line of ants is swallowed in the hills . . . This alluring proboscis of land has always been a convenient stepping-stone for people going somewhere, all wreaking their own havoc and even murdering the very nature they once worshipped. Pyrrhus lost a whole army here, routed in the forests, and there were once lions, boars and bears to be hunted, and even the Bourbon kings left their *lazzaroni* for a while for the love of the chase.

Perhaps Gildo was right and I will lose my bet, for even panting is becoming a useless encumbrance, and the memory of cool river-filled shoes is a vanished luxury. Each mile is a different shade of brown, peppered with pale chalky stones or streaked with the cracked beds of dried-up streams, and here and there long-abandoned furrows and husks of old walls promise a has-been life. New stretches of earth dip interminably into more teasing folds, giving seconds of downhill relief before surging up again, breathless and leaden-legged, into a remorseless sea of rust-coloured rollers; on and on ... Then a sound from over a ridge, a white chimney surfacing, and a red pantiled roof, then the lime-washed walls of a *contadino*'s house – a coarse mat of grass shaded by the arthritic bend of old trees and brightened by the splash of new geraniums, a stampede of worried white goats bleating and bell-ringing as they run and a clutch of untidy staring children. The owner appears, stern and brown-faced, to be puzzled and watchful a moment before hailing me over; and in no time an earthen jug of wine is set on the old wooden table in the shade and the children scamper off for glasses. We drink a silent toast beneath the old olive tree straining at its knotted bark, and as time stops the children circle round warily, joined by a perplexed audience of rabbits, hens, dogs and two sad-eyed oxen wandering over to watch. The wine is cool and yellow and no doubt strong, but my throat hardly tastes it; then he pulls out rough cheroots from a pocket and offers me one, and the clean air turns blue with floating smoke and my lungs scorch. He rolls another one purposefully, tipping crumbs of loose home-grown tobacco into his palm and rolling it in a leaf before handing it over with a swift lick.

'Twenty thousand lire the *quintale* [one hundredweight],' he says, and spits a long way towards the rabbits, 'that's all they pay me. Then they sell it for fifty thousand, or they throw half of it away because they say it's sub-standard and pay nothing.' He spits again, not quite so far: 'They never give the bad stuff back though – oh, no. They always keep it . . . They sell it in Africa.' He tells me about his two grown-up sons in Venezuela, and about the oldest of those left behind to help – a lean child of fourteen called Peppino who stands close, eagerly fills my glass each time I empty it, shoos his young sisters away jealously and cries angry orders to the inquisitively approaching animals. A wiry man-child, schoolless but eager to help, with sturdy brown bare feet, listening with anxious eyes as we talk. He says he wants to leave too, perhaps to follow his brothers to South America or to a big city where the money glitters, and there is food and television and plenty of prosperity. His eyes brighten as he explains his dream, and his father grunts. 'So, who'll be left to work the land?' he says. 'Nobody! They all want to go to the towns and find money . . .' a sudden gleam comes to his eye then fades as if he too once had a dream. 'Some Milanese people came here a few years back,' he remembers. 'They were in jeeps and lorries and had lots of maps, and they took measurements with instruments, and they talked about building a big road.' He gives a sigh. 'This land would be worth a lot if that happened, but it was a long time ago now.'

I'm full of wine and friendly warmth as I watch evening start to move in, and have to rise unsteadily to depart; then he pushes another cheroot at me and tells Peppino to take me up the hill and on to the path to Eclano. I thank him for his kindness, which he waves into nothing, and Peppino hovers and hisses a polite '*Venite*,' waiting on the withered track, and as I turn to wave I see his row of sisters gazing after us from the lamplit door.

He pads ahead of me with youthful eyes piercing the growing darkness, and quiet easy strides that own the path and challenge each gully and dominate the gentle bends. He knows each shadowy tree and recognises comfortable boulders here and there against the darkening sky. Then he slows in front of me and his piping voice drifts to a whisper as we breast a ridge: '*Questa è la valle dei morti,*' and he tells me softly how every year they find human skulls in the fields and hundreds of tombstones 'too big for a man to lift!'.

Another valley of the dead, and another sad smile in the darkness. Is this Pyrrhus' lost army after the last hopeless battle for Benevento? Or the hoary Lombards murdering the fading soldiers of Byzantium? Or a Norman slaughter of papal followers? Or some Angevin extravagance to decimate a rebellious war-lord? Death here has long been a commonplace. Would they could leap from their feeble graves to roll their battle cry through the hills again, and pierce the dark with helmeted eyes of blood red and the hideous clash of their brandished steel ... Peppino knows they are there, and hurries on in silence while I gasp behind. 'Do you believe in ghosts?' he whispers once, very quietly, but never slackens his pace to hear my answer.

Then we breast a dark slope and I see the glow-worm lights of Eclano winking through the darkness. '*Ciao,*' he whispers, and I am suddenly alone. All I hear is his soft feet pounding into the distance far behind, as he races for home and safety over the hills of skulls and bones.

ELEVEN

Eclano

I should have known things would change. After the clutter
and dusty restlessness of Capua and Benevento, actually
identifiable by dots on maps, I have arrived where cartogra-
phers have given up. Aeclanum doesn't exist any more: it
is called Mirabella now, or sometimes Le Grotte, or even
La Colonia according to locals; before which its name was
Aquaputrida, and before that Quintodecimo, being fifteen
Roman miles from Benevento. These details I have gathered
from the formidable lady who runs the only inn, which it
has taken me twenty minutes to find, as it is not an inn at
all but a house where people drop in to sleep. For company
I have nine telephone engineers, and we are sharing a room.
Her welcome is hardly auspicious.

'Good evening. Have you a room?'

'Perhaps . . . Where are you from?'

'England. Is there any chance of a bed?'

'There may be . . . Why are you here?'

'I'm just travelling – looking for Roman roads, remains.'

'We've got remains . . . Are you a professor?'

'No. Will I be able to sleep here?'

'We'll see . . . Come in,' eyeing me suspiciously and
scrutinising my dusty features with quiet contempt.

'. . . And the price, *signora*?'

'The same as usual.'

'But I don't know what the usual is . . .'

'The same as you paid before.'

'I haven't been here before.'

'It's whatever you paid at the last place.'

'Ah . . .'

The matter is settled and we will doubtless argue in the

morning, but until then I will take my place in the dormitory, to endure yet another night of communal horrors.

Sleep should be a private occupation, and like sin should have no accomplices, for it is fraught with unseemly possibilities that are best savoured alone. And the same applies to the preparations. Now that the carnal chumminess of schooldays is over, and the comforting breath of adjacent bodies in the dark is not necessary, one expects solitude, and dreads the reawakening of those memories of juvenile exposure. Not so the Italians: the sharing, the involvement, the voluble and corporate bond must be active twenty-four hours each day, for being public people in all things any kind of isolation is antisocial and the aberration of madmen, wild beasts or gods; even bedtime has to be part of life's endless performance. Every inquisitive explorer encounters the great good-night drama sooner or later: Fynes Morrison was so put off by his chamber-fellows that he warned any traveller to 'always have his sword by his bedside'; Evelyn had to have a young lady removed from a bed before he could occupy it (after which he contracted her smallpox); and Osbert Sitwell's father declared war on all occupants of south Italian dormitories by erecting his mosquito net with as much fuss and noise and for as long a time as possible. The worst aspect of these nocturnal communes is always the snoring; and when at last sleep comes one's companions all have a lemming urge to get up before daybreak with operatic enthusiasm, behaviour which might just be tolerable had not most of them arrived half-tipsy anyway long after midnight and convinced they were still in the *bottiglieria*. Such dormitory nights have a habit of being short.

In fact things aren't too bad, for the telephone engineers depart *en masse* at six, and I follow soon after, leaving one comatose body by the door, grey-vested with hairy, barrel-brown arms across the sheet, snoring loudly. 'It's the foreman,' whispers the *signora*. 'He goes an hour after the others to check what they've done,' though what precisely that is remains a mystery to her; all she knows is that they have been staying for a month and have no plans to leave, and the foreman pays her the money every week.

Outside the dawn air is briefly crisp, with the early sun sucking up the dew and cleansing the land into unusual sharpness of detail, as if drawing a tight skin across the ribs of the mountains to give every fold a short identity. Dark olive trees are foreshortened, standing out bold and clear, and the corners and roofs of the houses are new and sharp. A few moments of freshness touch the wandering stone stairways that crawl up between the walls, and etch the bulging ironwork balconies casually strewn with loose wigs of unbrushed flowers. The stone walls are earthen or painted white, all the plaster cracked and festooned with the faded peel of old advertisements and overhead strings of wire disappearing, and some have slatted shutters clipped back to open their eyes; lean cats watch over walls as doors start to open. Beyond the few houses a flat plateau reaches down into a valley, spreading itself smoothly in a tablecloth of land that doesn't belong to the uneven landscape.

Beneath that miniature plain are the roots of Roman Aeclanum, rased to the ground by the Greek emperor Constant II when he was challenged by the Lombards for the ownership of southern Italy. They didn't have bulldozers in those days, just venom and spite enough to eliminate what was there before, and leave an expanse of carefully tilled fields and olive groves, falling away in shallow steps, blending a host of dull colours, all beaten down and impressively final as if nothing had ever existed. But the earth is still littered with its battled fragments, surfacing after thirteen centuries as I wander over it: shards, pot-handles, splinters of gleaming glass – for it was a centre of glassmaking – crusting the furrows and popping out round the roots of trees. It was important enough to have had its own bishop until the Byzantine holocaust; one of them was excommunicated and banished for daring to express his views on Adam and Eve's behaviour in the Garden of Eden, for unlike St Augustine he felt certain the couple must have enjoyed some pleasurable sexual intercourse. Otherwise . . .?

Yet another network of Roman roads diverged here, the Herdonetana striking off east towards the Adriatic, while the Aurelia Aeclanensis went south-west to Reggio. An hour of idle walking kicks up little but a flotsam of shattered pots round a desolate stump of house wall partly excavated; then in a carefully cultivated spinney there's a locked wooden shed acting as a store for less wieldy remnants, and surrounded by some vandalised stumps of Roman pillars rising from the grass. 'He's away,' say the children playing in the shade when I ask for the *guardiano*. 'He was here yesterday, and he'll be here tomorrow, but he's not here today. He's digging at Muffeet.'

Digging at Muffeet! An unromantic-sounding place, and why at Muffeet, why not here? They shrug and start laughing; Muffeet is more interesting, they say, it makes rude noises and terrible smells – and they fall mirthfully in the grass holding their noses. Dialect – I should have known! Sir William Hamilton visited a curious inland volcano called Mephitis, sunk into a recess and bubbling like the Phlegrean Fields; Swinburne was taken to the Moffetta, where a most nauseous smell assailed him and the water 'spouted up as high as our heads'; and Lear sniffed the gases of 'Le Mofette', watched by his guide who wouldn't go within a hundred yards of the 'accursed eccentricity'. It's down the road past Frigento, the children tell me, five miles further on; so with brief farewells I hurry southward out of Aeclanum, already feeling the gentle burning of the sun and seeing its first distortions rippling on the empty road. Distant banks of hills line up on either side, channelling me towards the south, shadowy in grey obscurity, randomly scratched here and there with an ant's-egg inlay of clustered white houses, compressed and bedded or balancing on a crest of vertigo. A pair of shapeless villages rear up on the highest peaks of all, streaked by sunlight and proud as rival cockatoos saluting each other; they are the lovers Trevico and Guardia dei Lombardi, and their off-spring are two humbler villages in the valley below, Fri-gento and Nusco, each one on its small pubescent mound of hillock waiting to grow up. That's the story anyway; Trevico still trails her white bridal gown of tiny houses down the slope, while broad-shouldered Guardia dei Lom-bardi yearns everlastingly and reaches out for her.

Otherwise the land is of crumpled parchment carbonised by some unchronicled holocaust: the muddy phlegm of a giant and expiring volcano, spewed out and fossilised, but still bubbling out its last poisonous gasps at the deepest point in the valley. Here and there at its outermost edges accessible patches of rich soil throw up the juxtaposed greens of tomato plants, the red of peppers, the wavering yellow of corn and the uneven sludge of cabbage fields; and sometimes straggles of pert-tailed white goats are tearing out tufts of coarse grass.

The heat and the remorseless rhythm of walking start to burn all colours into one, while the haze dims the sparkle of Trevico to dusty grey; in the foreshortened distance a clutch of untidy houses grapple together incestuously like winter snails, clinging desperately to a cone of land as their ragged rooflines claw round a white church tower. It must be Frigento, still two or three miles off, climbing on top of itself for safety – Lear's 'miserable little town' where he had hoped to stay with the *gran signore* Don January Redflame who, he was told, was 'all money and all heart', but instead had to make do at the 'palpably disgusting' inn.

A Vespa draws up beside me. It is Franco Gallo, the storekeeper from the shed at Aeclanum, who prefers to call it a *'museo'* and himself the *'custode'*. He has been alerted to my morning enquiries by the customary whispers of cross-country telegraph, and is now pointing for me to mount his pillion seat. Unfortunately it is only a metal luggage rack, and we bump together in hideous discomfort over three excruciating miles, sometimes avoiding the ruts and pot-holes, but more often challenging them, as if to test the efficiency of his shock absorbers. It is a posture that the basic framework of man is not made for, that turns assets into hideous liabilities. It is a Schoenberg symphony of agony; with no footrests and no chance of communication, I can either leave by falling off or stay on in bouncing torment.

When it is finally over we are a mile beyond Frigento and slowing beside a haystack in a field, where he has to wheel the machine from under my bowed legs; but the thigh pain has suddenly become unimportant, for the air is sickly and suffocating, heavy with waves of rancid sulphur biting behind the nostrils, forcing my mouth open in fish-like gasps. Somewhere a grumbling cauldron is boiling dry, with dismal eruptions of pops and belches and farts, a distance away but massively strong and menacing as if a leviathan were in the last throes of drowning. Eyes smarting, we run down the field towards the noise to pause at a cliff-edge overlooking a half-mile expanse of grey mud, most of it pale and crusted but broken in places by dark pools of softness where glutinous bubbles rise like popping eyeballs and hiss as each pustule bursts. It's a geological frustration venting its intestinal complaint with ulcerous groans and gastric hisses, and on the point of suffocating us. But Franco has seen a half-asphyxiated hawk, and darts away over the grass to retrieve it, flapping its feeble wings as he carries it back by its legs. Another victim of Lear's 'well filled ornithological necropolis' where he counted crows, larks, sparrows and eight yellowhammers, then deliberately inhaled the 'noxious vapours' from the strongest point possible, and regretted it for three days afterwards.

I feel it too: raw nostrils, and a light stinging high up inside the head and the mouth forced open greedily; but

Franco waves that all is well, for before midday and again late in the evening the poisonous fumes hug the ground – they only rise dangerously during the heat of the afternoon. Then he points to where, far below us, a slow-motion group of men is digging into a section of crust, working their way deep into a slimy black pit beneath the surface, one of them standing apart as overseer, sparkling in a wide-brimmed white straw hat and tubbily wrapped in the dishevelled and rumpled robes of a cleric.

It is Padre Giambitto – a Vatican eccentric and purloiner of antiquities, a holy *tombarolo* doing a little excavation on his own. On seeing us he waves and rerolls his flapping sleeves to his elbows, then blows a piercing whistle, and finally starts to scramble up the grey cliff in our direction, his priestly smock open from neck to navel and offering flashes of dazzling purity as he half-hitches the flying folds around him. He arrives gasping and sees the hawk. 'Get rid of it,' he urges Franco; 'the men are coming up. They caught one before I arrived this morning; they cut its beak and talons off then let it go. Bastards . . .' he waits to count the men up over the ridge while Franco hurries off behind us on to a hillock and throws the huge hawk up into the air like an old pullover, where it flops for a befuddled moment then strains away, slow and drunken on giant wings that thrash weakly as it skims boozily over the grass into a hollow. The *padre* counts the diggers up, as stern and unsmiling as a bored schoolmistress with kindergarten ducklings, then pats the pouches of his cassock and turns quizzically:

'Welcome to Amsanctus,' he beams, 'the home of the Fury Allecto, daughter of the night. Virgil's "*Locus Italiae medio, sub montibus altis*" . . . We're looking for the temple of the malaria goddess Mephitis . . .' He pauses to tidy his cassock and laughs. 'D'you know something? The Fascists used to test gasmasks here in the war: whole battalions would march down in droves wearing them, then pass out like flies.'

We walk up the hill towards the haystack, where I see the maidenly bulge of an old Topolino roasting in the sun, which he assumes I will wish to ride in, just as he assumes that Franco will want to race him on his Vespa. It all happens in a matter of moments – but the route is not back towards Frigento. It is rapidly southward, in an uneven chariot race, the *padre* singing and talking as he drives, not caring much which side of the road he's on nor even which gear he operates, trying them all at unnecessary intervals or on a whim, or just wishing to bury the pursuing Franco in more dust, which he does frequently, turning with a delighted chuckle to survey the sandstorm behind, then having to heave the bouncing Topolino off the verge and grab at his excited straw hat at the same time. I gather we are going to his village to see his collection of excavated treasures, but most of his conversation is lost in bursts of miscellaneous opera, or the rubbery bounce of wheels in pot-holes, or the rattling flap of his open cassock, or just the hot wind buffeting through the open sun-roof. Mercifully we slow a little, for some snake-like twists into the village of Rocca San Felice, though the diminution is barely noticeable; trusting completely in his creator he slides round a maze of bends with confident horn-bleating glissandos, before at last he hauls on the handbrake and bounds out through a white archway and up some steps fumbling for his keys.

The gasping custodian joins us, suitably Sahara-caked and with weeping eyes, as we enter the cool of a shuttered study, exuding a staid Victorian calm and lined with dark bookcases, wooden cupboards, heavy old tallboys and long blanket chests. Opening doors and drawers at random, he half flings objects out before going on to the next outlet: first the shutters, then a leather-bound St Non in three volumes, then Pratilli's *Via Appia*, then Hamilton's dramatic folio of Vesuvius, followed by sheets of Piranesi as the dust clouds fly, and then a spillage of bursting envelopes hit the floor with the dead chink of old coins. An eye-consuming chaos of antiquity emerges, a picnic of archaeological indigestion that spreads like treacle round our feet as tins and boxes are rattled and out pop rings, bracelets, necklaces, pendants – all green and old; and drawers open, lined with paper and filled with lamps, pots, votive statues, calices, all faded with ancient colours hiding in datelessness and made paler by his rape. Or is it rescue? He has over five thousand coins stuffed into envelopes, and more in jars and boxes, all dug out of the sanctuary of Mephitis in the space of four years: Oscan, Greek and Roman, with crude emperors' heads or symbols of dolphins, lions, wolves, bulls, or serpents from the lost towns of Locri, Herakleia, Velia, Siris and Cumae; five gold pieces showing Alexander the Great; an Oscan coin marked VETULIA; and a boxful of Roman ases. The walls too are lined with pre-biblical shapes – spears, javelins, demonic green helmets and crumpled shields – and more drawers tumble out the additional bedlam of combs, mirrors, glass bottles, axe heads, earrings, old nails . . .

'The Trevi Fountain of Magna Graecia,' he beams. 'Those who passed by wished for a safe return, so they offered gifts to the goddess: a tribute, like your Peter's pence, or a form of indulgence – buying your way into heaven, pagan blackmail . . . *Plus ça change*. Virgil said it was another entrance to the underworld.' He rubs his hands smiling, his eyes free from guilt as if completely at home with his ancient and modern calling: 'About thirty coins today; nothing interesting . . . but we've found the temple further up the hill to the west, out of the wind; and the priests' living quarters further up still. It was called Aqua Sancta because the springs of water were crystal-clear, and they still are . . . a shrine on the main route from north to south.'

A pause for imaginative reflection. Yes, the southern

Greeks of three thousand years ago must have drifted northward by filtering up along all the old tribal paths and animal tracks, first favouring some and then others, until a popular consensus of routes was established towards Paestum and Cumae and the Capuan Etruscans and the productive Samnites, gently civilising everyone as they went. Then after three or four centuries of dissipating their energies in internecine squabbles, and the easy enjoyment of warm and voluptuous decadence breathed by the soft Ionian, they became the easy prey of the puppy Roman Republic as it flexed its muscles and stretched greedily southwards. All the outward beauty of Rome was inspired by these thoughtful Hellenes, with their gentle genius and vision and imagination, while the northerners provided the savage muscle.

The archaeological litter gets so frantic and deep that the floor is impassable, the museum custodian watching with confident pride as if it were partly his (which it probably is), and chuckling on about the old shepherd Pasquale who is the rival tomb robber and has been selling things off for fifty years at least – usually to the same German who comes down every year. This June he gave him eighty thousand lire – about £50* – for over a thousand coins. 'We have his car number,' he says, almost secretively. 'He's an antique dealer from Hamburg, *un uomo eruditissimo*,' and I wonder for a moment if another padlock on the shed at Aeclanum might not be a good idea . . .

But the *padre* is engrossed; grunting excitedly, he is spreading maps out on the floor as if preparing for cartographic Pelmanism; they are grey at the folds and foxed, showing outlines of unrecognisable Italy, with serpents of Latin calligraphy and bold designs of sea-horses and puffing angels and decorated scrolls saying ITER VENUSIUM, INTINER-ARIO ANTONINO, TABULA THEODOSIANA, HOLSTENIUS, VIE

* in 1960

ANTICHE. My mention of the Appia has fired his imagination and he is impatiently patting flat the resistant bulges: 'Tratturi, tratturi' – sheep paths – he mutters, 'follow the old drovers' paths where they moved their sheep and cattle from pasture to pasture . . . the big migrations. Those are the old Roman roads . . . come, I'll show you.' And the three of us perform a high-stepping flamingo dance through the Gordian muddle, bundle into the Topolino again and slither back down the village hairpins. Out on the open road once more, above the winded complaints of the wheels hitting pot-holes come snatches of minestrone conversation . . . Santoli sold his collection to Ferdinand of Aragon for four hundred ducats . . . That's Fontana Rosa; it took three German mines to blow up one Roman bridge . . . The postman here walks thirty kilometres a day . . . In winter the snow is a metre deep . . . The old landowner lives with a girl of fourteen; we call him Don Disgraziato . . .

But this Jehu has only just begun. As the roadway in front of us bends gently to the left he ignores it and drives straight on, careering on to the expanse of withered grass without slackening speed, and heedless to the outraged complaints of the baby Fiat as it responds like an infant Hercules, and after a fractional adjustment of temperament and a brief scream of wheel-spin starts to gobble up the bumps and mounds and ditches, and race across kilometres of wizened pasture like an angry mouse on a sports day. When we eventually stop to get out we are in the middle of a tratturo, a grassy pathway bordered each side by untidy scrub lines of wind-blown bushes and rocks about thirty yards apart, with long views on all sides over wandering plains and a sea-swell of land dunes scorching in the sun, and the broad old pathway dipping and rising ahead into the far distance. It's an ancient trade route from north to south, he says, still used by the shepherds for driving huge flocks along twice a year, but once used by travellers and pilgrims and merchant caravans, throngs of slaves and far-flung squadrons of expanding armies and bands of brigands, and perhaps by a few Pythagorean disciples or a Swabian body-guard of twenty thousand Saracens. The *padre* hasn't fin-ished: intoxicated by this new excitement, he bundles us in again and off we scamper down the track, swerving to avoid patches of rock and assaulting the ditches and billows in confident frenzy, the dips and dives shaking us off our seats like orgasmic jellies. '*Ecco!*' he announces as we expire in the middle of nowhere beside a pile of stone which, on examination, is the huge vandalised slab of a Roman sarco-phagus, and now a tumbled rubble of shattered marble. '*La Tomba Luparielli*', he announces, stroking a few faded details; it sits there against the hedge in grey petrifaction, jagged and askew, dark with resentment at being disturbed.

His enthusiasm is over; it expires as rapidly as it was born, and he drives all the way back to Frigento at a furious pace, to deposit me by the only inn, not even waving as he tears away in a cloud of dust with the shaking Franco beside him. I enter the only possible door in the burning line of houses, cooled by the dark and ominous interior which is unused to visitors and obviously little changed since Lear's day of palpable disgust; then I sit myself near the one other diner who is hunched painfully over his food. He is certainly not a local, for the moment I am seated he welcomes me as an audience for his caustic observations. He is a dentist from Rome on an obligatory tour of duty in the Mezzo-giorno and loathing every moment of it, and, in the fearless way that Italians can start animated conversations without being introduced, announces that what Italy needs is the return of the German Army.

'At least things got done,' he says, 'and there was organ-isation and backbone. Just look at that road outside: it's not even fit for a horse and cart. They just patch it up every year with some rubbish from a mafioso contractor who's somebody's cousin; and the workmen are all layabouts who've never seen asphalt before; and this year's mayor blames last year's mayor, so they all go out in the fields for a shoot-out and kill each other.' He sighs angrily, sucking at his soup with vehemence and looking for a non-existent napkin. 'It's hopeless ... we're not ready for democracy. There's no discipline and nobody takes orders. I never thought I'd hear myself saying anything good about the Fascists and Nazis, but my God! ...' He tails off in exasperation, desperate to regain the sanity of the north where at least he understands their brand of dishonesty, with its more sophisticated code of manipulation and a suaver type of *sistemazione* used to get round the weakness and instability of official institutions, and the corruption and unreliability of the law. He can't see that here it's exactly the same thing, though less smoothly tailored – a more rustic and ramshackle orchestration of anarchy that serves just the same purpose: to circumvent laws, to oil the administration generously so it functions defectively for personal profit. It has always been the same; it is the Italian way of life everywhere, the invention of endless ruses to defeat boredom and discipline, and to join the great conspiracy of self-preservation. But his bitterness is so savage that I fear for his patients, particularly as he only has one small attaché case of instruments with him, and his instructions are not to bother with fillings, but only with extractions, each one for a thousand lire. I chew thoughtfully on my fried donkey steak and imagine him working off his frustrations in some iron-disciplined Teutonic torture chamber in the back streets of Frigento.

Then suddenly Franco joins us, breathless and dust-stained and still full of animation from the morning's joy-ride, and with him a companion, large and puzzled and hesitant, growling in uncertain bursts of rough dockland American. More wine is ordered as I slip the new arrival into the lists with the dentist – the despotic patriot versus the return of the disillusioned *émigré*. And the ex-New Yorker is soft and realistic as he explains what he did for ten years in the

New World: he worried and got ulcers and exhausted himself because everyone was forever rushing around chasing money and women and cars and status symbols, and they were all shouting 'Take it easy, take it easy' and dying from heart attacks . . . He gives a big shrug of his shoulders. 'So, what's the point?' he says quietly. 'No one shouts Take it easy here. We just do it all the time. It's no problem.'

The dentist has no answer; the sublime escapism of the Theocritan idyll has long since left his imagination, as has that blissful sense of idleness and ignorance which warms and then peacefully emasculates these children of the sun. It is an inner spiritual contentment some people know nothing of, and is older than any religious testament. You can call it what you will: hopelessness, fatalism, a philosophy of resignation, or a national impotence and passivity, even the equatorial virus of everlasting boredom. It oozes southward from Naples like mud, wave after wave of delicious and masterly inactivity. Which is why they scream for change in leaders, kings, ministers, governments, just hoping something interesting will happen; then they hate what they have produced and want change again. They did it to Savonarola, Cola di Rienzo, the Bourbons, Garibaldi, Mussolini; they do it to royalty and prime ministers. It's more of a national sport than football: Crown him, then Off with his head. They're 'soft people', said Mussolini, 'only capable of singing and eating ice-cream'. 'Beat them and beat them and beat them.' No wonder they strung him up. Perhaps they'll do the same to the dentist after he's taken their teeth out.

He leaves, silent and unconvinced, as some locals enter, wishing to play cards privately in a corner, arranging themselves slowly as if for a ritual and muttering in dark voices, then watching carefully as glasses and a two-litre flagon of wine are placed on the table among them. The cards are dealt in funereal silence, broken only by the odd mutter from one or other of the dried-out mahogany faces as it scowls round suspiciously; then all their shoulders start to roll restlessly. *'Andiamo,'* says Franco quietly, standing up, viewing their cautious movements of discard-and-take-up in the corner, seeing how slow their play is and how all eyes are lowered intently.

'Andiamo,' he says again, and we walk out into the white heat being thrown off the baking walls, and into the washed silence of the dusty street where nothing is moving. *'Passatella,'* he says quietly. 'It is illegal . . . all grudges and insults, and it usually ends in violence; the winner of the first hand has power over all the others, and can ridicule or humiliate anyone he likes, usually by making him drink too much . . . or not letting him drink at all. *Andiamo.'* So we leave another sign of the boredom and resentment born out of the stultifying heat, something that Levi saw at Eboli in the 1930s when the peasants played it at night, eager for power over each other – not a game but a tournament, he called it, full of 'repressed rancour, hate and rivalry'; Roger Vailland wrote a whole novel about it to show how violence and death can follow a simple game of cards. It is not our kind of contest, of fairness and shaking hands, but a private war waged with hatred and ancient malice, filled with loathing and a lust to control and dominate each other. Their desire to overpower and humiliate boils every day on the brazier of this romantic land; and while we rush down from the north to bathe in its sun-kissed love and idyllic pastures, they drown each other in blood and desolation. We see what we want to see – the superficialities; we miss the ugliness, suffering and misery, where no one has faith in anyone else, and jealously whispering Iago is always king, and behind the bright footlights the stage is dark with despair and death.

Evening starts to come. Franco has left me sitting by the roadside in the shade of some whispering eucalyptus trees, with promises to return later. There is a party tonight, he says; a baby has been christened and everybody must celebrate. That I am a stranger and totally unkempt doesn't move him remotely. 'The party is for everyone, anybody who likes to come' – a more generous and welcoming view than our icy privacy, and a mark of their dreamlike craving for universal happiness. I listen to the ceaseless rattle of cicadas as they machine-gun each other in the sun like toy terrorists, while the oven glove of air folds round me, and the over-cooked land crackles on all sides as if it were burnt-out pastry. Some of them don't seem to feel it: there's a man trudging along hard furrows half a mile away scattering seed; and the vague tinkle of a sheep bell somewhere suggests that there must be a lurking shepherd. The heat washes memories of the morning into dubious ribbons of fantasy that only half happened: the dust-caked Franco on his energetic Vespa, the jovial robber-priest with his treasures,* the rancid stench of Mephitis, Don Disgraziato in his elegant farmhouse where he keeps figured Greek vases and an underage mistress. 'He's the local tyrant,' Franco told me. 'He rents out his hundreds of acres in small parcels to the peasants, who take three hours to get to their plots each day, and then surrender half their produce in payment. That's why they're all Communists.'

And now the heat is going at last; it softens magically as if a hotplate were switching off and cooling in a quiet hiatus of indecision. There is balm for the last hour before the ball of sun dives into the earth, and Franco draws up again on his Vespa. 'It's not far,' he says, smiling as I poise delicately on his luggage rack, almost ready for the rough roads that will lead to the family *festa*. We arrive at a farmhouse down a track, where all is strangely quiet and there are no preparations, just two empty stone-flagged rooms and anxious adult relations waiting with shy relieved smiles,

* Unfair. Padre Giambitto gave all his finds to the authorities before he left the area. See p. 319.

assuming everything will happen eventually. Celebrations such as this are not arranged in the south, they germinate by word of mouth; the potent genie of Arab fatalism still dwells in the corners of their minds, and everything will happen if the Almighty wills it. They have learnt long since whom to depend on. Through the rooms into the enormous vaulted kitchen the scene is different: elder sisters and cousins and aunts and two earnest grandmothers are scurrying like gremlins behind the scenes. They have baked an array of cakes and biscuits, and one of the crones is busy making her own pasta, kneading it, rolling it and showering it with flour, while two half-pointers slink silently through all the legs, looking for scraps. They want the sausages: hundreds of misshapen oversized udders hanging from the ceiling, obscene chandeliers of finely minced meat mixed with herbs or crushed vegetables, stuffed into gossamer tubes of intestine, and all of it done here on the farm. I tell them what little I know of humane killers and abattoirs and the RSPCA, and they smile sympathetically. 'Povere bestie,' they say.

Rapid twilight thickens to a remorseless curtain, thrusting dying breaths of daylight downwards into black; hesitant youths arrive at the door shy and awkward as they troop into the long rooms, their farm-hardened bodies restless under washed shirts and brushed trousers, their weathered faces tortured by formal cleanliness. As they grow in an apprehensive line along one wall the father appears, desperate with a tray of tiny liqueurs, which they take as he passes hurriedly; then the girls arrive, bare-legged and doll-like in fresh and spotless dresses, and touching hands for comfort they range themselves with fastidious timidity along the opposite wall, all eyes down in desperately serious non-recognition. They know each other, but custom forbids any sign of it – and, who knows, things may have changed since yesterday. They shuffle in an uneasy, earthy suspense of disciplined apprehension till an accordion wheezes from one end of the room to impel movement, and the line of males advances obediently towards the girls, who all tense as they are seized – with some mild scrummaging and chivalrous roughness – before being led out for a clumsy pair-dance. The boys are field-men, used to mules and oxen without rhythm, and are quickly outstepped by the girls, who are bright in movement and eager in agility, their muscular legs with heavy clogs delighting in exercise, and soon beating out a feverish rhythm on the hard stone as they all circle the room in a snaking ritual, sometimes leaving their partners a foot away and sometimes closing for a polite formal contact.

It beats on jovially, the evening's introduction, but there are too many men, which means the young unallowed sisters have to be called in from peeping at the door, or from chasing the chickens outside; so these scrawny pupae of nine and ten are scooped up into the throng, stiff bodies jiggling tentatively or feet not touching the ground, carried patiently by brown arms that whirl them and drag them over the stones, their bodies willing yet resistant with fear. But not for long; they master it faster than the men, and skip and gallop in no time with impatient frenzy and staggering whirls. A pause comes for another tray of liqueurs to pass and sweat to be wiped, but the drink is only for the males, who welcome their superiority; then the accordion restarts, followed by a quiet shuffle of partner change, and faces start to soften in recognition and smiles as if an effervescence of excitement is warming the dance and releasing their primitive springs of natural energy.

As it began, so it ends: with hardly a word. The cakes had come out and so had the biscuits, and the doubtful elders had passed them round; and the baby had been brought out to cry, swathed in yards of bundled white, and peepingly yearned for by the girls. And then I'd been shown a grandmother's majolica plate to admire, produced from a recess behind the kitchen – a mammoth tureen of multicoloured ornament, blazing in old blue and gold and orange, swirling with elegant heraldic beasts leaping in combat over crowns and castles and coats of arms, a massive porringer over two feet in diameter, incandescent with memories of eighteenth-century banquets, the rustle of crinoline, the haughtiness of liveried footmen poised like high-chinned toads and the polished elegance of mazurkaing couples in flame-lit velvet ballrooms. A chastened and silent memento of those southern aristocrats who held on to the bitter end, and still danced and feasted all night as the last of the Bourbons reeled out of Naples, and that self-loving little commoner from the islands was rabble-rousing. It is now a useless appendage in a back room at a peasant barn-dance.

Outside the darkness is hard and terminal as the girls drift away, whispering spectres sucked up by the hungry night, followed at intervals by the men. Silver stars glitter above the hush of still trees and a dog howls in a field, wailing its anguish like some projectile loosed from hell, and a hovering youth says the bus will soon come to take me back to Eclano. He is worried about his *fidanzata* in Rome, he confides, whom he met on holiday two years ago and hasn't seen since; but he knows she likes him because he has written to her mother and aunt who've both told him she loves him. He pours this evening's heart out in the dark and tells me of his great concern for her virginity and wonders how to be sure of it from a hundred miles away.

'If she's not true to me,' he says, 'the relationship will be over.'

'Oh dear,' I commiserate, and ask if the same condition applies to him, but the idea strikes him as quite absurd.

'Necessity,' he says, 'is an overflowing pot.'

'So Saturday whoring in Benevento doesn't count?'

'How can it if the heart isn't involved?'

'Supposing she does it too? Without using her heart either?'

'Pah! that's impossible,' he snorts. 'Girls always use their hearts.'

I ask when the bus will come and he says in five minutes, but we wait for fifteen under the cold stars as the silence grows deeper. He shuffles restlessly and has an idea it may be later on some evenings, but promises to wait with me anyway and I mustn't worry. The warm tar of night starts to stick like a damp bodice – a prison of unutterable darkness taking revenge on the blaze of day – and our ears stretch for the groan of a leviathan in the distance. But all is quiet, and he fears the timetable may have changed. 'It always comes at ten o'clock,' he whispers softly, so dark I can't see him.

But it doesn't come. Then he knows it must have broken down somewhere, and I know too that I can shake off my paralysis of not wishing to appear ungrateful and can thank him and tell him I must start walking. 'I'm sorry,' he mutters, 'it is sure to come if you wait . . . I know it will,' his tone slightly grievous as if it's partly my fault anyway. So I set off alone into cavernous darkness, as he slips away behind into a silent memory and to a home somewhere in those hidden fields, letting me count my own footsteps quietly as they beat back towards Aeclanum.

TWELVE

Bisaccia

Communion with a recumbent pig under the shelter of a cemetery wall. This one is an excited pig, trying to explain something in between comfortable wriggles in the mud. He obviously has opinions and much to say: a delighted squealing sphere of pink globosity, and positively adenoidal at the pleasure of my company. Perhaps he mistakes me for an old friend, for seldom have I been made so welcome or met such a vociferously symphonic hog, not even at killing time, when tones usually rise an octave or two. It must be the early-morning hour of his solitary sunbathe that brings on such porcine effervescence.

He is certainly not the only pig that lives in Bisaccia, far from it: the beastly place is full of them and they clearly outnumber the humans. They walk contented and free through the streets and alleys, they amble nonchalantly in and out of open doors, they stand flapping quizzical ears as they scrutinise each passer-by; masterful and confident, they wander everywhere and snuffle everything with the authoritative air of ownership, giving brisk approving quivers of the tail. They are obviously town pigs, and most probably house pigs too – none of that nonsense about fields and sties: these are the domestic variety who live with their owner-friends and share their life-style. This one has obviously had a marvellous night and the memory of it is making him ecstatic.

My admiration of him – or is it her? – is soon shared by a passer-by, an upright lady dressed in regulation black, sturdily bearing the usual enormous pot on her head, so well balanced she has no need to touch it. She tells me the pig is hers, part of her family of animals which she proudly enumerates as two oxen, one donkey, two sheep and a lamb (the lamb is for sale), twenty-three chickens and this pig and another one; and they all live at home with herself, her husband, her son of twelve and daughter of nine. And as well as that, she goes on, they have five and a half hectares of land which yield thirteen *quintali di grano* each August, and when they've sold four of them it leaves nine to last them the winter – which works out at one and a half *quintali di grano* each month. 'Now you see why we're Communists,' she says, and strides away.

Yes, the walls make the fact darkly obvious, even the cemetery; the grey, pointed curl of the hammer and sickle is daubed everywhere – some faded, some new – and the slow-moving men are as hunched and sour-looking as old Siberian trappers scowling into a useless wasteland. There are no young men among them, or very few; two thousand of the males are away working in France, Switzerland or Germany, somebody tells me, leaving the place to the old folk so they can shuffle among the pigs all day or sit endlessly in their doorways staring at the signs and the old writing on the walls opposite – POPOLO TI AMO, VIVA L'IMPERO and LA FEDE E VOLONTÀ FASCISTA HANNO PIEGATO LE COSE – sunken and misty but still clearly there. An odious place in an uncouth wilderness, was how Lear described Bisaccia, full of 'half-naked children, dogs and dirt'; and in the absence of any civility whatsoever, he hurried away from it with his rebellious mule driver. It hasn't changed much.

One wonders how it could have started, this silent town, so medieval and mouldy. Could it have been Roman Romulea, or a Greek settlement Latinised to Vis-Acies, as some would think, or just Bis-facta, having been rebuilt after an earthquake? A more extravagant view is that it was once renowned for its production of knapsacks, *bisacce*, 'decorated in many splendid colours'. But there's no such brightness today among its brown and brooding walls, and the boorish resentment of its inhabitants giving sullen stares that want you to go away. It gloats over its own misery and in the wallowing of its pigs that trundle everywhere like bubbles of pale flesh. And there are chickens too: they vie for numerical superiority and are more acute in scavenging through the litter, and when chased by children know exactly which doorway to flee into – but there is so much of appetising interest between the cobbles that they are soon back again.

Some thoughtful polliphile seems to be advancing the cause of the local hen, as there are fresh posters on the walls announcing POLLI COLTURA; these lead me to a small building which might be a disused school, where a white-coated chicken attendant is standing over an incubator containing twenty-five impeccably yellow Easter chicks huddled in sawdust. As I am his only audience I suggest that perhaps the people of Bisaccia have already found their own ways of ensuring the continuation of the species, but he assures me that such theories are not his business; the whole project has been paid for by somebody in America, and the Consorzio Agrario di Avellino has decided to use the funds by teaching the Bisacciesi how to rear chickens. A most noble gesture, were it not for the fact that *polli-coltura* has obviously thrived here successfully for hundreds of years without the help of science. The expressions on the birds' faces indicate how well they have got the problem worked out, and how they must never let an eyelid droop in fatigue or sickness lest they be deemed ready for the pot. For a commentary on the astuteness of these tenacious bipeds one has only to refer to the pages of Norman Douglas: he well describes their epic talents for multiplication and self-preservation in the face of overwhelming odds.

Campanian evolution being full of curious quirks, long before this plague of pigs and chickens Bisaccia was famous for asparagus 'of such great beauty', according to Doctor

Donzelli in 1677, that it was sent as gifts all over the kingdom 'and some way beyond it'. Mention of its excellence was even made a hundred years earlier – 'sitque Bisacta suis clarior asparagis ... ' – in the very year that Tasso arrived to stay with the local lord, Giambattista Manso, who (the scant archives of Bisaccia record) had the privilege of sampling young ladies the night before their weddings. If all went well, the chronicle states, the ceremony was permitted the next day; if not, she was sent to work in the castle kitchens till she improved. This fleshy ritual of enquiry only ended when a comely young man took his bride-to-be's place one night, and 'ad un certo momento' plunged his dagger into the master's heart.

Where all this took place is not absolutely certain, though there are the remains of a castle on the outer edge of the town, most of it hidden in a jungle of undergrowth and leaning trees, and those parts of it that are still standing are as decayed and uncared-for as the town itself. Concealed by its cloak of vegetation, it still whispers enchantment as if containing some fairy-tale sleeping beauty embalmed in cobwebs within its walls, where grappling ivies and brambles have launched their invasions, creeping towards mullioned windows to choke everything to death. Rain is doing the rest, and a few rusty notices warn one: DANGER, KEEP OUT, FALLING MASONRY, as if assigning it to imminent collapse.

But I am not alone. Some ancient retainer has appeared from the bushes and is pointing upwards, urging me to look. 'Tasso, Tasso,' he whispers, scribbling on his palm as if providing an explanation, '365 rooms . . .' and expands his eyes in saucer-like wonder, demanding I should believe him and his fantasy of one chamber for each day of the year. 'And Queen Giovanna of Naples stayed here too – la regina cattiva . . .' Where didn't she? I wonder. That energetic nymphomaniac must have slept in every castle in the kingdom (if all those guides were to be believed), lovingly whispering her prowess as the female Casanova of the south. No building of mention fails to echo with the rustle of her undressing and the fever of her steamy breath. But the old man has run out of anecdotes; he wishes he could take me inside; it is too dangerous, however, so instead he leads me away through the undergrowth, which in the bygone days of lords and barons was once laid out in formal gardens, till we emerge scratched and dishevelled on a cliff-edge looking westward and to the north. Below us is a plain that reaches to the horizon, brown and sun-baked, where the dust of a mule-cart or the flash of a sword blade could be seen for miles; while the castle itself lurks in a fold of ground behind us, hidden by trees and waiting to surprise any enemy that its scouts might report, who could then be slaughtered as they came up over the ridge.

But I've had enough of it; the hatred in Bisaccia is uncompromising, and they have no wish to speak. It is a mountainous promontory of sullen depression, and any enquiries about crops, fields, mileage to market or land ownership draw little from them but turgid silence. What plots of workable earth there are among the rocks and hillocks round about seem mostly abandoned. The stagnation of sentiment is such that no one will sell, lend, barter or co-operate; no person will share with his neighbour or try to halve the work; members of the same family will go off independently to scratch at different hillsides. 'A futile endurance, remote from history and time', Levi called the peasants' existence, and even Douglas could see it was a life of 'miserable revolting destitution' when he wasn't otherwise occupied. The crabbed old women sit in their doorways jealously shielding their day-long occupation, which is sieving lentils or peeling tomatoes or shedding corn-cobs or weaving chair-seats, and they never look up but just grunt inimical and gloomy mutterings. The hour hand of time has stood still here for years, and nothing can move it.

Fascism made an attempt in 1930, when an earthquake destroyed part of Bisaccia and all of nearby Aquilonia, and a new town was built further away called Aquilonia Nuova – but nobody wanted to move. Not even the Emperor's bombastic munificence could penetrate their apathy. MUS-SOLINI È MAMMA he wrote on the walls, but few believed him, and the granite shells of his grandiose vision – of long avenues with pale upstanding houses and shops and even schools and a church – are still there, five miles away, a little damp-stained now and unearthly empty. The few families in residence are ill at ease and walk round uncertainly as if lost in artificial and rootless space; for real life must be organically generated by the magic of Mother Earth: she is the only power their poor spirits really understand and worship. Her moods and foibles, her blessings and bad tempers they can appreciate, but not the interference of *Homo sapiens*.

I must go and see this dead town of Aquilonia, the tumbled ruins they call Paese Vecc' – The Old Place – where the goats and lizards and rabbits live among a graveyard of fallen buildings, strewn down the hill in a cascade of architectural crockery, limp shoulders of houses overgrown with grass the day the earth trembled and scattered them headlong into the valley to decompose slowly like so many corpses. I find a soft spot beyond the wind to dream among the giant hulks of old brickwork . . . of Greek coins that bear the legend AKADUNNIU, the ancient settlement, long since disappeared, that was the forerunner of Aquilonia; of Hannibal routing Fulvius Flaccus; of the noble Caracciolo family who were lords of this manor, one of them murdered by Nelson in the Bay of Naples; and then of the mysteriously named Carbonara . . .

As the silent hillside sweeps down towards the silver lake of San Pietro, shimmering in the sun like fractured glass, and the wind starts to beat against the dismembered limbs of the old town, I wonder if it may not have been some dying curse of the Bourbons that threw this whole area to the ground – this being the original seed-bed of the great revolution. Or so it is said by local historians (though no one will ever know), who maintain it was these woodcutters and charcoal burners who were the first of the Carbonara agitators to set about plotting against the government and taking mysterious oaths of anarchy, fomenting discontent by sending secret messages as far south as Sicily and north to the Alps. Even Byron got involved in these well-intentioned knots and groups and hierarchies that whispered revolution through the land like a thousand peasant Brutuses, as they invented passwords and signs and codes and mumbo-jumbo oaths of allegiance and barbaric rituals of initiation – some even calling for murder. But being born conspirators and useless organisers, mayhem soon followed: as each intriguer spun his own web and private armies roamed the countryside to settle old personal scores, arguers and doubters were drowned in blood, new leaders appointed overnight and squabbles, riots, rivalries and skirmishes became a daily diversion. The Aquilonia area alone was supposed to have three hundred thousand Carbonarists in its parish, led by a group called the Good Cousins: overnight they rounded up everyone they thought might be a Bourbon sympathiser and threw them over a cliff. Or so some of the locals say, repeating cloudy tales from their grandfathers, but no one really knows. It's all verbal tradition, and there are no precise accounts of the fragmented anarchy which swept the south in those years. Hilton has made an attempt in *Brigandage in South Italy*, Count Maffei has tried to chart some of the muddy waters in *Brigand Life in Italy*, and Maria Graham has provided several tales.

And what has changed? They were killing each other a hundred years before Garibaldi and a hundred years after him; they did it while a poet sang: 'In the balmy garden of

Italy, bondage is no more.'* And they're still doing it now.
The partisans disposed of each other in the war, the Mafia
still does it, and there are enough secret brotherhoods and
Masonic lodges today to fill a telephone directory. It is what
Barzini calls the invisible and perpetual Italian anarchy,
'spontaneously regulated by secret rules and customs'; it is
a plague of parasites and a network of conspiracy that deals
in greed, power and death, with tentacles that reach from
the bent peasant in the field to the inner sanctuary of St
Peter's. So what Lampedusa said would happen, did: 'In
place of the lion and the leopard they will have the hyena
and the jackal.'

For Italy is a quicksand, where real revolution is impossible and where each attempt drowns in its own miasma of
ignorance and ineptitude. There were Garibaldinis (good)
and Garibaldeschis (bad) and the Carbonara bands didn't
even know what they thought or whose side they were on
apart from their own – anti-Bourbon one year, anti-French
the next, anti-Bourbon five years later, anti-neighbour for
ever and usually anti-Pope, and then even anti-Piedmont.
And Sicily didn't know if it was part of Italy or an independent island, and nor did Sardinia, and King Ferdinand didn't
know which constitution to have, and even Garibaldi got
in a hopeless muddle and ended up back in Caprera.

This week a farmer of Aquilonia has had all seven of his
cows stolen in the night: an empty pen was all he found,
and lorry marks in the mud. So he went off to Nola to see
people who 'knew things' and eventually met *il capo*. 'I'm
sorry,' the great man said. 'It wasn't us. Aquilonia's not our
area; you'll have to try Foggia . . .' But in Foggia it was just
the same, and they suggested he ask in Potenza or even
Bari. And in Potenza they said he ought to try Naples
because they all move around so much nowadays . . . so he
gave up and went home.

* This was D. G. Rossetti's father, Gabriele Rossetti.

The lake below has turned black in the rising wind; cloud banks of impenetrable grey have cloaked the hilltops behind and are sinking down like fog. A wooded slope to the south is veiled in mist, tree-tops are lost in a ghostly vapour, and as the darkness flows swiftly in and the wind gives haunted sighs, all points of the compass vanish and compress, swathed in serpent tendrils of hostile nimbus crushing the land mass. I need shelter before the storm breaks; but it is too late, and it seeks revenge for my unkind thoughts about pig-filled Bisaccia. For this is no sanguine or experimental deluge; it is a *noyade* of devastating penetration, tipping out of the sky like buckets of sea water and flailing everything in its path with the joy of an inquisitorial torture instrument, soaking me in seconds with torrents of ice-cold visitation running down my chest and back, till chill pools form on the skin and weld damp particles of clothing to unaccustomed pieces of flesh. The rocks turn to tropical cascades, pathways to rushing brown mud, and silence into a hissing roar; running is instinctive but nearly impossible in liquid trousers that have suddenly become urgently possessive.

I rush to the first sign of shelter – half an old cellar with two walls and a corner of ceiling with pools of water growing rapidly on the floor, the roof cracked and showing breaches of sky – and shuddering in a cobweb corner are two waifs of shepherd children: a boy and a tiny girl, both drenched, the girl wearing clogs that bubble over with water each time she moves. With infinite wisdom in their big eyes, they assure me in whispers that it is certain to rain till nightfall as this is the first storm of the autumn; so we all stare shivering and defeated at the grey hiss of the elements rushing past and at the deepening pools on the floor as more arteries open in the ceiling. The wait is dumb and miserable and stretches towards the dark of evening; but then a lull comes and the infant shepherds file out without a word to merge for a grey moment with the ruined stumps in the drizzle before sliding away out of sight, leaving me nothing save their sharp cries in the mist calling to their storm-soaked sheep.

My host is not pleased to see me. He wasn't from the start anyway, but now that I bear half the water of Aquilonia as a gift he is less than welcoming. 'You'll catch pneumonia,' he says emphatically and with a hint of pleasure, to which I agree whole-heartedly and suggest, through rattling teeth, that a little warm water might be useful. But he shakes his head solemnly: there isn't any, nor is there a fire, nor is there warmth of any kind; the stove will be lit when it's time to cook supper. It's my fault for going out anyway; sensible people would have stayed at home . . . I remember what he said last night in one of his rare moments of conversation, when I asked him what people did in Bisaccia:

'We are all born here,' he said, 'so we stay here waiting to die.'

Another morning of excommunication, so I board a dilapidated bus to Calitri, which is over on another hilltop and is certainly not on the Appia. But what matter? Bisaccia is rotting with the plague and with mountain malcontent, a gutter of putrefaction and bilge water, while Calitri looks white and welcoming in the rays of early sun. It has much to be pleased about, for it is recovering from yesterday's *festa*, and there are still loops of coloured light bulbs strung along the main street, huge patterned haloes of pinks and greens tucked into lampposts and the tops of trees, and the gutters are white with lollipop sticks and the dead tails of streamers. Even the dogs are jaunty in their celebratory sniffs, and the people walk in a sticky daze of euphoria, their eyes still happily glazed, as if moving through air that is warm and heavy with post-consummation contentment. The bandsmen are obviously staying another day and are confidently strolling the streets, some arm-in-arm with satisfied young ladies; the old folk are sitting on the escarpment wall like a row of grandfather swallows, happy to have made it through for yet another year, and gossiping quietly about the old times.

Calitri is ancient Galestrum; it rests on a pinnacle of hill overlooking a sweeping plain and is virgin white. Everything about it reflects the sun – the walls, the stairways, the arches, the roofs flattened behind gleaming parapets to trap the rain – and the bell tower thrusts up like a blazing minaret; all is gentle and pillow-soft, even the stepped alleyways nuzzling between pale façades and disappearing in cobbled labyrinths towards cool shaded heights pierced by cardboard cut-outs of azure sky. The houses have multiplied into a coral reef of carelessly sculpted crusts, rearing in any shape or direction that pleases them, and clinging like suckling babes to this eyrie that towers over the Ofanto Valley.

And I have seen the rarity I came for: an old lady untouched by time and still in traditional dress – a long, wide-bustled skirt as dark as charcoal, a blouse of alabaster white with the sleeves and collar puffed up in lace and a delicate half-moon bonnet perched on the back of her hair and tied on with a crimson bow. Then there are three of them, all with walking sticks, sedately owning the road with their bent anachronistic waddle, ignoring everyone and equally ignored as if they were nothing but passing ghosts of a previous incarnation. This trio of ancient sibyls, all aged decorum and elegance, totters towards the square with a dignity that spurns the new and barbarous and is anchored in old dreams. And soon they will die – and the past with them – these wizened freaks of backwardness rustling with such graceful retrogression . . . soon they'll be thrown away.

The beating sun brings a thirst that can only be slated in some cavernous *bottiglieria* underground – of which Calitri has a number. Amid sips of a most powerful and giddy wine

I am asked most courteously why I am here. '*Perchè Calitri?*' murmurs the old gentleman, a kind and leathered face cracked by a thousand storms and blasted by sunlight, with deep listening eyes. It is hard to explain, I tell him: a Sibylline mystery, a call, voices of inner restlessness – have we not all some plaguing virus nibbling within our bloodstreams, diseased imaginings and secret madnesses? To dream them is only to regret the things not done. And he hears me with nodding comprehension and distant wisdom, as we deeply drink each other's health, smiling with pride at such a host of fairy tales – about a promised land, and knights on chargers, and kings in battle, and popes doing princes to death, and ancient gods at war, and where the sun always shone and everyone was everlastingly beautiful and always in love. '*Sì, sì,*' he nods, and we lift our sparkling glasses yet again to touch in mid-air.

To this paradise came many hopeful travellers, seeking never to arrive: Coryat with his *Crudities*, Fynes Morrison with his sword, Lascelles, Sandys, Hill, Evelyn and pilgrim father Chaucer; and other erudite wanderers like regal Swinburne dropping cards on silver salvers, angry Beckford railing against the Holy See, gentle Ramage floundering through woods and muddy rivers, ruin-loving Eustace steeped in ancient Greece, and the dashing Keppel Craven. Men of vision and unfathomable passions came – Milton and Shelley and Browning and Coleridge and Wordsworth and Swinburne and Wilde; and the carnally explicit had to come too – Charles James Fox who 'couldn't get a fuck' and Boswell who usually could; and the staid, superior, distant chroniclers – Ruskin, Scott, Hazlitt, Dickens . . . and Reynolds, Burney, Turner, Inigo Jones . . . shall I go on? A pause for liquid and for another flagon to arrive from the depths. The French sent Stendhal, Montaigne, Barthélemy, Montesquieu, Dupaty, St Non, de Musset, Duclos, Bertaux, Lenormant; and the Aryan raiders Archenholz, Goethe, Winckelmann, Riedesel, Gregorovius, Wagner, Mommsen

– all loving this golden sunny land, each dipping into the easy, private pleasures of a secret paradise while counting Angevin corner-stones, Roman busts, Salentine lizards, magic madonnas and cures for the evil eye; some dying of malaria or living for the first time ever, others fighting with assassins or fighting for Garibaldi. All drawn by this magic lodestone, this testament of beauty – even the women: Ladies Knight, Miller, Morgan and Montagu thieving birth-day-present lumps out of Herculaneum; tempestuous Blessington who did anything but idle; Janet Ross who cooked; and Elizabeth Browning who wrote poetry. His jaw has dropped, so we refill our glasses. 'Not women too?' he disbelieves. Oh yes, I assure him, we always export the mad ones, like Florence Nightingale, Mary Kingsley, Isabella Bird, Hester Stanhope, all over the world; Gertrude Bell too, and Freya Stark; and no one cares if they paint or faint, make love or music, strike attitudes or suitors, strip for Canova or sleep with Mussolini. No one cares about anything here; that's the whole point of being a promised land – it is all so unexpected, so completely accepted, so comfortably eccentric, so permanently promising . . .

But I have lost him; his crusty face has become a blur, and I am not sure where I started. Somewhere far away in the Bible . . . Edens, Nirvanas, Valhallas . . . beyond that last blue mountain perhaps . . . Then his face bursts forward out of the winy mist, almost in focus, steaming somewhere towards me. But you didn't have Christopher Columbus did you, or Marco Polo? And don't forget Julius Caesar . . . *neanche Messalina* . . .

An appropriate moment to leave wine-soaked Calitri with its gracious old women wrapped in their own cocoon of time, as I dream of other travellers' visions with a touch of sadness. There is so much one will never know: the burnt memoirs of Byron, the diaries of Burton, the journals of d'Annunzio . . . Did Philip Sidney come to Italy? Yes. Did

Donne or Webster or Marlowe? A useless tumble of inebriate thoughts as the bus rattles back to Bisaccia, that backwater of mountainous and wintery discontent where the men are downcast and the ill-natured hags are forever crumpled in their doorways, fumbling at leaves of fennel with bony blue fingers. Autumn is on its way; a crisp wind is claiming leaves, rattling the untidy lines of washing and whipping chickens' tails up like can-can fans. We won't miss each other.

THIRTEEN

Melfi *1*

Melfi is a town with problems; one is whether or not it should become the capital of Basilicata's third province. Some faceless authorities have decided in a moment of idleness that the earlier arrangements made by the Greek Basileus in AD 930 are no longer adequate, so the region is in the midst of internal reorganisation. Everyone knows this to be a pointless exercise – save that it will keep the loafing hive of bureaucrats occupied with months of argument, mountains of paperwork and new puffed-up airs of self-importance. Paper and forms are manna to them: without them nothing exists and nothing happens, so you must always have plenty with you. Exhortations to take this all-important issue seriously are liberally pasted on to every available piece of wall-space. CITTADINI ... MELFITANI ... AMICI ... PATRIOTI ... COMBATTENTI – plenty of words for the same thing, but they attract singular lack of interest from a wise population well used to such time-wasting administrative exercises, and fully aware that nothing will ever change; except that as usual some different pockets will become well-lined along the way.

Another problem is the plaque, which no one ever sees. The great worrier Theodor Mommsen insisted they should put one up as long ago as the 1850s, which they finally managed in 1922, apologising for the *'incuria delle amministrazioni del tempo'*. Nothing fancy: just a discreet tablet on the town-hall wall, which by some circuitous route throws more lustre on Dante than it does on the Germanic emperor who made the town his capital:

IN QUESTA ANTICA CAPITALE DEL REAME DI PUGLIA
ILLUSTRE PER ARMI, INDUSTRIA E FREQUENZA DI POPOLO

CARA A FEDERICO II DI SVEVIA
ITALIANO PER NASCITA, GENIO, ARDORE DI LOTTE
CHE NE RINNOVÒ I BALUARDI E LA CINTA
FURONO NEL MCCXXXI PROMULGATE LE COSTITUZIONI
PRIMO FONDAMENTO DELLO STATO LIBERALE
PROFETIZZATO POI DA DANTE . . .*

By the end of it Frederick has come off second-best, and
the famous Constitutiones Augustales is merely a paren-
thesis which, had it endured, would have been the Magna
Carta of Italy, the wisest document since Justinian, said
someone – the whole constitution for the kingdom set out
with all the administrative, legal and procedural details
drawn up by the Emperor's first parliament: laws, rules,
hierarchies, regional authorities, all the formalities, controls, means of communication, codes of practice and rights
of appeal. An epic work of wisdom and fairness, now
forgotten, which was shredded by the papal and Angevin
sword. But at least the place basked in glory then, the
capitale del reame and Frederick's favourite city, where he
lived in splendour with his whole court. And one can see
why, poised as it is on the highest point of a ridge of
undulating hills, and commanding infinite views on all
sides over the gently receding corrugations left by the final
seismic convulsions of Monte Vulture as the Mediterranean
was born. Its cold crater glowers blue-black in the distance,
nursing its teeming litter of wart-like hills spread round
about in a cast-off skirt, with Melfi triumphant on the

---

* In this ancient capital of Apulia
(Renowned for its warriors and the greatness of its people)
So dear to Frederick of Swabia
Who was Italian by birth, victorious in many battles
The builder of our ramparts and walls –
The great Italian Constitution was decreed in 1231,
The foundation of a fair and free way of life,
Carried on in the works of Dante . . .

highest fold: smooth and dominant, curved like a crouching lion's back and crowned by its long-abandoned castle. Today it glows gold and black in the autumn sun, and is completely forgotten.

Which raises a third problem: that the man I spoke to in the State Tourist Office in London had never heard of it.

'You mean Amalfi,' he told me.

'No,' I said, 'it's called Melfi: one of the old capitals of Italy. It has a castle and a famous sarcophagus, and Prince Doria owns it now, and Frederick used to live there, and there's a book by Malpica which says it has good roads, beautiful buildings, a fine cathedral and gracious squares . . . in fact, it is one of the most beautiful and celebrated towns in Basilicata.'

'Ah,' he said closing his books emphatically. 'We don't do Basilicata here; you'll have to ask in Naples.'

So much for north and south. No one ever goes south of Naples if they can help it – They're Arabs down there . . . Saracens, *ladri, negri* . . . And so much for officialdom when taken off its guard, that strutting and omnipresent evil, with its claws into everything, licensed not to care what it says, and wishing you to disappear as quickly as possible – or else so misleadingly and effusively helpful it summons up an army of such persuasive and argumentative eloquence that you end up missing your train. Talk, that's what they want: yards of it, like spaghetti, or dismissive ill-mannered grunts. You can never tell what's coming, that's the problem; having perfected the art of the unpredictable they may give a curt shrug or a circus extravaganza of operatic enthusiasm. You never know till it happens.

There's no choice today though; everyone is sour and morose, as if the contagion of the south were on them, shiftily shambling through the narrow streets with hang-dog looks and baggy, ill-fitting trousers as if drying uncomfortably in the sun after half drowning in some Lethean lake, still damp with drips of darkness and distrust.

The weight of resignation distorts them: grudge, despair and heavy-heartedness provide a southern shapelessness never mentioned in guidebooks. My search for an inn through the cobbled lanes is followed by forests of peeping eyes behind the uneasy twitch of beaded curtains. Will it be the 'utterly filthy' one that Augustus Hare found here freely admitting pigs and chickens?

Instead there's a grim dame of the mountains, firmly seated in a chair behind a *locanda* door, who half lifts her hooded eyes and lets a shaft of cobwebbed sun streak off her skull-cap of jet-black hair slipstreaming behind her to a fearsome bun. 'No food,' she mutters with relish, not moving, 'and no coffee for breakfast either.' After which the Devil himself peeps out from behind her chair and glares eyefuls of undiluted hatred at me, puffing his anger out through blocked nostrils, before creeping from the dusty recess to cross himself urgently against my alien influences. It is her hunchback son, divining more about me than I know myself and not liking what he finds; for *il gobbo* has magic powers and is privy to unspeakable secrets, he can see into the future, commune with the spirits, talk to animals and foretell disasters; on good days he will find you buried treasure and pick the winning number of *il lotto*. So never underestimate or despise a hunchback south of Naples, for he may decide to exercise revenge. His exorcism now is to pace the creaking passage outside my room from end to end, interspersing his patrol with uneven gallops and bursts of sprinting in the hope that they may hasten my host of imported evils out of his territory to plunge down Melfi's mountainside like a Gadarene herd. Do his sudden bursts of speed mean he has caught one? I wonder, and I enquire delicately from his mother how long his metronomic vigil may continue. But she – southern simplicity itself – says that as long as her son is happy then she is too. So with that matter comprehensively explained, all that remains is the question of food, as evening is approaching.

Does the *signora* happen to know ... could she recommend ...?

Rocco does considerably more than run a restaurant; he is also a gangster, a follower of the nineteenth-century tradition of brigandage hereabouts that provided such legendary figures as Crocco and Ninco Nanco. Lying, cheating and stealing have long been part of his nature, like many bright southerners repressed by northern hatred and denied opportunity or hope by intricate webs of favouritism and bureaucracy. So he joined the Mafia long ago and went to New York and killed a man; the courts gave him thirteen years in jail and then a ticket back to Italy, where he continues to operate quietly on the fringes. He was framed of course. 'Jeez ... Never seen the guy in my life,' he complains, which is often the bad luck of the underling; though he still drives up to Naples once a week to see Lucky Luciano and to collect a few orders for the neighbourhood of Melfi – cigarettes, lighters, whisky, a camera or two, a box of watches, sometimes even a gun. 'Everybody has one tucked away somewhere,' he says, spitting in his newly laid sawdust. 'I'd kiss the floor to go back there. You can buy a copper here for five hundred lire ... the law in Italy is made for imbeciles.'

La legge in Italia è fatta per i fessi, only idiots obey the law; the fact becomes obvious after twenty-four hours: smoke where it says NO SMOKING, go in at the exit, park in forbidden zones, challenge one-way streets, ignore red traffic lights. Law-breaking is a prime necessity of life, one of the essentials to existence. It's their 'wonderful anarchic spirit', says Stuart Hood; the 'running sore of Italy', says Barzini: their inventive skill and charm at weaving in and out of all regulations and controls so adeptly, thus perpetuating the underground anarchy that causes so much of the suffering and injustice filling the land. Nor is it a recent phenomenon; Samuel Rogers said the same in 1815 – 'a land where laws are trampled on, and lawless men walk in the sun' – though in those days he referred to the uniformed bands of brigands who virtually ruled vast areas of the south, men like the Vardarellis who controlled Foggia, who had persuaded the King in Naples they were peace-loving vigilantes and had even been given a special uniform. After years of looting, extortion, murder and other abuses Keppel Craven saw them all wiped out in one day by a troop of dragoons, 'while watching children howled and women tore their hair out'.

Nor is that the half of it: Maria Graham tells some interesting tales, and so does Strutt, and the poor old Scottish banker Moens actually got himself kidnapped for over a hundred days in 1865. That was the great age of abduction, when countless travellers disappeared never to be seen again, and there were impassioned letters in *The Times*, and angry questions in Parliament, and diplomatic cables were exchanged, and English and French warships were anchored off Salerno waiting to receive released hostages and sometimes their captors. For no one knew what was really happening, and even if they did things would be different the following day, as the release of south Italy meant an explosion of uncontrol and anarchy and taking revenge on anything, be it royalist Bourbon or Piedmontese or Cavourite or Mazzinian or Sicilian secessionist or Neapolitan republican or just a passing traveller. Moens' account is an interesting read for any student of Italian brigandage, with tales of eating snow and mouldy animal intestines, and walking for hundreds of miles in complete circles to avoid pursuers who didn't even want to catch the gang anyway. He hasn't much good to say about the forces of law and order in the new Italy – things were a good deal better under the Bourbons is his view – and nor has his frantically searching wife in her journal, having witnessed secret policemen arrest one another for suspicious behaviour. One can't help wondering at the end of it all what

might have happend to the mass of photographic impedimenta he carried with him everywhere, even to the summit
of Etna: perhaps it is still in a Calabrian cave somewhere.
He is one of the few writers to put forward a sympathetic
and constructive view afterwards, an objective appraisal
that suggests possible solutions and describes the collusion
between the brigands and peasants, united in their hatred
of authority, and how they bargained over the supply of
provisions and signalled to each other all over the mountains by bird-calls and axe-blows on trees. He is amazed too
at the incompetence of the authorities and the pursuing
soldiers, suspecting they could have found and released him
earlier had they wished, and he actually feels sympathy for
his captors in their struggle against the vacuous and insen-
sitive inactivity of those in power.

His wife also makes some forthright observations during
her hundred days of waiting – on children of six working in
mines, monks who go shopping in horse-drawn carriages
(one of them she met was building an aeroplane); and after
being chased down the road by an angry hotelier for not
paying her bill remarks that the only way to get on at the
Italian hotel is to bargain beforehand: 'Those who pay the
price demanded are despised as well as imposed upon.' Wise
words indeed, and even wiser ones on the role of the Italian
female in society, having noticed how the peasants trotted
home on their donkeys after work leaving their wives and
daughters to carry the harvest back on foot: 'I thought of
some of my countrywomen who are so fond of contrasting
the status of their sex in England with that of their sisters
abroad, based solely upon the charming external politeness
they have received from a Frenchman or Italian in some
ballroom.' A sensible and perspicacious woman; and a book
much underrated.

Women, beauty, biological magnetism, the fatal attraction
of hims and hers – an appropriate matter to consider now

that darkness is closing in; it is the hour of the *passeggiata*, and the bright human fireflies are darting among the trees. I have fed on a mountain of Rocco's well-buttered spaghetti and his bread and cheese, and have drunk his wine, and now that the heat has gone from the sun into early twilight the tree-lined avenue outside is alive with slowly passing bodies on their ritual journeys of evening incitement. First come whispering groups of softly walking girls, all hand-in-hand or arm-in-arm, slenderly neat and erect, with young jauntily beckoning bodies coyly wrapped in clean coloured dresses but letting their bright skirts swing from teasing hips. They move noiselessly, with trim and eye-catching expertise, innocent provocation in their stately breasts and smoothly sliding thighs as they sparkle in the half-dark like tropical moths, flowing forward in tantalising steps, dangerous sweetness in their eyes and the primeval huntress in their cat-like tread. Glowing embers of an evening rainbow beneath the trees, they mingle their bright and spotless colours and laugh softly, oranges, blues and emeralds with scarlet, cornflower and gold, all fused into the same motion as a kingfisher on the wing. Their heads are high with long hair thrown back in confidence as they let the sight of their limbs ripple and rub on the gaze of the watching men, who fall in behind to follow at a voyeur's distance, sharp-toed and sharp-eyed. This tribal ritual of courtship and amorous dalliance is agonisingly chaste, as if an Eden of childlike Eves were wooing the serpent, watched by a tumescing tribe of Adams made dumb by their enticements but slinking forward narrow-eyed in delirious expectation. Each one of them makes the same chemical response: short heroic Hollywood waddles, shoulders inflated into a boxer's hunch, cognisant smirks that signal the size of his invisible virility and the muscular power in his Olympic loins.

It is a curious phenomenon, this mating business in Italy, full of contradictory manifestations: sometimes chaste and sometimes barbaric, and either dreamily divine or impurely pagan, but always dominated by the outward show. For the appearance of it is more important that the reality, and just like some Gothic cathedral its exterior must predominate and overpower even if the interior is bare. Hence the frenzied scenes of palpitating lust that pantomime through the summer cities, when car-horns toot at wriggling rumps, love-howls echo down narrow streets, necks swivel like idiot roosters, tongues hang out like drunk St Bernards, and tight trousers tighten further still – affection with an erection, someone called it, a grotesque exhibition of mental foreplay and of teeming schoolboy-nocturnal imaginations running riot. But after this braying overture to orgasm the curtain never rises ... everything shrivels into vestal solitude just as the stars come out to approve the failure, for barking dogs don't bite, and *post clamorem homo italianus tristis* ...

And all of it is pandered to most graciously by the light-hearted ladies, with no little sadistic pleasure, for it flatters them and tortures the males; so they taunt his obsession for manliness and his trumpet-blasts of professed virility, and they love his frustration and stupidity. They know just what his bellowing means: the pain of an overfilled sperm bank and an inflated sexual ego.

We have all helped perpetuate this myth of a priapic land filled with Casanovas and Don Giovannis, where only bedroom conquests count, where the great centre of pilgrimage is St Penis, and where the armies of unloved flock each year with hopeful organs of veneration all aquiver. The truth is different. They are among the worst lovers in the world, and it is nothing but *bella figura* – a vainglorious rodomontade obscuring a vacuum. They only do it because it looks manly, said one expert on Italian love habits; they're obsessed by fear that anyone should doubt their virility, said another – and was requested to leave the country.

So do not be taken in by this vapour of amorous humbug, the everlasting boosting of pubic egos, nor by candle-lit spaniel eyes, nor the vanity of fitness performances prettifying the beaches on summer days. It is all narcissistic – self-loving exhibitionism. I have dried a victim's tears more than once, and been privy to many closet confessions about the brevities of consummation and fidelity.

It is for this the female seeks her revenge, for all the veneer and falsehood, and the shame of having her own *bella figura* destroyed so quickly, after all the hopes and the youthful excitement of arousing as many sighs and erections as possible. And then, after settling for the ultimate *figura* of marriage, she endures his unquenchable thirst to display his continuing manliness during her metamorphosis from sylph to suckling mother and on towards pasta-fattened flesh; so decides to take a lover. No tantalising this time, just a regaining of self-esteem and a private renewal of her own lost *bella figura* and desirability. So she wins the game in the end; and while the men all think they run the relationships and control the country, it is the women who run the men.

So it is tonight: the age-old game of gods and goddesses, Priapus rampant but Venus dominant, a silent ballet of dancing devils on ego trips of orgasmic fantasy pursuing a clutch of moonlit graces who lure them on with swirling webs of temptation, diaphanous and out of reach.

Beware then, you moist-thighed northern maidens with lonely hearts, lost in dreams of dark-eyed Ferrari romance. Love here is rapid ravishment and slow unhappiness, a night of flame and years of ashes. Forget a warm sensual heaven laced with stars and the tune of deep-throated nightingales; flee back to the cold ethic of the north, where it is safer to be born of a stockfish and live than to die from the rebellion of a Latin codpiece.

*

An unquiet night between damp sheets that are far too small, one of them half covering an unyielding straw mattress that crackles harsh protestations at every move. And there are plenty of them. Apart from fleas and other uninvited company, nothing is less conducive to sleep than a cold bed laid on straw: it suggests noise even if there is none. I listen in vain for the sweet notes of the nightingales that Ramage heard here, but the shrewd birds have departed long since; instead there is the ghostly creaking of young *gobbo* playing exorcist and sentinel outside my room, flitting along the passage like a wounded bat. And so I read . . .

Although the Castle of Melfi has been ruined by the earthquake of August the 14th, 1851, at least one-fifth part of it having been thrown down, namely, the towers of the outer side, with much of the modern palace, the great gallery, the rooms occupied by Il Signor Lear, the other gallery, and all that side of the building occupied by the family: yet, notwithstanding, no person who was in the castle at the time of the earthquake perished . . . the campanile of the cathedral fell down to one-third of its height . . . the octagonal church, and the great Casa Manna . . . exist no longer. Such is also the case with the Town Hall . . . the Palazzi Aquilecchia-Aranea, Severini, and many others. Thus it is too . . . with all the smaller houses in Melfi, which are all of them destroyed . . . and at the first shock of the earthquake there perished in [a great taverna] 62 individuals, and 25 horses; this building is now literally a shapel s heap of stones. Not more than 840 persons were killed in Melfi.*

* From a letter by Vittorio Manassei, 1852, in Lear.

Details of the terrible earthquake which took place in
Melfi . . . reach Naples but slowly . . . The morning of
the 14th of August was very sultry, and a leaden
atmosphere prevailed. It was remarked that an unusual
silence appeared to extend over the animal world. The
hum of insects ceased, the feathered tribes were mute,
not a breath of wind moved the arid vegetation. About
half-past two o'clock the town of Melfi rocked for
about six seconds, and nearly every building fell in.
The number of edifices actually levelled with the earth
is 163, of those partially destroyed 98, and slightly
damaged 180. Five monastic establishments were
destroyed, and seven churches, including the cathedral
. . . More than 700 dead bodies have already been dug
out of the ruins . . . I proceed to give a few anecdotes
. . . 'I was travelling . . . within a mile of Melfi, when I
observed three carts drawn by oxen. In a moment the
two most distant fell into the earth . . . Shortly after
. . . the third car was swallowed up . . . I found [a man]
stupefied – he was both deaf and dumb; the boy
appeared to be out of his mind, and spoke wildly, but
eventually recovered. The poor man still remains
speechless.'*

Melfi, and all around, present a singular and
melancholy appearance . . . people wandering about
stupified, men searching in the ruins, women weeping,
children here and there crying for their parents, and
some wretched examples of humanity carrying off
articles of furniture. The authorities are nowhere to be
found.*

Such are three accounts of the Melfi earthquake of 1851.
In spite of the absence of 'the authorities', it should be

* From the *Athenaeum Journal* of 13 September 1851, in Lear.

noted that the King himself was there within days, directing
the rescue and relief work in person, and that he made a
private donation to the town of two hundred thousand
ducats; and all the time he was there he knew that his
youngest son lay dying in Naples. Furthermore, he dismissed a senior regional administrator for misappropriating
funds during the period, and pardoned any escaped convicts
from Melfi jail who had stayed in the town to help.

Such a display of royal humanity doubtless helps to
explain why Melfi briefly became an active centre of anti-
Garibaldi sentiment in 1861, and for one whole week led a
pro-Bourbon uprising. It was started by an old soldier of
Francis II's army, who rallied the people to take up arms
and persuaded the Piedmontese National Guard to defect,
then released all the prisoners from jail, had portraits and
busts of Garibaldi and Victor Emmanuel publicly beheaded,
draped Bourbon flags from all the windows and had a
thanksgiving mass celebrated in the cathedral. And such
was the people's joy when they heard that an 'official'
Bourbon general was on his way with an army of reinforce-
ments that they 'strewed the entry to the town with
flowers', and held another thanksgiving mass in the main
square. But this general was called Carmine Crocco and his
first duty on arrival was to collect donations from every
household, 'to maintain the holy cause', thus relieving
them of some thirty thousand ducats. And on the following
morning he announced that as Unionist troops were on the
way he had better leave immediately. 'Such is the instability of human beings in time of revolution,' comments
Count Maffei, describing how quickly the Melfitans found
tricolours to fly from their windows again, and made their
effigies of Francis II and Maria Sophia look like those of
Garibaldi and Victor Emmanuel.

At last a visit to the remains of the castle: the rooms long
gone where Edward Lear sampled 'princely subtleties of
luxury' in a suite filled with gilded mirrors and furniture,

old oak chests and older armour. He was even served buttered toast and *caffè* for breakfast – would it were so today! The straw and the *gobbo*-scamperings in the night must have blended eventually into a narcotic; and now, dusty-mouthed and cramped, I have been sought out by a guide – for news travels fast in these remote and hilly townships, especially of inquisitive strangers nosing into bypaths of history.

It is Signor C—, an anxious and bespectacled schoolmaster, who is the town's Honorary Inspector of Archaeological and Historical Monuments – a prestigious appointment conferred on him by officials in Bari and Salerno, for which he is paid nothing, but has responsibility for Melfi's entire cultural heritage. If any local person is stupid enough to show an interest, they think ... Small wonder he looks worried. What am I doing, and why am I here, and do I speak German, and where have I parked my car, and searching looks of suspicion and disbelief at my wandering innocence. Just the Appian Way? Why, it never came here anyway. It was over to the west, near ... but now you're here, *signore* ...

And so to the castle, heading uphill through the narrow streets towards the wind, as the houses tail off rapidly near the heights, where odd walls stand partly dismembered; and then black against the sky rears this battleship of a broken building, as if marooned on a sandbank as it rushed over the rolling waves. Dismal ravens float silently out of the funnelled towers on outstretched wings, and hulks of crumbling wall sag like the drooping shoulders of a spurned and too-old lover. Young saplings have rooted in the cracks, and the tumbled stones have been roughly dragged away to make piled-up cairns or goalposts. 'What fools we are,' he says, staring at it, '*ignoranti* ... arguing about a new capital of the province while this goes on falling down every day. A royal palace where popes have slept, and Robert Guiscard and Hildebrandt, where Frederick wrote his Constitution and his book on falconry. They think local politics are more important. We've had twenty different governments in as many years and nothing has changed; while here two ceilings fell in a month ago and no one has even been to look.' He has my sympathy. If it's south of Naples forget it: a little hand-out for the palace at Caserta perhaps, and Pompeii can look after itself with all those visitors – anyway it's only half excavated and nothing has been done for fifty years and a lot of the stuff gets pinched; and Herculaneum? who wants to unearth a library of old Greek and Roman texts, a few more bronzes, another bakehouse or brothel? Keep all tourists north of Naples. *Italia Nostra* says it all: a tiny quarterly pamphlet no one ever reads, pleading for a little sanity and dignity when it comes to matters of history and the isolation of the south and a neglect amounting to vandalism. Perhaps there'll be a meridion dawn one day . . .

We approach the looming Norman keep, scarred and sad, as our feet scrape over tumbled stones. 'A royal palace,' he mutters in exasperation, 'and I've just got the last of the squatters out – twenty-seven families.' We climb together over banks of grass, through an archway, into a courtyard strewn with boulders and fallen masonry, then enter a chain of rooms with pitted earthen floors where the final shreds of plaster on the walls show swirls of long-faded colour, and vaulted ceilings curve upward to massively hewn bosses. And then the two rooms jaggedly open to the sky, and he stares up sighing and kicks the fallen rubble. 'So you see, *dottore*, the Soprintendenza delle Belle Arti is in Bari, and Antichità is in Salerno, and between them they can't decide which category the castle is in, art or antiquity – so nothing happens . . .'

We move across a second courtyard, ghostly in its silence, where spirits of dead paladins seem to whisper from the walls, and he unlocks a heavy door at the base of a tower to usher me through. Dimly I perceive a long rectangular room, ill-lit by high cobwebbed windows, vast enough to be a banquet chamber, its floor dark with the congestion of heaped-up stones and builders' rubble and time's long detritus, a narrow aisle picked through it like a mountain path to balance on as we advance. Good God almighty! it's a carpet of Etruscan urns on either side of me, reaching from wall to wall, with dark mouths open as my eyes slowly acclimatise – Greek, Roman, medieval – stacked in rows with military precision and all agape, with fat plain bodies or figured thin ones, some with elbows, arms, rims, lips, waists, necks, some squat and clownish, others tulip-elegant. And heaped among them a feast of marble heads, limbs and torsos, weapons and helmets and ornaments . . . and majolica dishes and terracotta reliefs . . . and languid against a wall two chariot-wheels . . . Sadly he raises an urn shaped and painted as the wide-eyed owl of Minerva:

'You see the problem, then. They won't even give me a cupboard to put it in, not even wood to make shelves. I've asked the Mayor and written to the bishop, but nothing happens. Upstairs I've got boxes of Doria family papers going back to 1532 . . . and the farmers bring in more stuff all the time – after they've sold the best of course. *Siamo tanti ignoranti . . .*'

Words seem superfluous: another minute tragedy. Yet who requires another antique storehouse, when the real world outside is full of wars, starvation, slavery, torture, death, and fifty thousand souls give a final gasp each minute? But why not use it if we have it? Enrich the experience of the living just a little by seeing the beauty of the past. Acorns may become oak trees one day, even in this blighted land of *ignoranti*.

We step outside into the fiery sun, grinning down its torture and bouncing it off the courtyard walls. The school-master squints into it, pointing upward. 'That's the tower of the Seven Winds,' he says, 'where Frederick had his study and did his writing; and there's a room I haven't found yet:

it must be a dungeon. I have a letter written in 1290 by a prisoner who says the sun only shone through his window for ten minutes each day, and only in June. It must be on the north side.'

We walk down into Melfi's midday heat, where the sunlight bursts off the grey and yellow walls like the clash of cymbals, and the oven-breath of God is cooking the stones. The stifling narrow streets wrap their manacles of revenge on us, bouncing discomfort off the houses and sucking it up from the cindered cobbles so that breath is stillborn. Fierce light turns all into blurs and blinks of cellar black or paper white like the gutted corpse of a zebra, and everything is quiet and still as a midday graveyard. Noon, death and silence have coalesced, and nothing moves, just a flattened dog testing his scorched ribs gently in expiring pants, stretched as a shot hare, and stone chickens, paralysed like sphinxes, too hot to blink. Even the aged crones have shuffled away like wise old spiders, leaving their black doorways empty, and the flies are scorched senseless and drone in with slow exhaustion for a drunken ride on my face.

The schoolmaster seems oblivious, skipping over the frying-pan of stones and barely panting. He is too busy complaining about Melfi to notice it is suffocating me. They have an asbestos-like insensitivity to the heat, this tiny tribe of possessed individuals. There are all too few of them: most collapse all too readily at the first sting of the sun like stricken seaweed. He is rushing me downhill and across a road towards a metal garage door which is levered open by pulling on a chain; it rattles up screeching painfully on unoiled joints. There is blackness within, a cool pool of darkness – a fresh waterfall of comfort to bathe in – and a square, grey shape lonely at the centre, gathering a slow whiteness as if smiling at the birth of light. The famous sarcophagus of Melfi is better than any in Rome, said Lenormant. Its cloudy outline turns to clear-cut curves of frozen marble alabaster – a host of frosted figures parading round the glacial tomb, fifteen of them, as if on eternal winter guard. Who is she, this quietly sleeping girl-child with one arm at rest behind her head, gently surrendered to her maker? And how did she die (probably in her twelfth year)? Nobody knows. Road menders found her not far below the surface between here and Rapolla a hundred years ago. Perhaps the much-loved daughter of a Roman provincial governor, perhaps the young wife of a senator or general – the gods and heroes closed round her in arctic jealousy are saying nothing except that she was very precious. 'It used to be in the town hall,' explains the schoolmaster, 'but people thought it was part of the furniture: they leant on it and kicked at it, and children wrote their names on the marble, so I had it moved here.'

One steps back from it with a little wonder, a tinge or awe that death can be made to look so beautiful, and to last for so long.

We stand ready to brave the sun again as the metal gate squeaks down, returning her to darkness. 'Come,' he says excitedly, 'I'll show you the Venusan Gate, where Frederick came in after hunting . . .' But this withering furnace of yellow dust is too much, and the flies are back again, my face drawing them like a magnet. Perhaps *il gobbo* is off duty and I might snatch a little sleep to make up for last night; so I bid him a grateful farewell. He removes his glasses to give me a final smile. 'Be kind about Melfi if you write about her,' he says. 'She is not all bad. Some of us love her very much.'

FOURTEEN

Melfi 2

Waking up at teatime for a second day combines heaven with hell. One scratches upward from depths of drowning towards daylight again, uncertain whether the world deserves this second chance. But the morning violence is over; daylight has become soft and liquid, almost friendly; a suspicion of oleander and rhododendron hangs in the balmy air; even the muttering voices are quiet, no longer battling against the heat. It is as if some kind fairy has flown across the sun, calming its rage; and when I reach the doorway even *il gobbo* attempts a testy smile from the curled-up comfort of his mother's chair; and she too has suddenly become afflicted with an overwhelming desire for conversation.

His brother will soon start at Bari University, she tells me, and will study engineering. Italy needs engineers, she continues, and the examination results have just come through from Melfi's Liceo Scientifico. He was one of the lucky ones.

'Good, good,' I beam. 'Well done. I'm delighted. How many passed?'

'They all did.'

'All? Excellent! Every one of them?'

'Yes. All eleven of them . . . the whole class.'

'Wonderful,' I exclaim, 'what marvellous results. Everyone must be very pleased.'

'Yes,' she says, dropping her eyes with half a smile. 'Only three of them took the exams, him and two others – the only ones in school that day.'

'Three? Goodness! What happened to the other eight?'

The hopeless shrug comes, and a little sigh; the eyes vacant and resigned. She has an admission to make.

'Fortune . . .? Call it what you like: one of those things. Sick on the exam day, perhaps, or a family crisis, some *incidente*. So the teachers write letters, or the school officials . . . explanations are made; they know people . . . telephone calls, *sistemazione, come sempre.*'

Not bad at all. Seventy-five per cent slipped through the net on nods, winks, favours, secret signs. She does it too, no doubt, to get her *permesso* for the *pensione*; she knows someone somewhere. Anything to beat the system and avoid the right channels: it is much easier to start a system of your own, and it always has been, right back before the days of brigands. As there's no way through the bumbling bureaucracy, go round it. What did Chitarella say – The first rule in playing cards is try to see your opponent's hand? Precisely. Never be honest: it doesn't pay. Better to lie, deceive, fiddle, swindle, crib, steal, pull a multitude of strings. But on no account be stupid enough to stick to the rules.

Rocco agrees, at suppertime when I've wandered down, looking for those hips swinging along the avenue, but it is too early . . . 'If you're honest today,' he says, pointing his fingers like a pistol, 'you may as well be dead, and it is the same the world over.' His voice is matter-of-fact: no feeling, no moral questioning, impervious. 'Here. Do you want to buy a good lighter? Dunhill?' The two *carabinieri* in the corner don't even look up; they're slurping orange-speckled entrails of spaghetti off their plates with gusto, expertly squirting it inwards through their lips, as if an albino's innards were being sucked into a vacuum cleaner. A salesman is on his own in another corner, studying a newspaper intently; *Do not disturb* is written all over him, *I just want to get this nightmare visit over*. Somewhere else there's a burly farmer gnawing at something, coat off, muscled like an ox, cramming bread into his mouth and swilling it down

half-chewed with wine while he grunts to himself. So Rocco
flicks the lighter and wanders over to the *carabinieri* . . .

Hopeless! Incomprehensible! What on earth is one to do
with them? Lawrence wanted to know. A nation seeking an
identity, and lost in the process; all on stage without a
producer and not quite knowing the plot. No one has found
one for them yet . . . Mussolini, Garibaldi, Caesar, not a
single pope nor a king or emperor . . . even poor Gramsci
gave it up when they split all his Communist cells up into
pirate gangs and cliques and camarillas. Italians would
undermine anything, was his view: they're their own worst
enemy. 'Yorick's skull with the worms in it' Ruskin called
them, hating their behaviour as much as he loved their art,
surveying them with Popkins-family contempt and certainty that 'everything not English must be wrong'. Self-
destructive, then? A deep-seated wish that nothing should
work? A desire for death? That is what Lampedusa thought:
'They've borne the weight of other people's civilizations for
twenty-five centuries; all they want is to forget and to sleep.
Their sensuality is a search for oblivion; murder a search
for death; languor a search for rest. But their vanity is
stronger than their misery, so they call it pride. Really it is
blindness.' He knew them better than most, and is probably
right. He is the only Italian to write about his own people
truthfully. A book worth reading; but no answers are given.

I dig at the plate of pasta Rocco has brought over,
thoughts definitely morbid. I suppose this must be the most
central point of unwanted Italy, I am thinking, when the
commotion starts: something like a small explosion is
occurring at one of the tables. The ox-like farmer has turned
round, almost burgundy-faced, half chewing as he splutters
out:

'We were better off under the Bourbons.' At least he has a
sense of history. Eyes glowering furiously, he addresses
everyone, anyone, no one in particular: '*Ladri, ladri,*' he
shouts at all of us, chest heaving like an angry bull and

leaning forward, 'filthy capitalists . . . They buy my grapes
for twenty lire a kilo then sell them in Milan tomorrow for
two hundred. Greedy exploiters! Profiteers! Villains!' But
no one looks up. There's no surprise; or perhaps he chose
his moment badly. Usually a public outburst like this
would start a quorum; everybody would have an opinion,
and in no time there would be a tumult. *'Quattro bambini,'*
he carries on, rather louder, addressing everyone: 'four
children, and my wife, and all our beasts, together in one
hovel . . . while they have Alfas, Lancias, big apartments.
All we get is bread and cheese for lunch, and potatoes for
supper . . . *stronzi, banditi,'* voice edging up the scale. And
having uttered his emphatic challenge he waits a moment
for it to be seconded or taken up, but no one offers. Instead
there is a pained silence of embarrassment while he goes on
waiting, then snorts and turns back again to his supper,
whereupon a thought obviously strikes him. 'They paid me
today,' he says out loud. 'This is my first meal for months,'
spearing at his plate angrily. It has all been too much for
him – specially the lack of sympathy – and he needs a walk;
so he gets up, hoisting at his bulky trousers, and makes for
the door, where he pauses looking out, his shoulders still
heaving with emotion in the silence. 'Hey!' he calls out,
turning his head. 'Hey, Rocco,' and his huge face is now
radiant with jubilation, poverty and thieves forgotten, 'I bet
you never saw rows of arses like this in New York.'

Now the man who does not contradict himself at least
once a day is a fool, said La Rochefoucauld. He is also boring, and probably completely insufferable. Hence this galaxy
of Mediterranean madness, this universality, this total
inclusiveness. Italy is all things to all men, and it embraces
the whole of humanity: it touches every nerve and cell; it
is Wotton's 'paradise inhabited with devils'; it is also hell
and full of angels; it is all the world and *Homo sapiens*
complete. You can't be one person in Italy: you must be
several, and bring your own contradictions with you and

make the most of them. It is a land where the blinkered wither and die; for life is many-splendoured and restless, totally inconstant . . . Or else you should not come at all.

It was not a good night. I was debating departure from Melfi, toying gently with alternatives, and waiting for *il gobbo* to start his evening run. All was suspiciously quiet. Everywhere is Roman, I thought – Calitri is Galestrum, Forenza is Ferentum, Montemilone has a Roman aqueduct and the northern Atellans built another Atella down here in the Punic Wars – but I really ought to go to Rio Nero and see the lake. That was where Lear found a Barbary ape at the dinner table when he stayed with the Rapollas, and afterwards his hostess sang fifteen songs with 'terrible energy'. God preserve us! One of the penalties of travelling armed with letters of introduction is that you never know what you may be letting yourself in for – dressing for dinner, washing up, compulsory tennis, kissing people . . . (Ramage thought kissing his male host rather objectionable.)

Uproar outside the window, clamour, battle stations! The Boche have landed! Cry Harry and St George! Two peasants have met in the alleyway, who haven't seen each other for fifty years. Roars of gladness go rocketing up the walls, bouncing, amplified by the narrow space, turning voices into bellows; noise is squared, then cubed, then four- and five-powered. Thick wodges of it deluge the dozing brain, which fights back weakly through the clatter of donkey hoofs. Preposterous: it's one o'clock. The hoofs are pattering like falling biscuit tins, while the men shout each other down, smother each sentence with a louder one, outdo the latest noise, compete for decibels. They're warriors clubbing each other to death with vocal organs: stones, rocks, boulders of sound, then a whole mountainside – *Oori pangi gangio, Poori onio pangi, Ora mango ponio* – ripping the darkness into infinitesimal black shreds, then joined by

howling gastronomic donkey-squeezes, 'Hooya ... hooya
... hooya ... waaaaaaah ... hoo-hoo' straight from rusty
bellies, euphoniuming it into the tortured night, killing it
stone dead, murdering it with umlauts, diphthongs, vowels,
gutturals, nasals, glottal stops, surds, sibilants, sonics and
phonics, and whole palates, skirls and stridulants soaring to
a nightmare heaven ... sweeping over me in a sweat of
impotent anger.

Then clippety-clop, final whistle, enormous emptiness,
void, a gaping black hole, an even louder silence. That is
night-time Italy. Hooray for Mr Murray, you think; stupid
old fool: 'If you can't conform to their customs you've no
business to travel in foreign countries.'

The bus is about to leave for God knows where with its
restless passengers numb and silent, waiting for the last
one, obviously a regular. Villages, more villages, and out of
these mountains, perhaps towards Venosa. The chat won't
start till we're on the road, and then it will bubble like a
witch's cauldron – with some darkly spicy ingredients too,
no doubt, a stew-pot of local secrets. On he gets, panting
hard, swirling his black cassock and smiling the good
shepherd down the bus as it jolts off, and the man beside
me crosses himself and gives a mutter: 'God to women;
Devil to men.' Then he spits between his knees on to the
floor very slowly, grunting afterwards, 'Visiting his family
in Rio Nero ... start another baby.' And why not? Better
than one or two of the alternatives. Popes have had babies
after all, and done more to virgins than just sanctify them.
Almost all the priests have children round here, said Levi
at Eboli, and no one is concerned ... My neighbour is,
though, and continues muttering as we bump along on
exhausted springs.

Blocks of ugly country roll by, patches of eyesore, half-
grown, half-dead; withered fields tangle in and out of grey
leviathan rocks and charred remnants of tree-stumps. There

are ridges, dips and slopes, and little hills that slide down into uncharted valleys – mixtures of green and brown where the sun chokes everything to death or burns it at the stake, or else life is clogged by invasions of untended vegetation. It shines vindictively. Be my crematorium, it says; let me brand you with hatred, singe you to the bone . . .

For this was all forest once. The village populations here trebled from three thousand in 1730 to nine thousand in 1750 as outsiders flooded in to cut down trees. It was one of the southern centres of the timber trade: ships, forts, homes, roads and bridges were all built out of the forests that darkened the slopes round Monte Vulture and Monte Michele; the woodsmen blessed their good fortune to find their land so rich. And they still do, the moment any national or regional authority starts a much-needed programme of reafforestation: they can't believe their luck, manna from heaven – it has happened again. And zap! within hours all the saplings are neatly stacked up as logs behind the houses ready for winter. *Carpe diem*. Tomorrow is a more distant matter altogether to a southerner; it only exists when it arrives. '*Crai*,' they tell you, in bastard Latin (*cras* – tomorrow), mixing sighs with their firm resolutions, for to them Tomorrow is synonymous with Never.

The same state of confusion hasn't yet spread to the womenfolk as we disgorge at Rio Nero, a leftover touch of Spanish Aragonese. It is washday, and Amazonian lines of them are at rows of stone troughs in the square, their sleeves up, their biceps bulging as the water turns milky grey, and their chatter goes up to heaven like a cloud. It is obviously their occasion, the female coming into her own; today they are Goliaths of the washtub. They knead, pound, bash, squeeze, grind, with huge enthusiasm and huger muscles, as the waters of their enjoyment spout out crystal-clear from old lions' heads in the wall, straight into trough after trough afloat with bits of fish-tailing Ophelias – shirts, sheets, trousers, dresses, pantaloons, vests, covers, curtains

– all wrung or hammered into submission by sinews that burst with compressed energy. My word, what aggression! The all-in wrestling of giant laundresses helped by one or two sturdy apprentices. Kill the garment! – laughing with satisfied resentment – wring its neck, pump the air out, smash it, gouge its eyes, tear its fingers, beat it, drown it, squeeze its last gasp of life on to the stone, break its back, then chuck the screwed-up corpse into a basket. And up on to a brick-like hip and away, hate consummated.

The reason for this violent exhibition, I gather, is a strike by the men. They have refused to go to work on the farms: not today and not tomorrow, unless their rent is reduced. It happened last year, and the year before; there is not enough produce to sell to pay the landlord, so the ragged fields are empty. The Prefect did something twelve months ago apparently, by cutting the rents in half; and now they've all been off to see the Mayor, and they want the same thing to happen again. Meanwhile they're standing about in doorways, shaded from the sun, and having withdrawn their labour are watching the laundry. The village of Leonessa, down the road, has a strike on too. Nobody was being paid regularly at the sugar factory – just enough to be going on with now and then. The management wanted them to sign a proper wages agreement, but they couldn't read it, so nobody signed, so there weren't any weekly pay packets, so now there aren't any workers.

'Don't you help them?' I ask the priest passing through the square. 'They'd sign if you explained it.'

'Yes, they would,' he replies, 'but not the men. They think I am part of the government.' Is he priest political or priest religious? No one really knows. It doesn't worry him being semi-ostracised: he's always busy, he says, there when needed, but some disputes don't require his interference, especially the political ones.

'Come and see the church,' he says, suddenly struck by the fact that I must be a *rara avis* in these parts – a tourist

— and strides off across the square again, not to be deflected. Apparently it is thirteenth-century. This seems unlikely, but you never know; perhaps some stony corner of it goes back to the Normans. Inside it is whitewashed all over, splendidly bright and hygienic, and he displays it proudly, even the plain glass in the windows: the most candid and artlessly boring holy interior ever seen, a triumph of all things insipid. And again there are niches for Disneyland plastic, Snow White and her seven saints, Happy, Sleepy, Bashful . . .

I smile my polite amazement, whereupon he takes out more keys and beckons me through a doorway to a vestry, stony and bare save for a huge square stack of curious shapes leaning against a wall, all dark and grimy. He indicates the pile calmly, which on closer examination proves to be old oil paintings, thirty of them heaped up together, ancient and mouldy, thick with dust, the blackened canvasses coming apart only with difficulty. 'They've been here years,' he tells me, 'long before my time. No one knows what they are or where they come from, perhaps from one of the castles. Do you know anything about paintings?' I decide I don't — not enough about those, certainly — and replace them gently, no doubt consigning a lost Doria collection to another few years of perdition, or leaving the Caracciolo inheritance to the beetles and termites. Perhaps all those lost Caravaggios are in Rio Nero, those gone-for-ever Giorgiones, those missing Solimenas and unknown Raphaels . . .

I ask him which road I should take to the lake at Monticchio, and he points: 'Down that path,' he says; soon it grows leafier and more thickly wooded as the road slopes down towards the eye of the crater, and through the densely packed trees that proved too difficult to cut down and carry off in the vandalising days of the eighteenth century. Massive oaks and beeches crush shoulder to shoulder, and with them are chestnuts, elms, maples, ash and hornbeam, and ferns, shrubs, creepers tangle through and round them like a wild nature garden, with head-high leaves of wild rhubarb and sumach, where bees and butterflies hover in clusters over swags of columbine or soar to pink clumps of frangipani (there are 977 recorded species of plant on these slopes), and on each side there is the rustle of ancient wildness. Once it was the haunt of wolves and wild boar and stags, and there are records of wild cat and tortoises.

Then the lake emerges – or two lakes in fact, split by a causeway where the road crosses, one surface metallic green, the other silvery black; which is not a trick of light but a quirk of nature, and when local storms arise – which they do quite frequently – both lakes turn rusty red. Their depths have never been finally ascertained, I gather, indicating that the beds of the craters are rough and treacherous. And there are actually bird-songs, muted and cautious. A perfect paradise, you think: sun glinting on the golden-green carpet of foliage spread round you luscious and thick, the incandescent splash of flowers, the mysterious stillness of the waters ... But wait! 'One seldom finds a spot of agreeable ground in Italy that is not covered with a convent,' said Addison.

There are two of them, both abandoned and one of them completely in ruins – the inmates of each either caught by malaria or trapped in winter by the snow – empty since the 1860s. The earlier one is San Michele, overlooking the smaller lake, and was built over a grotto once inhabited by Basilian hermits, probably in the ninth century; but then it was taken over by the Benedictines and then the Cistercians and then the Capuchins; and in between times they became restless and moved over to the other lake and built the Abbey of San Ippolito; finally they deserted that one too. Though there is talk of something being done about them ... plenty of talk. San Michele has ancient mosaics and frescos, which Bertaux says were painted in 1059. To ensure a happy marriage newly-wed couples are encouraged to visit San Ippolito and ring its bells, though I am not sure on whose instructions, nor could anyone clarify the matter. 'A custom, a custom,' they said, but I wouldn't if I were them: the roof might fall in.

They are also building a hotel – indeed it is nearly completed – with a terrace that overlooks both lakes where you can eat your lunch or dinner and admire the medieval view. Lunch wasn't being served when I arrived – RISTO-RANTE CHIUSO – but the juke-boxes were alive and well.

And finally the statue ... We all know Pope Nicholas II came down to consecrate the first abbey in 1059, and assume therefore that the huge white figure dominating everything with arms aloft in benediction over both the lakes must be he – or is it? Possibly it might be San Giuglielmo d'Avercello, who was the first of the holy fathers to take up residence, but there is one of him already at Montevergine. Or it could conceivably be Fr Felice da Marsico, who was in charge of building the abbey; or San Vitale (one of the original Basilians) perhaps? But he was Greek Orthodox ... It is none of them. Instead it is San Giovanni Gualberto, a little-known Florentine, who never came near the place but was passionately fond of trees, and is the patron saint of the Italian Forestry Commission.

FIFTEEN

Venosa

Venosa is different; it has wide streets and real people, unlike those sour mountain Melfitans oppressed by the darkness of the rocks which surround them. Today it is bathed in a pale warm light that glows along its streets and laps against the white and ochre walls of the houses as if washing the people towards happiness. And just to encourage them Horace is standing in the main square as a reminder of their birthright, and a spur to joviality. What a pity they have made him look so serious, with a brooding face and a deadly earnest expression; he is even holding a scroll of odes as if it were a roll of lavatory paper. They've no sense of humour, says Baudelaire of the Italians, and certainly the perpetrator of this artefact didn't have one; a mixture of melancholia and Mediterranean tummy were his idea of representing the poetic soul. Life, decreed the local muse of authority, is a serious matter and never funny, so they gave him indigestion. Thank goodness there is something more appropriate in the town library, where a quite terrible oil painting hangs, but at least he has a mischievous bucolic grin and some vine leaves in his hair.

Contented people are strolling everywhere, soaking up the sun in comfort as they walk along the broad pavements, or sitting peacefully under trees to pass a few hours and wait for the *banditore* to bring the news. He comes round twice a day with a drum he beats to quell the noise before his announcements, thrusting it out proudly on his hip. Today his messages are mainly culinary and domestic: anyone wanting olives should go to the Piazza del Castello where they will be justly and honestly sold excellent ones by Signor M—; delicious fish and squid have arrived fresh from Taranto and Signor P— is in the square now offering good prices; the new Necchi sewing machine will be demonstrated in the market at six this evening; the film in the school-room on Sunday will be *Bandiera Rossa*. Then he rings a bell, or sometimes blows a bugle, to signify his newsletter has ended; and off he marches, drumming his way up the road to the next stop, striding straight through a street football game as if he were blind to its existence and could will it to pause – which it does, only starting again when he's safely passed, whereupon it gathers renewed ferocity and the smaller team members start to collapse again in agony or grief, either ignored till they crawl away through the dust, or – if worth it – are kicked back to life and made to continue. The full-throated yells of the small unwanted as they stagger off echo round the buildings and have more to do with life's inequalities than with pain.

In spite of those truculent bellows Venosa is all smiles, and there are gracious palm trees lining the roads to signify that this is an oasis of rest and pleasure. Doubtless the routed Roman Army found it so when the remnants fled here from the ignominy of Cannae, falling upon this warm breast of land in exhaustion. It spills out like a soft tongue over two gentle valleys where there are toy houses of *masserie* shining in the distance, white and genial, on the sides of soft curving hills that liquefy towards the friendly horizon. The inhabitants are composed and dignified – 'grave, self-respecting folks', somebody called them – with slow unhurried footsteps as if quietly self-assured, and they look you in the eye evenly to show they are on equal terms; no more of that obsequious doffing of the cap or standing in respectful immobility as they did when Lear strode past them, sketch-pad in hand.

Mommsen was here too, tenaciously exploring its ancient history, loving its ruins and spending months trying to unravel its tortured past and make sense of all its broken buildings. They made him an honorary citizen for his pains, and still keep drawers full of his notes and observations carefully locked away in the town hall. But he retired baffled in the end, unable to reconcile a once-flourishing Roman *municipium* of twenty thousand people with the four thousand he found himself living among.

Less patient with it all was Douglas, who called it 'an infirmary for mutilated antiques' and said it was twice as dirty as Lucera. Had he been a trifle more forbearing he might have paused long enough to delve into the unseemly life of one of its princes, Carlo Gesualdo, who was doubly famous, as a musician and as a murderer. According to *La Storia della Musica* he was as great a composer as Monteverdi, and his madrigals contain 'an atmosphere of delicious sadness and expressions of deep, passionate and limitless desire' – all of which came violently to the surface one night when he found his young wife in bed with her lover, and promptly murdered both of them. As it was the abundantly amorous age of Aretino's widely distributed pornographic sonnets with Giulio Romano's instructive illustrations, and as the twenty-year-old Maria d'Avalos d'Aragona had already outlived two wealthy husbands, and was still considered to be the most beautiful woman in Naples and known to be warm-blooded and obligingly companionable, he might have seen what trouble lay ahead. However, rumour has it he was more interested in music and his young male attendants than in his wife's misdemeanours. Though when it became abundantly clear soon after the wedding* that he was a *cornuto*, and when he was then given some facts and figures about it by his uncle – who only provided them, apparently, because his own advances to the lady had been turned down – the prince decided he

---

* On this occasion her dowry was eighty thousand ducats, and there was a coronet of diamonds and pearls, and a parrot of pure gold among the presents.

should do something. So he rushed into the Cornigliano Palace one midnight and stabbed her and the Count of Ruvo to death. As the entire cast was related in some way or other to the highest nobility in the land the matter caused quite a stir: Tasso wrote sonnets about it, and spicy accounts circulated about the amount of blood, the position they were caught in, Maria d'Avalos' last words and the fact that the count was wearing a chambermaid's nightdress.

While the courts upheld the prince's actions as being fully justified, and allowed him to retire to the country and get on with his composing (advising him at the same time to watch out for vengeful relations), divine justice took a different view and from then on 'assailed and afflicted him with a vast horde of demons' — a polite euphemism for acute constipation, which could only be overcome if he were stripped naked and flogged by one of his servants who was kept specifically for that purpose. Furthermore, it is recorded that the family troubles didn't really end there. One of his sons, by a previous marriage, so disgraced himself in Venosa that the inhabitants had to write a letter of complaint to their protectress, the Duchess of Gravina. 'Don Antonio has broken into almost every house, rich and poor alike, and violated the women, not only at night but often in broad daylight. If the servants try to stop him he either threatens them or does it to them, too. At the moment, he is boasting that he has cuckolded every husband in Venosa.'*

At the moment I can sympathise with him, for Venosa has a most markedly carnal atmosphere: the women move

---

* The present Prince of Venosa lives in Rome and, I am informed, requires English lessons. Applicants should be able to explain the difference between timber and lumber, and should know whether it is better to invite a person to dinner or for dinner. Useful additional qualifications would be to know which end of Bond Street is the more fashionable, and whether Gerrards Cross or Stoke Poges are acceptable suburbs of London for an English nanny to retire to.

their limbs with lustrous and full-bodied provocation as they walk by, staring you in the eye and taunting you with the summer fullness of their breasts and the promises whispering in their thighs. Every movement, look and gesture has an unabashed aura of things physical, the older ones strong and giant-hipped as if their legs had been opened by years of eager child-bearing, the young ones proud and untried but full of watchful glances that offer untold dreams of the pagan heat smouldering under their marble-smooth skin. These must be some of the 'wild animals' that Levi saw 'with desire oozing out of their eyes' and who thought of nothing but love-making; or the 'little goddesses' that Ramage found were marriageable at the age of twelve. You can't help watching as they pass: their movements spread deliberate breezes of desire, and their eyes, full of ancient appetites, burn dark as coal.

For Venosa must be none other than Venus, and these her handmaidens, left over from a bygone age when all the strengths and weaknesses of human nature had their own deities. Even the shape of the land is an offering to her; for a mile beyond the town it gradually narrows to a bulging point of cliff where nature, or man, has made a cleft. Rumour has it that this was the sacred spot where Isis was once worshipped, then Mithras and later Hymen and Venus; and there is still a circular stone altar not far away, which the pious will tell you is the Stone of Friendship, where bridal couples come to take an oath, but which others will say is the base of a giant phallus which once rose to heaven, and in more happy times this was a *campus venereus* where all the unmentionable rites of procreation used to be practised as acts of worship.

But I have found the best way to make Venus look ugly. It is to go into the back streets and catch her unawares at her toilet, where muscular mothers are sitting out in the sun on chairs and holding their erstwhile delectable offspring across their laps while they search for fleas. Here sprawl the dishevelled buds of Aphrodite, heads down, silent and uncomplaining, while nimble maternal fingers scavenge about their persons for foreign bodies, and on finding them crack the offending parasites between their fingernails with a dextrous squeeze before flicking the corpses away into the road. The whole operation is accompanied by nonchalant conversation and offhand chatter, as if they were putting their washing out or gossiping over the fence, while their fingers rake eagerly through shoals of flowing black hair down to the hard whiteness of scalp, and scour back and forth in a relentless treasure hunt.

Judging from a faded graffito on a wall claiming that DDT was last used here in 1946, the bugs have had plenty of time to get their wind back. There are other messages, too, considerably more recent – L'ITALIA È DIVISA IN DUE: ITALIA RICCA E ITALIA SCHIAVA (There are two Italies, the rich Italy and the enslaved Italy); LA CHIESA È LA MALATTIA BUBBONICA (the Church is like bubonic plague); YESTERDAY'S FASCISTS HAD BLACK SHIRTS TO THEIR WAISTS; TODAY'S FASCISTS HAVE THEM TO THEIR ANKLES – all of which suggests there is plenty of bitterness about the centuries-old tyrannies and injustices they have been subjected to by every kind of authority – civil, military, ecclesiastical – and about those of today and how they would love to shake them off. But the only way they can ever do so is by moving north or emigrating – the timetables of the passenger steamers from Naples to New York are displayed outside all public buildings – which they sometimes manage, singly or in small groups, for concerted and unified action is not in their nature. Except in their one invincible trait, a passionate and stubborn resistance to all authority.

Judging from the pictures on the walls of the inn, its owner must be a Fascist, for they are all photographs of the splendid preparations for war, and the greatness of the forces that were going to recreate the Roman Empire. Mussolini is there in several of them, being cheered by lines of hat-raising soldiers, waving imperiously from a balcony to an infinite crowd and watching enthusiastic infantrymen bay-onetting sacks of straw. There are formations of aeroplanes wheeling in the clouds, tanks thundering over sand dunes, smiling gunners loading lumps of artillery and staff cars full of upright officers giving the Fascist salute. There is also a picture of a young subaltern standing by his machine gun and smiling proudly as Il Duce shakes his hand. That one must be the innkeeper.

He still believes it could have worked. 'You let us down,' he says bitterly, 'you and the Americans ... At first you understood what we were doing and supported us, but then you changed your minds because we wanted a bit of empire too, so we had to turn to the Germans. It was your fault we ended up fighting you – not ours,' and for emphasis he shuts my passport in a drawer and locks it firmly. I am obviously to be a hostage, part of his revenge. 'Then afterwards instead of building on the structure Fascism had left you dismantled it and gave us a puppet government nobody wanted, like you do with all your colonies, pretending we're all going to be British sportsmen and play fair ... But what's happened as a result? Nearly fifty different governments since the war, and the Mafia running everything from Milan to Messina. It was better under the Duce; he stamped the Mafia out ...'

'But wasn't it Italians who murdered him and strung his body up by the feet in Milan?'

'They were Communists, Bolsheviks, partisans ... not real Italians. The same happened to Caesar: stabbed in the back by his own people.'

'Not really comparable, are they? One killed for being too successful, the other for complete failure?'

'He was a giant, *signore* ... Good-night, I'll have your bill in the morning.'

Perhaps it's for the best; though I agree in a way: he was

certainly a giant – as a showman. Anyway, the innkeeper is having trouble with his drains and particularly with a new lavatory being installed on the first floor, which is such an unusual object that people keep popping in to examine it. Passers-by can inspect it, too, as they've had to remove an outside wall to get it into position, with the result that when they practise flushing it everything cascades straight out into the street. Probably a tribute to those Calabrian immigrants in New York who used to rush out into the countryside at weekends just for the pleasure of dropping their trousers alfresco again.

To glean local wisdom in south Italy, says Osbert Sitwell, apply to the pharmacist. This one, in fact, is the ex-pharmacist – which, he explains over a cup of coffee under a friendly palm tree, all came about through gambling. Everything went reasonably well until a year ago, when his luck changed, and in a moment of desperation he wagered his whole business – shop and contents – and inevitably lost. So now he is reduced to spending the mornings in the library among the other literate *disoccupati*, reading the newspapers, then drinking one small cup of coffee for two hours in a café, and then in the afternoon he sleeps . . . At which point in the story his eyes stray wistfully towards some of the passing women: '*Una gallina vecchia fa il buon brodo*,' he sighs gently – An old chicken makes the best soup – then explains how his wife and family left him after his misfortune so now he has no one.

I'm having trouble, too, with some of the unusually fair ones, and the melting motion of their slender serpentine thighs that just suck your eyes along with them.

'Unusual isn't it,' I enquire innocently, 'to have so many blondes?'

'Ah, it was the Germans in the war,' he explains, 'with their husbands away the women here went mad – one of those unfortunate undercurrents of history that follow invasions.' Insane or coerced? I wonder glibly, thinking how little one knows about what really happened and how many secrets may be hidden away here under the surface; for the Italians have little taste for books on war or campaign memories, and prefer to leave such accounts to foreigners like Iris Origo or Norman Lewis. When their own kind do it, like Curzio Malaparte, they feel ashamed.

He is surprised that I should wish to see the castle, a monstrous and ill-kept edifice in his opinion, which he passes every day and hardly notices, as it is overrun by local families who have had homes there from time immemorial. 'There's talk of it being turned into a museum one day,' he says, leaving his seat with reluctance, as he knows it will cost him something to sit down again, 'but they've been saying that for years ... They're thinking of displaying Dottor Bricese's collection there. He keeps it in his house at the moment, so no one ever sees it: elephant tusks, suits of armour, black figure vases, Roman glassware, prehistoric arrowheads ... He and his father used to pay the peasants one lira for anything they found, but he's old now and has forgotten what one lira is worth, so they don't take him things any more ...' and his voice fades uncertainly as if he has said too much.

So we arrive at the Del Balzo castle, which was begun in 1470 and is nearly all there, and now plays host to numerous Venosa families who have designated most of the downstairs rooms as communes for chickens, goats and children and a puppy or two, and decorated the walls with their streams of washing, and placed old chairs and tables out in the courtyard so they can sit and chat in the open air as the sun goes down. I am anxious to see those 'fearsome dungeons' where Lear saw 'mournful records' scratched into the walls by despairing captives, and am eventually led down long, winding stairs into damp and inky blackness by a willing urchin hugging one of the puppies to his chest, and pausing so I can light matches every few steps of the

descent. The air is icy and fetid as we stumble our way
along passages, under arches, past long-bricked-up alcoves
and down even darker steps, closer to the rustle of rats, and
I start to spy faded scratchings on the walls; at which
moment there is an agonised howl in front of me and a
scrabbling of petrified feet as some earth-hugging presence
passes inches away, wailing in agony as it makes for distant
daylight, while my guide gives ghoulishly delighted
chuckles in the dark. 'Dogs don't like it,' he says, 'they can
see the *fantasme.*'

How many can they see? one wonders, tortured spirits
locked up in this abysmal darkness from those far-off days
of plunder and annihilation begun by the Sforzas and
Medicis, then continued by the Venetians, Aragonese and
Turks, when the Renaissance form of Balkanisation was
smash and grab and gratuitous cruelty that left nothing but
ghosts and faded epitaphs of despair.

It is much the same at the Abbey of the Trinity, which is
two miles out of the town and significantly placed on the
point of the Venus triangle. The *farmacista* is in need of a
rest and more coffee, so shows me the direction. 'Just past
the amphitheatre,' he waves, 'you can't miss it . . .' And
indeed you can't; for it stands like the bones of a giant
carcass, dark against the sky and rotting in a wilderness of
grass, where gaunt tubes of old pillars mourn their solitude
between half-built walls, and mullioned windows gaze
empty into the wind, and stone arches leap on their way
into open space. Though this time it was not savage
mutilation that caused such wreckage, but sheer fatigue;
for the Normans conceived it as a royal mausoleum before
moving their empire away to Sicily, then the Benedictines
found its completion impossible, as did the Knights of St
John of Jerusalem to whom it was handed on. Thus it
remained half-finished, and so infuriated Lear that he called
it 'a disgrace to Venosa' and doubtless sketched it (he was
still with the Rapolla family and their Barbary ape, dining

off cuttlefish, playing chess and discussing Walter Scott).
And so it remains today, just a grandiose skeleton open to
the elements, with half-frescoed chapel walls, lidless tombs,
stumps of headless eagles, blurred shapes of lions *couchant*
with time blinded faces and the dancing streak of lizards
across dusty rock, where tufts of grass sprawl out of
masonry cracks between the scored names of occasional
visitors. It has a legendary nascence: a prince fell in love
with his own daughter after the death of his wife and
wished to marry her, which was sanctioned by the local
bishop on the condition that he built a church first, and
used white of egg instead of cement. One wonders how
many years of eager labour went into it before he lost
interest or she found someone more suitable. In fact, it was
to have been Robert Guiscard's triumphant monument after
he and Hildebrandt had driven all the predatory Greeks,
Lombards and Arabs out of south Italy, but with the
changing fortunes of war and fading dynasties it was all
forgotten. And it still is, in spite of the government having
recently set aside thirty-eight million lire for its care and
upkeep, as I am told by a bent old man half-heartedly
scything at the grass.

'I do it for the visitors,' he explains glumly, 'but all they
ever do is laugh and steal things; some piece of stone goes
missing every weekend. There's a mosaic flooring over
there which I have to keep covered under a foot of soil; we
left it open in the summer to show them, all patterned in
white, red and gold, but by the end of a week half of it had
been put in their pockets and taken back to Venosa. They
think it's a lucky charm and will keep off the evil eye . . .'
Then he shows me the Stone of Friendship standing in a
patch of newly scythed grass, and pats it lovingly with a
gleam in his ancient eyes. 'From the Tempio di Venere,' he
murmurs wistfully, as if the old spirits living here have
been telling him their unholy secrets . . .

He passes these on, later in the evening, when we meet

again beneath the sign of the *frasca* back in Venosa – those withered bunches of vine leaves that hang their hospitable thirst-quenching greeting above the doorways of every wine cellar, and have done so since the days of Horace. For the *farmacista* has suggested we should make a tour of them; and there in our first descent into Venosa's bucolic underworld sits the *custode* of Trinity Abbey, who in return for a litre of wine is eager to tell us all he knows of the shameless goings-on that took place there in days gone by, and of some that still do in the darkness of summer nights – because he has heard the voices, and peeped from his window, and witnessed the terrible scenes of ghostly figures dancing in the ruins with nothing on, and leaping and cavorting and . . . like rutting goats in the moonlight. And a whole litre slips away easily among his stories while all the room listens, and another litre is called for as we creep away.

They are all the same, these subterranean *cantinas*, dark and rough-walled, filled with hard-drinking men of the fields with coarse nutmeg faces scored by sun and wind into whirlpool wrinkles, nodding at the *farmacista* with knowing eyes as we enter each one. 'My turn, *professore*,' he insists as the flagon arrives filled with dusty gold, but my hand is there before him. 'Ah, I've had to give money to my ex-wife today, you understand . . . and my three illegitimate children. Next time then . . .' As he lifts his glass to drink he eyes the faces at the other tables and leans forward whispering, 'A tomb robber in the corner. He bought a perfect marble head off a farmer last month for twenty-five thousand lire [£15]. It was second-century, and so good the Soprintendenza heard of it and sent an inspector up. He told him it had been stolen, but actually he'd sold it in Rome for 325,000 lire,' and we smile our complicity as we drink his health and everyone else's in the glowing peace of evening. Then he leans forward again: 'Did you know the Jews overran Venosa in the fourth and fifth centuries, and we have the biggest catacombs in south Italy?' – pausing to fill our glasses – 'And we had a famous Norman prostitute living here, Sant' Agnese,' draining his easily and signalling for another flagon. 'A priest was caught making love to her, and was burnt at the stake in front of her eyes; and she was so upset she repented and founded a convent where she spent the rest of her life in solitude.' He smiles and starts on another glass with barely a pause, 'And have you heard about the monks at Rio Nero? Really? Well, if a girl got pregnant by one of them she had to stay at home for a year then go and work in the monastery kitchens. So you can imagine how easy it was for the Abbot to get cheap labour . . .' winking furiously as he reaches for the emptying flagon.

Then on to another one, down uncountable steps into unsteady darkness, where the faces this time are crooked and over-cooked like burnt rice pudding; and as soon as the wine is poured off he goes, about Horace insulting some Roman nobles who were visiting Venosa. '"No poet should be shoeless and go round bare," they told him. "All rich men are pompous and full of air," he answered,' and all the faces round the walls seem to grin in agreement. So he swallows some more and starts on their nicknames: 'That's Sette Minestre who eats too much, and there's Quattr' Gatt' with spindly legs, and Rub' la Nott' steals, and Bomba farts, and Carese gropes people . . . Drink up, *professore*, let's have another one; soon it'll be time to sing, like the old inhabitants of Venosa did to scare away Atilla the Hun.'*

Somehow we reach a fourth, floating to it on bubbles of air, reeling in lovely liver-spin, swelling our golden hearts. And the rows of goblins and swaying gnomes on the walls split and multiply like amoebic wine-spooks, and his syllables bounce softly on the air-waves as he asks for another flagon. 'You know about *"il santo membro"*, *professore*,

---

* The *farmacista* should have known better: Attila never reached the south of Italy.

don't you?' he whispers, ' – they call it San Cosmo's big toe now – and the twelve foreskins of Christ? No?' but forgets to tell me, remembering instead the prescriptions he used to write out for the men to have bigger and better ones, '. . . and why we call *il Vaticano "il Vaticulo"*?' but he can't remember that either, except it's something to do with homosexual priests . . . because the flagon is already empty.

Staggering, we make it to a fifth, a puddle-filled catacomb lined with moving walls of nightmare trolls and leather pixies grinning like baby birds drowning in a quagmire, a choir of muddy faces shouting for help, and he prods me somewhere in the middle as the wine arrives: '. . . Five hundred husbands away in Germany, just think of that,' squinting with a stew-house bend and leer, 'So how about it then?' and up tips the yellow specimen bottle again, and down goes another suffocating glassful . . . and all those thighs like wild mares swimming across my eyes have become sunken corpses, and Aphrodite's kittens shatter to lice-ridden scraps of dismembered doll . . .

Then we float half hoping on skinfuls of golden posset into Venosa's hopeless darkness, as it wobbles towards us then backs away. We lurch in pursuit of it for miles and hours till we fall into the amphitheatre, two leg-bent nightjars tottering in silver-cold moonlight to listen for the sighs of a thousand ghosts twittering in the owl-eyed saucer of rubble, where rats scuttle in the rocks and wandering winds whisper in the grass, where the same old stars give timeless blinks to ten thousand vanished people, where muttering voices trickle back to find their buried bones, where the tumbled stones heave at our out-of-focus visitation.

Daylight, in high romance, can creep in through latticed shutters like melting butter, or it can tear its entry in rapine fury through a scramble of shouts and transistors – which is Venosa's version of chanticleer: bleating machines with bright Tokyo grins helping each individual to drown the silence. Quiet is ugly and must be done away with, because modern gods have said it is a part of nature and therefore ominous and evil. So one wakes to the charge of cacophonic bulls goring each other into submission, volumetric invasions decimating the enemy, portable roarings that swell the ever-stretching balloon of morning till it ought to burst.

I tiptoe down the dusty road away from this power struggle and wash at an obliging fountain, struggling to clear the lens on last night's ending, but it stays obtusely dim, so I pray quietly that I've lost the *farmacista* for ever, and amble off southward down a lane that may go where I'm going. On the other hand it may not, and it would be wise to ask at one of the small huts or one of the cavernous openings in the tufa cliff-side which have wooden doorways cut in them suggesting habitation. Then there's movement ahead in a shadow, where an old man crouches at a bench pumping a roped pedal with his left leg, and bending forward to tease a pudgy ball of clay flat into a circle as it whirls round, then easing the edges gently upwards till they fold into a curving urn that grows tall and slender under his fingers as if he were awakening a swan in slow motion. It's done in two minutes; he stacks it behind him with an army of others, an immaculate multitude of flowing curves and hopelessly open mouths disappearing into darkness.

'You can have any you like for fifty lire.'

'Thanks. Is Gravina this way?'

'Yes, a long way . . . My father taught me to do this when I was six; it's the only thing I know how to do, but I'm wasting my time: they make them in factories now by the thousand. Nobody wants mine.'

'How far is it?'

'Fifty kilometres maybe . . . perhaps sixty . . . I had six men helping me before the war, but now they just sit in the square doing nothing. That's why I'm a Communist. I was

Fascist then and loved Mussolini. I've got lots of heads of him in there you can have. I suppose we all make mistakes . . .'

'So this is the road then . . .'

'Yes, more or less . . .'

'To Gravina?'

'Roughly . . .'

I leave him starting to shape another one, slapping it down on the whirling wheel with an automatic movement, as I slip away past the last locked caves of Venosa and its tumbled stones of old yellow now starting to beat back fiercely at the sun; and I look out towards the plain ahead which stretches like a sea of ochre dust broken occasionally by rising whale-backs of wolfish grey rocks and sun-withered green. But there is no shade. Somewhere to the east, almost on the edge of eyesight, mystically shimmers a ridge of mountains uncertainly veined in soft colours as the heat licks it into morning life; and beyond that lies the Tavoliere plain, a lush belly of liquid green reaching from Foggia to Taranto, bordered by the sea. But this ahead is a crematorium, a combustion of dust, a salamander sheet of unending dryness where Venus once sat on a welcoming edge to greet the weary travellers.

I turn in case he's watching, and there he is; so I wave to him, thin among the palm trees, and he raises a hand slowly in distant salute. Then when I turn again he's gone.

SIXTEEN

Gravina

Inimical, I'd call it, that flat morning walk out of Venosa
into arid nothingness, crazily broken by buried rock-backs
too hot to touch, eaten into by monstrous weevils of time,
with sockets of nightmare eyes gouged out and staring like
a fossilised Polyphemus. Miles and miles of it, grimly still,
tilting away in cinder greyness to touch the sky at world's
end without a bird or cloud anywhere, leaving it all to the
angry sun – that implacable enemy that blazes his fury and
his hate because years ago they starved him by deforesta-
tion; so he withers it all to desert by way of revenge and
wants it to die. Which it does, slowly, every day – except
where dregs of soil have washed down gullies to be caught
in pockets and fed by odd drops of winter rain, and where
there's always a shack of old sticks and dried bamboo
throwing tiny shade on to a fragile handkerchief of
preciously nurtured earth, and where a dog lies sleeping,
and a wandering group of balloon-uddered goats tears at
rock thistles. Ahead I can see a whisp of brown dust along
the road, puffing up into a cloud as it gets nearer, and
pushing along behind an old donkey-cart sat on by a silent
staring man; the veil of it hides the bleached land a moment
before it powders away slowly and settles invisibly on eyes
and lips to coat them in more dryness. And somewhere I
saw a shepherd once, grey-draped like a standing stone and
watching me blankly without a wave, and his white hound
was chained to a rock and baying to reach me.

God, what a graveyard, all shrunk to this little measure
of stripped carcass. You battered old whore of the Mediterranean pleasured by millions and still alive – just. Once you
were young and beautiful and rich and you enjoyed the

bawdy weight of visiting heterogeneous civilisations and loved them doing it and wanted more; but now you're a raddled old ruin nobody wants, with that same soft-beating heart but dried-out, wizened skin and sunken eyes. All things to all men from Euboean Greeks to Nazi stormtroopers, a body to rape and pillage, a stepping-stone from here to there and back again, a willingly absorbent public convenience, a sun-clad temptress encouraging desire, and still at it – forever generating a hopeless sweaty love with your dried-out thighs – a sweet courtesan shrunk to an unsung skeleton.

And on it goes: beside a monotonous yellow-baked wall of mountains far to the east, a dusty, dwindling road ahead like a loose thread, winding through sinews of rock where paint-brush entrails of track have been made by goats and foxes, curling away into grey space to lose themselves in a cauldron of changing land-shapes where the skyline slides slowly in infinitely restless patterns. Then suddenly, hours later, between hillocks that don't quite meet, a dip on the left falls away to a valley of weak vegetation stretching in browns and greens to a fishbone line of trees that prick manfully upward beside a line or ditch or culvert. I scramble down to it over lumpish banks and loose stones, and plod away damp with sweat over hard-cooked earth newly ploughed, towards its furthest edge where a narrow stream as lost as I am wanders aimlessly through a cleft, too slow to sparkle. Small hills have begun to grow up alongside, and on one of them, black in the white sky, sits a jagged bastion of owl-haunted Monte Sevico where a Duchess of Taranto once murdered her duke for the love of a plough-boy peasant. Then shrill from side to side over the valley comes the cry of child shepherds calling sheep, and getting answers from others hidden on different hills as they banter and yell a high-pitched *stornello* contest* that trickles in the air

---

* This is an ancient form of vocal amusement, usually for lonely

like pan-pipes among the muffled bells, then dies into midday boredom as the untuned clunks mourn on. Somewhere I pass a silent figure sitting in a shadow of rock a stone's throw away, turning his face to watch like a slow gun-muzzle aiming. As the land creeps up to an eiderdown of hills again there's a square patch of meeting paths on the crest of a rise hubbed round a giant boulder, where there are goats bleating at a trough and a rugged man leaning and watching as he sucks at a long-stemmed pipe.

'Gravina?' I ask him, and he thinks, with deep eyes half hidden in ridges of oak-bark skin, and takes the pipe out still pondering, then says things in mountain-shepherdese which are darkly incomprehensible but jerks his head over his shoulder to a choice of two dusty cart tracks.

'Plaz',' he grunts, 'u' Gervas' . . . acca,' and sucks his pipe again to settle back into ancient cloudy thoughts.

I know what he meant now: Palazzo San Gervasio, a tired little town tucked off the southern road from Montemilone to Spinazzola, behind some hills and almost forgotten, half filled with shrugging fragments of people sitting in warm white dust in a crumble of houses. It's not as great as it once was: the home of Emperor Frederick's royal stables and stud farm, its rich terrain filled with prancing bloodstock presented by Arab princes, where long-legged foals grazed before their shipment far beyond the Alps. And here was commissioned the fabulous treatise on equine care and disease, *De Medicina Equorum*, which Manfred completed

---

occasions, in which two people exchange conversation or repartee in song, very often without seeing each other. By its nature it is supposed to be non-serious; most forms of amorous, *risqué* or insulting dialogue can be exchanged without fear of reprisal. In its purest form it is extemporised poetry of three rhyming lines, each of a certain metre. It is a beautiful, and chilling, experience to hear a spontaneous example of it echoing out in the normally silent mountains, though unfortunately it is fast disappearing.

after his father's death. But it's not royal now; 'Maybe it was,' they say, 'who knows?' They mutter things in obdurate monosyllables, then turn away and leave me to look for a bar and lemonade. Perhaps it's because he was a German, I think.

So I turn to matters more ancient and Horatian, and mention a Bandusian Fount which was either somewhere nearby at Banzi, or was a flight of poetic fancy and transposition to his arcaded gardens at Tivoli; it draws out a flicker of interest at last behind the bar, and starts a growled argument with two seated drinkers in a corner. 'It's that one down the hill,' they say, 'down there in the trees; it's the only one it can be . . . *Bandus'*, *Bandus'*,' and they laugh quietly at the name, wanting me to go away on an errand of invention and leave them alone again; for strange things disturb them and make them wary.

Out over the mounds I go, and down the undulating hill to the reported water-hole where the earth gets quickly sodden near a clump of luxurious trees, tall and lonely as sentries, surrounded with brambles and choked with overgrown bushes that hide a footpath; the slurp of my shoes in mud mingles with sounds of tinkling laughter. I pause to listen and it comes again, a most definite shriek of delighting nymphs as they dance in water and frolic in playful disobedience; so I burst through the embracing undergrowth to catch them at it, and surprise a peasant family enjoying a picnic. Barely a century ago they'd have fled up the hill in terror, like the Calabrian woodcutters when Ramage stepped out of the trees, but these are more sanguine, and beam an arm-waving welcome into their private paradise, spread round them on the grass in baskets and paper parcels and tilting bottles of wine cooling in puddles. Skirts are up over lard-white thighs melting in the sun, and fat paunch buttons are open to ease the eating. All is most public holiday merriment to be shared with strangers, and a loaf is waved in greeting:

'*Vuol' favorire?*'

'Is this Fons Bandusiae?'

'*Sì, Banzi, Banzi. Venite favorite,*' and the *capo di famiglia* seated splendidly on the grass nods out his knowledge, slaps the ground by him in invitation then tears at the yard-long loaf, and ripping the broken bit open stuffs blood-red circles of salami into it with his fingers, and holds it out imperiously to be eaten. Does one welcome the ruination of a private family picnic so at home? I wonder, biting it thoughtfully, studied by admiring happy eyes. Somehow I doubt it: congestion makes us jealous of reserved territory, and we treasure our rarities of aloof isolation; but not so these, who value bonds of affiliation and involvement far more than privacy, for it brings the comforting, secret warmth of complicity.

'*Grazie.*'

'Tourist?'

'Yes.' And he exclaims his triumphant 'Ah!' as if he knew all the time, and had arranged my visit personally, twinkling a told-you-so look at his wife, who smiles in obedient adoration and massages the nobbles on her varicose knees before drawing in breath and bawling for the children. They ignore it publicly with louder shouts of glee, out of sight somewhere in the water-logged bushes.

'*Italia bellissima,*' he says and belches, then reaches to tug a bottle from the mud, which releases it with a suctious plop of unwillingness, and waves it at me with its contents whirling like a misty aquarium of drowning crumbs, and they watch hypnotically as I drink. 'What more could you want,' he asks, 'than this *vita meravigliosa*, with its warm sun and blue sky?', and she claps her hands in pleased agreement, and rocks from her long-lost waist as if tethered to the earth like a deposited meteorite, then bawls for the children again without looking. And this time out they come, peeping from the bushes like woodland wisps with wide-eyed stares of quick appraisal, then scampering off again with wilder shrieks to chase deeper into the hidden thickets.

They give me goat's cheese oozing out of the bread in liquid gouts but poked in again with his fingers, and she smiles, '*Regina*,' and fits an imaginary crown on her head, and we all wear seraphic beams of instant friendship, as out plops another flagon from the mud to circle recklessly from mouth to mouth, and he tugs his holiday hat down to shade his eyes, and rolls his trousers up to cook his calves. We gourmandise in the autumn sun, surrounded by paper and crumbs and fruit skin and tilting bottles, grimacing with pangs of gobbled indigestion, hearing the distant flute-yells of invisible offspring, bonding ourselves to archaic Mother Earth again, and enjoying the abandon of an open-air banquet in a wild copse somewhere in an undisturbed world. Their smiles show a deep contentment of timeless understanding, and a simple prehistoric affinity with ancestral pilgrimages towards the womb – punctuated by solicitous mother-clucks to her brood, which she utters by instinct and which are instinctively ignored. While a few feet away in a brackish pool the forgotten waters of my make-believe fountain bubble away unaffected, and an uncaring decanter of history seeps anonymously through the fallen leaves into the thirsty earth.

Then they tell me how to get to Gravina. 'Down there,' they point when the wine is finished, and he starts to lie back for his perfect sleep, his unbuttoned stomach heaving happily and his face lost under a tent of newspaper; and she smiles me away down the path quietly so as not to disturb him. '*Vale Fons Bandusiae*,' I think, and '*Salve civitas Gravinae . . .*'

But if Gravina was Roman once it is not so now, in spite of the ancient road that leads there. Like all the others it is perched on a little cliff-top, with vertiginous grey edges tumbling into scarred ravines filled with half-sunk boulders. Its Roman ancestor could have been anywhere on these corrugated hilltops: perhaps at Botromagno, an uninhabited point two miles away, which is unusually dark with trees, all rooted in a stubble of shapeless and dateless ruins levelled to the earth; or perhaps it was Antica Silvium, or Plera, mentioned by Strabo and Pliny; or that long vanished staging post on the Appia from the Peutinger Table and the Antonine Itinerary. No one really knows which of these broken rock-peaks might be which, or where the road passed along these narrow gorges of scrub-scattered reef with their iron-grey surface of calcified intestines writhing in torture. A 'pickaxe' is what Gravina means today, a sharpened hammer . . . a mason chipping holes in rock life-sentenced among the stones.

Gravina's square is small and sunny and whitewashed on three sides; the fourth is the Church of Purgatory, which has a Gothic festoon of hideous gargoyles leering down at a lunatic on the steps mercilessly punching a small child – doubtless in just retribution for teasing him or tripping him up with a dog on a string or throwing stones – all watched by a cackling hag sitting on her doorstep and relishing the unequal struggle. Kick a man when he's down? said some tutting sportsman to an Italian once. So when else is there a chance to kick him? came the answer – which is a good deal more logical, after the fake banalities of fairness have been swept aside by bitter experience and you realise that anyway life is one long cheat from end to end with no one obeying the rules. Like those legends of courtly love that were dressed-up lechery, and those covens of squealing nuns pleasuring Renaissance priests and nobles. So we survey the massacre together, till the smaller one manages to wriggle free, with shouts that twist into laughter, leaving the idiot to stagger drunkenly on the stone steps, outwitted again, then lurching away out of the square in a hang-dog shamble. '*Al terzo piano,*' applauds the hag vocally, wanting more, '*al terzo piano*,' meaning in this southern vernacular that if you live on the third floor you are insane; as this is earthquake country that seems quite logical.

I wander away from her, as she prattles on about a priest who will knock it down if he can, bemused suddenly by such extremes and all those whirlwind possibilities conjured up in the superlative -*issimus*. What a weak invocation 'very' is as an adjunct to intensify meaning, but what imagined marvels can resound in those syllables *issimo*, as they open unexplored curtains of the mind and suggest realms of untold matchlessness. And how do they do it, this creation of brilliant extremes? These Urbinos, Palladios, Raphaels, Palestrinas, Dantes; and the most beautiful women in the world; and the fastest cars; and most excessive madness and fantastic cruelty and unparalleled vice, that scale all heights and depths imaginable with no difficulty – all born from some fickle and demon genius that sees things invisible and makes them real, and can talk to the hearts of angels or dance with devils in the rich transformation of dreams into reality. Where else would they build a Palazzo del Te or Villa d'Este? Where else would they crucify a bishop upside-down in his own cathedral? Who else would dare write of seeing hell and seeing heaven? What kind of people would kiss a madonna one moment then curse her in a darkened room the next? And where else would you find children dancing on piles of human skeletons, but in Gravina?

They are down under the town in caves, stacked away in grey heaps behind iron gates, where the precipice falls away from the ragged swallow's nest of houses perched at the top, and drops sheer to the ravine. These old burrows have been cut carefully into the rock, and are part of the neolithic warren that stretches from here to Matera, and beyond to Massafra and to the edges of Taranto, where half-men roamed in tribes to hunt each other, or demented hermits counted their fingers, or fleeing soldiers hid, or painters invented saints, or bandits buried money and bones. You reach them down alleys of hundreds of steps falling away past the buttressed walls of houses, so steep that donkeys slip; but beware of the urchin army that asks to lead the way, a motley array of baggy shorts and wide braces – for they thrive on unusual mischief, and having done with the lunatic for the day will look to you to provide amusement.

In fact, I am looking for a particular Byzantine chapel called San Vito, mentioned in old Murray; but they are unconvinced and make more interesting suggestions, which lie along a different mule path altogether and are round a corner under the base of the cliff. Here there are four or five long-forgotten caves, cut deep and black into the sinewy folds of the hillside, and all barred at the entrance. And there, beyond the rusty ironwork, pale in the chilling gloom, are mountains of human bones, heaped to the roof like the picked-clean refuse of a cannibal banquet or a charnel-house from the plague. A whiteness of spiderish ribs and grinning skulls and tangled vertebrae rises in a crisp risotto of ghoulish afterlife, packed tight in extravagant shapelessness. The slender gap between the top of the bars and the roof is enough to let this scoundrel army swarm inside like mice, starting to climb and dance on the brittle corpses so that the age-old bones crack and crunch under their slithering feet as they scale the macabre heights, pounding them noisily into smaller fragments. There are five caves to be similarly invaded, and each dismal necropolis so solidly packed with bones that these dervish corybants barely sink to their ankles in them, but slither on the tumbling debris of death as if kicking crust off a ski-slope, chanting, 'Saraceni, Saraceni,' above the avalanching sound of splintering ribs and crunching skulls. Their savage leaps of revenge are enough to crush the final breath out of any lurking ghosts.

I suspect, however, they may be dancing on the remains of their own ancestors rather than on those of the Saracens, who sacked Civitas Gravinae so horribly and thoroughly in AD 970. More likely these are the Gravinians themselves, or the corpses of their Lombard helpers who arrived too late, or the remains of a routine Norman rebellion, or the victims of an Angevin purge, or even the innocent and ignorant who dared resist one of Cardinal Ruffo's cleansing annihilations in the south. For some of these tumbling and shattered bones are still coarsely clad in shreds of rag and rotten sack, clinging to them in useless modesty, which some enterprising biochemist will one day analyse, adding a footnote to Gravina's history; until when the gleam of a distant battle will shine in the children's imaginations, and they will remain the lying legend of the vanquished *Saraceni*.

Suddenly the foot-pounding ceases, and with a scatter of chipped bones the fledgling limbs slither over the railings in disarray, as a dishevelled *guardiano* arrives, panting with exertion and, lacking the strength to shake his fist, castigates the futile bars and the dead inmates beyond between puffs of exhaustion. Would I like to see inside? he gasps, getting his wind back; but I have seen enough of porcelain skulls used as footballs, and cascading spillikin patterns of fractured skeletons heaped into pyramids of forgotten purgatory like the contents of a good day's work at Belsen or Treblinka. Quite enough for today, thank you.

I can recommend Zia Rosa's – thanks to the *guardiano*, who says he's vaguely related, and during our perspiring ascent back into Gravina finds breath to inform me that San Vito Vecchio no longer exists. A German professor came, he says, and chopped the paintings off the wall and took them away; but he can't remember when precisely. It must have been a few years ago, he thinks, and gives that all-expressive shrug that can fit into any situation and answer it. This time it is helplessness tinged with self-pity, as if to say, It's not our fault we have so many enviable possessions scattered all over the land. And he goes on to enumerate other chapels in caves which might have been just as interesting once: San Michele, Sant' Antonio, Sant' Agostino, Santa Teresa and San Bartolomeo. 'Don't tell any Germans then,' I say to him as we mount the endless ladder of steps, numbing the knee-joints, towards the eyrie of balancing houses perched on the knife-edge of rock or clinging to it like a crenellated wax-crust of old candles. For no one has ever come to this land except as an enemy, conqueror or thief, or sometimes as a passing traveller devoid of understanding. Except for Frederick, that is: he gave this town and the surrounding lands as a gorgeous gift to his favourite mistress, Bianca Lancia, in its days of beauty.

We hover together a moment in the relative flatness of the square as my aching limbs return to normal, and he innocently eyes one or two signs on doorways with a subtle suggestion of thirst; a most wise idea, for it is then that I hear about Zia Rosa and her children and her cooking and even her husband in faraway South America, and he knows she's a distant cousin of his by some roundabout connection – or perhaps it's through his wife or brother-in-law – and anyway what does it matter, as half the other drinkers seem to have a similar relationship. These southerners have a quaintly biblical attitude to lineage and consanguinity, as if hoping any tenuous kinship may unite them against chance oppressors.

She is tucked away down a warren of side streets, and is built like an Amazon queen, with hands the size of axe-heads, volleyball bouncing breasts and a laugh like a thunderstorm that shakes her hippopotamus hips and sears my ear-drums. 'Let's not discuss money,' she booms like a friendly belch of Vesuvius (a fatal suggestion) but with terrible eye-twinkling gaiety, as her body fills the room – which in Gravina is not difficult. Then when her *guardiano* cousin has fled she sums me up with undisguised relish. I

can only blench – for an army of Zia Rosas would have won
the war in no time: with their muscled chimney-pot arms
made hard by scything and the hugeness of their tractor-
tyre thighs swollen by pedestrian labour, men would have
turned and fled before them. They would have fought with
honour too: less for the sake of *figura* and more for the sake
of the real world and its values; for unlike her male
counterpart the southern Italian woman loves more than
just herself, and despises the idea that doing nothing is a
mark of distinction.

Her children lead me upstairs – all four of them, curious
and helpful – into a small whitewashed room with painted
shutters that open on to a street so narrow the opposite
wall is touchable, where cobwebs of coloured washing are
still strung from the graceful curves of one iron balcony to
the next, broken by the haphazard glare and tumble of red
geraniums splashing their blood-drops against the stone. A
babble of evening voices rises from the shadows of half-dark
rooms as soft as birds bidding each other good-night. And
then comes the mammoth Rosa herself, with a jug of water,
and as the view to her has never been romantic, she now
swells even larger with an appetite of indelicate curiosity.
Am I married? she demands, dark eyes shining somewhere
in her face. How many children do I have? Where is the
signora then? How long have we been apart? her voice
growing charged with emotion and perhaps, I imagine,
pleading sensuality. Do I enjoy being alone? she asks, sitting
on the bed, which bows obediently beneath her like a
hammock; and I glance at the door, having visions of the
mild and diminutive Dr Levi being dumped in the bath
every night by that raven-haired giantess of Eboli and
pummelled into submission. Somehow I must retreat from
the booming diapason of her shire-sized thighs and plead
incapacity; but, not being drunk or diseased, can only offer
that noble piece of work's shrivelled impudence as being

withered by exhaustion – which in fact means terror. So I pant, '*Esaurito*,' and mention my walk of thirty miles, and do some heavy breathing, and we talk instead: first of her long-lost husband who has only written one letter in four years, and then, when I mention the caves of bones, she talks of her buried children – three of them, she says, '*Sono andati in paradiso*' – and her eyes moisten in gratitude for their being with God and happy at last, not like us poor people left on earth to suffer in misery. She regards their escape from existence as a blessing, which is not exactly as we would see it, being conditioned to the misguided sanctity of unwanted life in an over-populated world. But their attitude is more realistic and has changed little over the years, as Mrs Martin found just over a century ago in Rome, when she noticed the indifference shown to an infant's death: 'even the mother evinced no feeling at all' she wrote home horrified, perhaps forgetting conditions in London.

The truth is that they have children to spare, as did the Victorians, and would be relieved to dispose of some, preferably for a small consideration; nor are such transactions as rare as you might think, in some desolate and downtrodden areas south of Naples (I suggest Battipaglia might be a good starting point), thanks largely to His Holiness, who would rather impose ignorance and poverty in this world and joy in the next on his swelling flock than update his priorities. Which only shows how right Addison was when he decided there was no people in Europe more miserable than the Pope's subjects.

As for tonight, I shall remain purposefully ignorant of where this Amazonian mother sleeps with her teenage sons and daughters, and shall obliterate all thoughts of bedfellows. And not just those fleshy damsels Boswell boasted of, but all those others on record too – pigs, scorpions, devils, dogs and cats and sometimes chickens and monkeys, and one or two youths and chambermaids and peasants and priests (for does not Montaigne mention innkeepers running up the road towards approaching travellers and promising them anything they wished, *'anche ragazze e ragazzi'?*) and, of course, bedbugs and fleas uncountable (against which the squeamish travellers of yesteryear protected themselves by carrying a sleeping sack with them everywhere: an over-sized pillowcase into which they could climb every night and, by tightening the mouth of it comfortably round their necks, hope to remain relatively undisturbed. A wise precaution in certain circumstances, especially if the bedding was loose straw; but in less Spartan situations they must have missed quite a lot of entertainment).

Gravina's morning begins at five, with the jolting drone of cart-wheels rotating on uneven stone and the fog-horn bray of agonised donkeys complaining to one another – a noise that spreads through the alleys with the insistent fury of a forest fire, and is joined in no time by bubbles of matutinal chatter as shutters clack open against walls to radiate the sound more thoroughly and evenly. Everyone is getting up before the stars have had time to rub their eyes, and I lie there hating all of it and feeling just like Lawrence in one of his moods of detesting all things Italian. Have they never experienced, I wonder, that deliciously subtle nuance of the sandman's stealthy creep along eyelids between sleep and wakefulness? Or do they have to erupt so precipitously into all extremes? It is part of the *issimo* problem again, I suppose – their natural eagerness for superlatives, their exhilarating secret of wanting to make every moment of life into a work of art. Though for the moment I could do with them being less creative.

I am watched at a lukewarm-coffee breakfast by four pairs of curious eyes, for Zia Rosa is already out in the road describing last night to the neighbours; strangers are rare in Gravina and their doings call for microscopic analysis. So I ask the audience what to see, and they can't think of anything except the castle – but who would want to go

there anyway? they add, except *innamorati* to be alone, or
boys to play football and spy on the love-making couples –
their knowledge of history leaping stupendously from
Caesar to Garibaldi as if they were a few weeks apart.
Nevertheless they accompany me, eyed jealously by others,
and we reach a bare plateau outside the town where the
shell of another Hohenstaufen stronghold stands, with its
broken towers and walls and a massive stone gateway
which the footballers use as the goal; here an Orsini prince
was battered to death by one of his serfs in the days of *jus
primae noctis*. And far below it there are dark underground
chambers with drawings scrawled on the walls by sad child
prisoners who tried to pass some time in amusement before
death. *'È una vergogna,'* announce my young companions,
relegating the pile to an ugly nuisance, another tiresome
article of landscape rubbish; so I suggest a walk across to
Botromagno, where I will reward them with five lire for any
unusual piece of stone they may find, subject to approval,
and excite them with the thought that there may have been
a town there at the time Jesus was born in Bethlehem.

Remains come in handfuls, which makes them laugh
with the thought of their imminent riches; but there are
only the same flaky shards and splinters turned over by the
plough each year or loosened by rain; whatever was here
and then destroyed, its extinction was accomplished so
thoroughly that not even the foundations are visible today.
They have to be dug for, and then emerge blackened by fire
as if some fanatic invaders had demanded total obliteration.
Here and there are half-filled channels and pits abandoned
by archaeologists decades ago, now the dusty home of
darting lizards that vanish in brown blurs from the corner
of the eye. But apart from that the town – whatever it was
– has been mummified for ever like so many others, and
barely has the dignity of memory. Even the handful of
preserved fragments in Gravina's tiny museum, which is

seldom open, bear the same evidence of wrathful demoli-
tion, for there is little to see save brutalised scraps of carved
stonework – though there are some coins inscribed with
the word SIDINON. Stamelluti, writing in 1870, reports that
a number of valuable objects had been sold off to Prince
Louis of Bourbon years earlier, including a silver goblet that
was 'miraculously decorated', and a golden serpent with a
button on its tail which could be pressed to make the whole
body wriggle 'and a forked tongue dart from its mouth, and
its ruby eyes roll wildly'.

No one will ever know the truth; for even destruction
itself was a work of art, part of the process of *issimo*
searching for sublime satisfaction – like those human
executions when the kneeling victim would have his temples hammered, his throat slit and his belly ripped open all
in one graceful movement. A curious manifestation of the
same artistic genius.

Out of nowhere an aeroplane passes, miles above in the
blue sky, a remote droning in a removed world, and the
children sing to it happily:

> *Apparecchio america'*
> *Gette' le bomb'*
> *E se ne va*
> *Scegl'te buon**

laughing at a hearsay figment of war, and an even closer
past they don't understand. They live so intensely in the
limited present that everything else is a succession of
miracles: the statue of San Michele in the church that
is not fixed yet cannot be moved (they've even tried rop-
ing it to a pair of oxen); an unknown father in Argentina;
the pictures they stare at vacantly on television all hours of
the day. Everything outside them is miracle or myth, and

---

* American machine Drop your bombs And go away Choose wisely the screen presents them with a convenient daily dose of visions that require nothing but their passive acceptance and semi-digestion. As a result of which they can hardly communicate except by signs and gestures and expressive movements – that whole language of inexhaustible pronouncements conducted in complete silence, which the fanciful say goes back to King Gerone's decree in Syracuse that none of his subjects should speak a word, in case they were plotting against him; though Lampedusa would say it is nothing but the silence of fear, and a deep hankering for oblivion.

But I am breaking their reticence down, by rewarding them for a few choice scraps of *'L'antica Silvium'* (or so this point is designated by the local historian Dottor Martini; though for verification one should turn to Volumes 6 and 7 of the bulletin of the Associazione Archeologica Romana). And now that the passing miracle in the sky has established a union of amazement between us, they are talking and singing songs to each other among the trees, chanting anecdotes of the region's love affairs, feuds and romantic adventures. For singing such songs makes the remarks unpunishable and beyond the reach of revenge or law; they are repeating them from memory or making them up, varying names and details as the stories go along, each one chipping in with a different verse or answer, adding titbits of embellishment to make the others laugh or to bring tuts of disapproval when matters get too Burnsian and racy – which, being human stories, most of them do. So in the scattered shade of old beech and chestnut the dry mountain rings with the songs of children, and the dusty landscape rolls away in infinite grandeur smudged by a midday haze, and my pockets fill slowly with *'la beauté des ruines'*, which Chateaubriand says is *'plus belle que la beauté'*.

SEVENTEEN

Altamura

One wonders sometimes about Mussolini, and whether it was all so despicably bad. Like most idealists, he probably had some of the right thoughts and intentions at first but then they all went to his vain impractical head, and the grandiose schemes were turned into another infamous 'tyranny tempered by disobedience of all laws'. One doesn't hear much about the early years when Puccini and Croce were on his side, equally depressed by disorganisation and anarchy, and when he dared call the population 'a nation of cowards' to instill some patriotic fervour, and said Parliament was 'a gathering of old fossils' and Catholics were followers of 'that small and insignificant Christ', and it was all for the sake of making Italy 'great, respected and feared', which he had promised as a young man he would do.

I am studying a notice on Gravina Station which states that in 1938 the country had over four thousand steam engines in use, but in 1952 only three thousand; also that there were fifteen hundred electric engines then and now only twelve hundred. So there is something to be said for those bad old days, it seems. The next columns, however, are less comforting: the rail system carried 167 million passengers in the year before the war, and just over a decade later 357 million, which is over twice as many people in fewer trains, an experience many of us have not enjoyed.

It is early sunlight and the platform is grey and empty, surrounded by a spreading backcloth of fell-like hills creased by jagged veins of dark gorges and half covered in bursts of scrub, all glinting green in the freshness of morning – for the station is in a defile a mile from the town. The children have come to see me off, friends at last, particularly

233

after last night's supper, which was a Zia Rosa speciality and reserved for special occasions – probably a reward for having taken them off her hands for the day. The *guardiano* was there, and there was dark wine almost purple and as thick as blood, with fiendish qualities that whispered ungodly messages to the senses and made every living creature an object of desire, filling the mind with 'thoughts not to be spoken of'. And then came a cauldron that contained a stew of Zia Rosa's own proportions, thick with meat-covered bones of various origins – lamb, chicken, rabbit, horse (and probably fox, dog, cat, guinea-pig and stork, as they too are recorded on travellers' menus) – into which the whole market place of Gravina had obviously been stirred – potatoes, beans, *finocchi*, lentils, cheese, tomatoes, peppers, macaroni, sage and thyme – providing such a harmonious compound that I took two helpings. 'Gentlemen, do not invest your money in diarrhoea,' warned Thomas Cook setting out for Italy in 1860, but no such thing happened, nor would I ever need to eat again after such a banquet. We dined like lions, with dripping paws and salivating dewlaps, applauding each new flake of succulence with such craterous sounds of approval that the room was filled for an hour with the lip-smacking counterpoint of our juicy pleasure. Then we fell back one by one with the disbelieving gasps of consummated lovers immobile in gratified exhaustion, and wordless sighed our magnificat of gastronomic satisfaction, while the amnesian wine lifted me slowly to a heaven where the children turned into angels and even Zia Rosa shone briefly with a lunar beauty.

That was last night. Now a goods train has pulled in and we are all watching the unloading, which is quite a performance as no one is quite sure what exactly has reached its destination; so manifests are studied and there are arguments and discussions and caps are removed to scratch heads, and as the sun inches higher and hotter, two rolls of

matting are tumbled down on to the platform followed by
three dozen stacking chairs, a crate of chickens and some
ferociously glinting tractor intestines. Then there are more
arguments and a search for labels, after which the chickens
are put back in and so is the matting, and the train draws
away with a friendly whoop. The landscape is empty again,
and the departing shape is now a statistic.

Eventually my train arrives, and as the clock has been
stationary at 4.17 for the last half-hour no one knows if it's
early or late, and as time is relative and inconsequential in
these parts nobody cares. This one is also the local countryside diligence that crawls along slowly enough for the
surroundings to remain recognisable, and stops wherever it
can to be friendly (I suspect it would do so by request if one
tried), heaped like a gypsy encampment with the scrambled
oddments of unclassified bodies that all know each other
and, as they are only going a few miles, have little wish to
be separated.

I wave goodbye as it sets off to continue its morning
trance, and am instantly in a world of rustic mothers
sheathed in silent black, bent boxes of fugitive vegetables
smelling of earth and collarless *contadini* with gnarled tree-
trunk faces sucking at ebony cheroots that smoke like Etna.
The slatted seats are filled with bulging packages straining
at labyrinths of string beside the latitudinal and Limpopo-
like buttocks of their matronly owners, and the air is
flavoured with cheese and garlic and sour eructations; but
everyone is happy. For movement like this is a brave
adventure that encourages expansiveness and diminishes
inhibition and, like the closed and secret world on ship-
board, suspends everyone in a daring limbo of irresponsibil-
ity, cut off at last from their roots, so that words, gestures,
feelings and opinions unutterable on land can be expressed
without reservation, and everyone's most intimate business
becomes common property. It's the same with the food:
first chopped with a well-thumbed knife or shredded by

hand, it is offered round in generous fingers of well-meaning kindness – sausage, bread, mortadella, cheese, cold macaroni – everyone part of the caravan family of coexistence and therefore equal, and a manifestation of that instinctive comradeship and sacrificial sharing among the peasants which Iris Origo talks of in *War in Val d'Orcia*. And we all rattle on, deep in each other's food and friendship and business . . .

I have caught an everlasting cold. It has lurked suspiciously round the fibres of the nose for days, and has at last decided those hours spent on Botromagno were the final straw and burst in a wasp's nest of retaliatory fury everywhere inside my head. Precisely at the moment I stepped down on to Altamura Station it struck; my voice disappeared and my eyes dimmed and my nostrils fused in conflagration, as I stared at the leaden shape of the platform getting emptier and emptier, and watched the turbulence of passengers running off the stage to leave me in a concrete void of wretchedness. 'Where is an *albergo*?' I croak to the ticketman in somebody else's uncontrollable castrato, my head full of strangled sounds, my eyes running straight from a funeral and my nose dripping like an open drain.

But Altamura is full: it is the week of autumn convocations and every bed is already filled with bus drivers or postmen or bank clerks or sheet-metal pressers or grape growers or goat fanciers. Even the huge Autostella on the edge of town – which I can't afford anyway, but being built for the relaxation of American servicemen away from one of their secret Apulian bases might just offer me that glimmer of comfort so longed for in adversity – is solidly overflowing. It's an oasis of transatlantic luxury, peopled with crew-cut Aryan giants crowding the foyer amidst Lilliputian onlookers. I turn to the gathering of curious youths outside hoping for favours, and beg them to find a room where I can be alone and nurse my gasping suffocation in solitude – for I feel like a dying cat clawing through fog at a warm-milk heaven – but all they can find is someone they know in the twilight zone of doubtful accommodation who will put a camp bed up in the passage; and as the front door is only two yards away, and there are numerous other visitors to come and go, I may as well be grateful.

It is at times such as these that one learns to be better satisfied with one's own country – which Johnson remarked was the overall effect of travel: when what is left of one's clogged-up mind is blackened by discomfort, draughts, ringing bells and a river of people, and one knows one has found a new definition of hell, and wonders if the others ever suffered like this: Nugent who called for fresh straw, Smollett who said beds turned the stomachs of muleteers and Sitwell who likened inns to tramps' doss-houses. We all have our personal thresholds of pain, which vary according to circumstance, and my state is entering that area of vacant numbness which precedes the breaking point. It must be stifled urgently with curative intoxicants.

Mercifully, among the warren of Altamura's ageless streets there exists Padre Peppe's bar, which is the sole purveyor of a secret and devilish brew, distilled on the premises and originally concocted in 1742 by a monk with a bent for chemistry. Nothing else is known of him save that he stumbled on this happy invention by accident in the course of his meditations on unripe walnuts and certain herbs and a pestle and mortar, which after the precise period of forty-five days gave the world a treacly brown liquid like syrup of figs. It first cauterises the throat (so you feel like Portia after her first mouthful of coal), then lies on the stomach a moment, till some demon ignites the fuse, whereupon it explodes dramatically, and finally pops the ear-drums. Five Padre Peppes and Smollett is a sour old smelfungus again and Altamura is ravishing, and you stare in light-hearted amazement at the rows of fake whisky bottles behind the bar – Capercaillie, Cock o' the North,

Black Douglas, Loch Lomond, Prince Charlie, White Heather, Bagpipe, MacTavish, Glenalmond, Pitlochry, John o' Groat's, Tartan, Edinburgh Tattoo – and are happily overcome with admiration for such inventiveness.

Decidedly mellowed by these caustic monkish vapours, I pause to wonder why more is not known of Altamura, one of the oldest zones in all Italy, its hilltop roots tangled in neolithic history, its megalithic walls and medieval streets and magnificently Romanesque cathedral, all spread on this dominating crest of land and swept by every passing wind, and 'riding the desert like a moored battleship', as Rose Macaulay would have it, or like a dark sentinel standing guard between the Adriatic and Ionian. Herr Baedeker gives it half a line: 'with an old Norman cathedral'; Mr Cook the same: 'Roman ruins, etc.' (where did he see them? I'd like to know); the *Blue Guide* generously stretches to one and a half lines; while Mr Morton doesn't mention it at all – which is something of a surprise considering its position and elegance and that it was once the capital of Basilicata (for a week), and before that Frederick II let the Greeks found a university here (later re-established briefly by the Bourbons), and the Jews founded a synagogue, and then came Cardinal Ruffo's bloody siege in 1799, which was either famous or infamous depending whose side you were on, Bourbon Royalist or French Republican.

It all happened at the time of the great revolutions in Europe, when Napoleon was liberating Naples from the Bourbons, and the Bourbons were being liberated from Napoleon by Nelson, and Nelson was liberating Emma from Hamilton, and Hamilton was being liberated of his post by the British government; between times Nelson was murdering prisoners, while Fra Diavolo was killing anyone he pleased, Chiavone was doing the other thing, and the English contingent (some three thousand) was leaving south Italy 'like startled hares'. By the time the King regained control of the situation the Altamurans had made up their minds to remain firmly French Republican – so Cardinal Ruffo was sent in to persuade them to reconsider. And it is here that the animated accounts start to differ: for according to the Republicans this Bourbon priest-general was 'foul in his youth, and even filthier in his old age' and he brutally shot an old man and his son kneeling outside the gates; while according to the Royalists he was generous, kind and forgiving, and he gave the couple his blessing. Objectively detached reporting never having been a strong point in Italian journalism – in fact, Barzini says no Italian can write honestly about Italy – one has to guess one's way through the sycophantic partisanship of the so-called accounts in the hope of arriving somewhere near the truth. For sheer tabloid sensationalism the Republicans must carry the day, with those monsters of licentiousness and murder, Ruffo and his aide Revelli, starving the town out for days, killing off any peace delegations, then leading in a drunken rabble of ex-convicts and defrocked priests, who after a few hours of butchery went straight to the Orsoline Convent, where they made forty virgins strip naked and sing the 'Te Deum' before preparing a banquet and then joining in an orgy. Any who refused were stabbed 'through the lower stomach', and the same thing happened at the end of the evening to those who participated, and in the mean time Revelli had kept the Mother Superior for himself and ultimately dispatched her in similar fashion.

Sacchinelli's account, however, is more restrained, and tells how Ruffo, after his peace offerings were refused, deliberately lined his soldiers up on one side of the town so that the inhabitants could escape from the other; then, when most had done so, proceeded to enter the town peacefully. It was only when the remains were found of some tortured Royalist prisoners that he began to lose control of his army, and in order to avoid a full-scale mutiny had to order the immediate distribution of booty. Sacchinelli adds that the Altamurans soon returned, and became so fond of Ruffo's soldiers that when the time came for departure they could scarcely be dragged away. Apparently by then they had returned all their booty and had spent all their pay, thus making Altamura to Ruffo what Capua had been to Hannibal.

You may take your pick.*

I've had quite enough of Peppe's anodyne fluid of venting warmth and concussive strength, and must go to meet the cathedral, which is a long way but can be forgiven as it is past some most elegantly sunlit Romanesque façades, curling balconies and near-Renaissance courtyards with graceful loggias and dignified stone stairways and baroque-shouldered doorways of splendid theatricality. All are still redolent with the air of departed patrician wealth and faded nobility, and restrained in their Olympian good taste – almost casually flamboyant, one might say. Yet it is an absurd mixture of shapes running into each other in mongrel accumulations of historical stratifications, like the meaningless patterns of pebbles on a beach bronzing in the sun – liable at any moment to throw out a mauve bundle of wisteria, or a coloured-bunting display of washing, or an unkempt forest of geraniums, or a spray of yellow japonica balls – and everything bursting with energetic untidiness and harmonious disorganisation. A geometric imbroglio of broken straight lines, abundantly decorated.

I kneel in front of the cathedral, not out of reverence but merely to point the viewfinder at the crust of intricate carving round the 'richest of Apulian doorways', with its wide-legged growling lions, kneeling caryatids holding up several tons of stone angels, Bible stories, serpentine acanthus leaves, virgin births and last suppers, all fusing themselves into a gromanesque riot of ringlets, Gordian knots

---

* Considering Cardinal Ruffo's gentle behaviour in Naples (much to the annoyance of pugnacious Nelson), Sacchinelli's more benevolent account is likely to be the truer one.

and interlaced proliferations, a lavishness of dripping ornament that soars in an encomium of architectural rhetoric
as if a stonemason had blown up a concrete meringue. Then
I am tapped lightly on the shoulder: 'Excuse me *signore . . .
si paga . . .*' A priestly shape is hiding the sun, a black blot
of avarice standing with hands in cassock-pockets and
waiting with firm expectation; so rather than begin an
unholy dispute, I bow to his thieving and away he whispers
up the steps on his loose sandals, clutching my lire and
disappearing like some beetle hurrying to ground with his
happy day's foraging.

Humbly I return to Padre Peppe's, where the barman
sympathetically likens religion to some curious form of
insanity; and after another glass of the monk's firewater we
agree unhesitatingly with Mussolini that priests are the
curse of Italy – words also used by Garibaldi, and every
leader since the days of Nero . . . And will be used many
times again.

'My God! You can't drink that dragon's piss.'

He is small, with pale skin and steel-rimmed spectacles
coating bright eyes, and is moving restlessly from one
short leg to the other as if embarrassed or animated by
perpetual motion; he has obviously been summoned by
the same telepathy that makes jungle Africans roll over
and die.

'Someone off the train told me,' he says, 'one of the
schoolboys, said you were looking for the Appia Antica and
le cose antiche. I'm the history teacher.'

'Drink?'

'Scotch . . . I'll show you Altamura. Goodness, you've got a
cold. *Orlandus me destruxit, Fredericus reparavit.* Mercadante was born here. Ours is the biggest cathedral in Italy
south of St Peter's . . . He carried out experiments on his
prisoners, early vivisection, to see how long they'd float or if
they'd explode when he boiled them – Frederick, I mean, not
Mercadante – brilliant person, German.' His eager staccato

pauses with a sharp intake of breath as the barman relates my cathedral adventure. '*Stronzi vigliacchi*,' he snorts, polishing his spectacles angrily. 'They've been stopping me using their library for years, so I can't write my history; no wonder we don't get any tourists. They say history should only be written by priests. All they do is sit up there, sniffing for signs of heresy and changing things they don't like in old books, destroying the rude bits – like when Contarini complained that half the houses dedicated to God for the shelter of virgins had been turned into brothels. Last year the librarian burnt some eleventh-century manuscripts because they mentioned Arnold of Brescia and were therefore unorthodox.'

He downs another whisky without flinching, and bids me follow him outside, through labyrinthine streets shaded like a medieval ghetto and then narrowing to cobbled alleys where eventually he vanishes gnome-like through a door and we are in his tiny 'history-room' with dog-eared maps curling off the walls, tumbled stacks of books strewn on the floor amid bursting waste bins, an invisible desk somewhere central but hidden beneath a debris of boiling-over paperwork, and whatever space might be left taken up with photographs. Miraculously, a bottle of whisky has appeared in his hand, together with two glasses:

'The real thing,' he announces, slapping it proudly, 'White Label . . . I have friends in Bari. It will do your cold good,' pouring carelessly lavish measures. 'You have to know the right people if you want anything: that's the rule in Italy. Do you know how much contraband comes into Bari and Brindisi each week? About a thousand crates. *Si deve arrangiarsi*' – You have to make the right arrangements – and his eyes sparkle with pleased complicity. 'It all depends on who you know; so next time you want to photograph the cathedral, just leave it to me; I'll send some children in to wave their willies at the priests . . .'

So the little history teacher is into it too: his own secret society. *Si deve arrangiarsi* (or *sistemarsi*): more fixing, more knowing a person who knows a person who can get it fixed for you – that same subtle code of insider-dealing that permeates Italian existence from birth to death, the whispered way of doing things in order to create an acceptable way of living out of chaos, because the law is unreliable, and official institutions are hostile and weak. So they operate a network of unwritten methods to overcome the uselessness of the proper ones; breaking the law becomes a necessity because it doesn't work anyway, and it's no use living according to the rules because there aren't any, so let's make some of our own – better ones, to our own advantage. And the result is a framework of carefully systematised anarchy regulated by mobile and hydra-headed formulae – but it works. It also defeats itself. It means proper law and recognised regulation can never come, because they can't get a purchase on a quagmire and keep sinking; so suffering, humiliation, hell and outrage for those who can't *arrangiarsi* will continue for a long time yet.

Three helpings of whisky and I feel I can take on anything – even my cold has been forced into oblivion – vaguely aware through my humming head that the *professore* is looking for something on his desk and scattering more papers on to the floor.

'*Ecco,*' he blinks owlishly through his spectacles, waving a pamphlet at me, 'the latest official guide to Altamura, which is produced by idiots in Bari who have never been here: "The Region of Altamura is famous for moorhen-shooting, *caccia di folaga*" – I ask you – no one's seen a moorhen here for fifty years. The tourist boards only want visitors to go to the best-known places: Castel del Monte, Bari and Alberobello to see the Trulli, or maybe the stalactite caves at Castellana; nowhere else exists . . . Look,' and again he dives amid the plethora of paperwork to find another booklet, slim and grey. 'See here,' he urges: 'stalactite caves not three miles away that make Castellana look like a second-hand-spaghetti shop; hundreds of yards of them: white ones, yellow ones, even red ones – *rarissime* – and stalagmites too, in the same cave, and some of them going horizontally, and one going in a circle – ' he throws the book down pathetically. 'An old shepherd found them and took us down two years ago, but does Bari want to know about them? Bah!' He sighs and looks sadly at the whisky bottle, which fortunately is empty, then reshuffles the papers on his desk. 'Come on,' he says, 'I'll show you something else that doesn't exist.'

Back in the narrow streets, where the walls are streaked by straining shafts of overhead sunlight, we push our way into more alleys barely one person wide, and then clamber through a gap in a building, over mounds of rubble towards a derelict doorway which is half boarded-up, but this doesn't stop him worming his way in. So I follow into the decaying and dust-covered rooms of a last-century *palazzo* with corniced ceilings and crumbling plaster fireplaces mummified by gloom, and he's far ahead of me, rummaging his way to the head of some cellar steps.

'Be careful,' he whispers, gingerly setting off down into the darkness; and as I follow the echo of his footsteps into the chill of stale damp air, the eclipse is complete, making my balance hover dangerously, and then rock violently, at the whispering sound of moving water. I sway uncertainly in the grasp of midnight blackness, till his torch-beam pierces the unknown; we are a foot above a sluggish lake, brackish and calm, out of which lofty pillars are soaring up into arches over our heads, where the vaulted ceilings are flaking away their gleaming patches of blue and silver. 'We're under San Nicola dei Greci,' he whispers, 'the old temple; but the priests won't let anyone see it. It's a place of heresy, so it doesn't exist, and of course everyone obeys the priests; what they don't know isn't knowledge . . .'

Later he takes me out to the Messapian walls, and pats the stones fondly. '*Ecco*,' he smiles, 'how did they get there? They're older than Homer. We're in one of the oldest parts of Italy, and nobody cares.' And he says the same thing at Il Pulo too – The Place Picked Clean – which we drive to in his old motor car; it is a vast, clean-cut crater made by a meteorite, grey and forbidding, over five hundred yards across and nearly a hundred feet deep. It's the home of Orco the giant, he says, the one-eyed monster who devoured women and children and threw stones at his enemies, and as real to the Altamurans today as any other gods – for there is not a dwelling within three miles, and only a madman would go near the place after sunset. Not a wit deterred by such nonsense – and anyway there's still an hour of daylight left – down the near-vertical escarpment he bounds, leaping over rocks with the ease of an excited rubber ball till he almost disappeares at the very bottom, where I join him, some ten minutes later, sitting on the gigantic boulder half-buried at the eye of the crater. 'One of the first altars in the world,' he announces, patting it affectionately, 'when our ancestors worshipped the sun and sacrificed each other to placate mysterious elements. Look – here's the hollow where they collected the blood.'

And there it is: a carefully ground-out saucer-shape at the centre, the receptacle of human sap, with a drain channel chopped out towards the edge. 'Now we'll make our sacrifice,' he announces smiling, 'to a real and better god,' and he draws from his pocket another whisky bottle, which he opens with a flourish and pours the first inch into the bowl. 'To Bacchus and to Scotland,' he announces, eyes twinkling happily as he passes me the bottle, 'and to the Via Appia. *Salute . . .*'

EIGHTEEN

Matera 1

My God, what a night of blowing winds and cracking cheeks. As if it hadn't howled loudly enough across Il Pulo in the afternoon, tonight it whistles under gaping doors and rushes down passages, straight into every cranny of my shivering skin; the deeper I shudder into the camp-bed, woodlousing it under the bedclothes, the more frustrated and hysterical it gets, just like a neurotic vampire. Then when I'm finally rolled up unassailable, nose snug in crotch, the bells start. They ring all night: clarion peals of jubilation for late arrivers, early leavers, button pushers or attention seekers – and most of these trample past or over me with operatic enthusiasm. So I sob quietly to myself through the wind-whipped sonic ecstasy, and moan inward paeans of hatred. 'Nothing of humanity left but the smell,' said Ruskin; though this time it is the bloody noise.

It must have subsided in the small hours, for eventually I slept. And now I have found the track southward, that the professor showed me yesterday, a dusty lane out over open country, completely deserted, which points towards the far-off blue shape of Lucanian hills, strung across the horizon like a growth of shadows. Bleak and sun-savaged with barely a powdering of earth round them, the olive trees writhe in age-old pain, then thin out in humiliating surrender to nothing as if scorched by the heat of some giant's breath where gasping birds can only give dry croaks of despair. Amid this timeless exudation brooding ghosts from mountain and desert search through the endless grey cairns of rock for their old homes and the tents they once pitched on the dusty earth; and in the distance two arches of Roman aqueduct rise like lost mastodons, blurred by the haze, and stalk away across the plain with their feet hidden in a shimmer of watery light. Now the sun is up and burning, flies have found an oasis of comfort round my face, and through them and sweat-drips and tangled lids the burnished warts of grey rocks pile up higher and closer. Some of them ooze upward to the height of cliffs, others lie like conical baubles thrown down by a team of colossi after playing nine-pins. Deep in some chosen crevices are hollows of grotto chapels, with faded outlines of figures on the walls, pock-marked by weather and mutilation, and with gashes for eyes where raiders have hunted for treasure.

Two hours of relentless and silent space, droned at by circling flies, and one begs for change. No wonder Trajan wanted a fairer and happier way where he could skirt the warm Adriatic beaches against the smiling blue of those tempting waves, instead of marching through this torment. The moment I have passed that lumpish grey mound over there of Murge Catena – thought by some to be ancient Sub Lupatia, and one of the final stations on the Appia – I shall turn westward towards the distant hills, where there must be shade and moisture. And perhaps there will be cool morning mists to curtain the rough parcels of land perched at all angles – and perhaps even a cloud may come, no bigger than a man's hand, lifted by breezes off the warm Ionian with promises of rain.

Matera's population has grown by almost a thousand each year since 1935, and now numbers forty thousand. It was hardly there at all when Luisa Levi saw it before the war, on her way to visit her exiled brother: she only found it when she leant over a cliff and saw the caves. And then she saw the children too, naked or in rags, with skeletal bodies and the wizened faces of old men, with flies crawling on their eyelids, and all of them begging for quinine. 'I felt I was in a city stricken by plague,' she told her brother when she met him, not far away, imprisoned among a desolate race of men and low hills of grey stony earth.

Much has changed in twenty years, but not everything. The caves are still there, in spite of efforts to close them; these are the famous *sassi*: hundreds of worm-holes bored into the scoriations of grey-green cliff, staring out like the eyes of a battered colander. The stream below them is much the same, swampy and sluggish and full of refuse. The children are still thin and wizened, with flies round their eyes, but only in ones or twos. For Matera has been a *cause célèbre*, discovered by politicians and journalists to be the *anus mundi*, where troglodytes live in subhuman conditions, miserable and impoverished relics of another age. So the Prime Minister has been to see it, and laws have been passed, and cries of 'Scandal!' shouted, and money has poured in from all over the world to help with the 'resanitisation', and the agony of an enforced metamorphosis has been thrust upon it. No one has noticed that some of the caves have television and refrigerators and hot water, and are lived in by contented people whose families have always been cool in the rage of summer, and comfortably warm in winter, for as long as they can remember.

So change is being resisted; the *mago* is still preferred to the white-coated doctors in the new hospital, the donkey is still better than the tractor, and nobody wants to move up into the new blocks of flats being specially constructed. As fast as the officials move in to brick up a cave, someone unbricks it the following night. And to hell with Law 619 dated 17 May 1952, they say, this cave-closing has been done before and never worked. And the quintessential power of the Italian family bonds together again in mute impregnability: the invincible force that authority has never beaten.

There they are then, and there they stay: history's obscene pock marks defacing an entire cliff. But not so when examined closely. Then they become a warren of creative genius that has turned a potential Gothic horror into a cascade of unbalanced brilliance, where tumbling jewel-dens splashed with colour are linked by invisible strings of alleys and by stairways that weave like tentacles. Bubbles of inventive shapes jostle and crowd, and additions, mutations, excretions, divisions battle in coagulants of sun-loving forms; there are myriad complexions of ochre and watered pink and dazzling white shapes balancing on each other's roof-tops; yellows and misty reds are tipped at forbidden angles on outcrops of cliffs, defying gravity. Long hairnets of mauve wisteria tumble from flat roofs, turrets and arches, cobwebs of tamarisk peep round corners, and jacarandas grow in roof-top gardens; there are shadows that run into medieval tunnels, and long streaks of sunlight on old balconies with regal balustrading balanced in space.

Each cave has combusted like a seed of coral over the centuries, and has multiplied crust-on-crust in chromatic exuberance, sucking in tints and colours and chewing on history, so that Norman pilasters nudge Venetian windows and warlike Moorish turrets touch Romanesque buttresses. Crimson peppers lie baking in the sun and domed, rain-thirsty roofs are spread with ripening tomatoes. Here wide-eyed children stare in wonder a moment, before darting like minnows into blackness sucking moons of melon; then a coolly naked pig walks by, pulling a wide woman on a lead as she balances a jug of water on her skirted hip. They both saunter down cobbled steps to a pointed corner where a coloured cart idles in a splash of shadow, coupled to a bony donkey with a wagging tail and a hang-dog head hidden under a straw hat.

There are two main cliffs of caves, the Barisano and the Caveoso; they meet where the plateau above comes to a point, where the medieval town started when the inhabitants had to put up defences and walls and climb on top of each other for safety. Hillocks and hummocks and humps of goblin-houses hug one another in heaps of worried abandon as they scramble upward towards salvation and away from death, fighting for air and blinding each other's windows. And it wasn't just Pyrrhus and Hannibal who came; it was sacked by the Goths and taken by the Lombards and twice rased by the Saracens in under a hundred years, then taken by the Byzantines and later by the Normans; and long before that there were the tribal Mateoli and the Myceneans; there is a bath-house with a frescoed floor somewhere down a tunnel, and the pillars in the cathedral were robbed from temples at Metapontum . . . So Matera is older than very old, and much worse than a maze and muddle, because it has been re-created countless times out of anything that was left, piled up and up on yesterday's rubbish – and now they are trying to do it again. So no wonder some of the old Materans are sick of it and want to keep their heads down in the caves, so things won't keep changing and nobody can interfere.

'Plonk!' A stone has landed on the earth three feet away. 'Plonk!' and another one. No, they don't like meddlers. They didn't like the Germans in the war either, so I'm told, when the caves were 'off limits' and called the Casbah: one or two soldiers disappeared down there. 'Plonk!' Some loathsome brat is playing medieval war-games from a high-up ledge where he's safely out of sight, defending his territory, repelling the invader – completely invisible. And 'plonk!' again . . . Bastard! Being defenceless and stoned is not amusing: the cranium grows thin, the body naked, the eyes useless; one feels massively vulnerable and unprotected, with a porcelain skull full of angry impotence, and rage and terror . . . Where is the little sod? And you look up and see nothing but rock, just like the olden days: miles of cliff-face going up to the sky and not a movement. 'Plonk!' Run for it; outflank the little bugger before a big one comes and smashes your skull like china – not easy with a hundred unseen eyes watching from caves and through cracks in doors and round edges of wall. Up we go, through a zigzag

maze hugging the cliff, to find him; but Materan children
can vanish easily into the entrails of old honeycomb for
nearly ever, and then pop out a mile away later like satisfied
moles, smugly innocent of the wanton bestiality they
showed a moment ago as part of their history. Or was it just
a childish game, using the cliff as his plaything? Or mistrust
of something he didn't understand, and so had to be done
away with? Who knows?

My audience isn't certain either. I have taken shelter
through a half-open doorway beneath an arch, drawn in by
the incongruous sweep of a Vivaldi trumpet concerto; and
the roomful of people all look up from the benches where
they are working – four men and a girl bent over tables
strewn with maps, books, charts and papers.

'*Salve*. I'm glad you've found us. The professor said . . .'

'Did he tell you? Are you the history society that looks
after the caves? Are you La Scaletta?'

'Yes. He said you were coming.'

'That boy nearly killed me – throwing stones.'

'He probably thought you were from the ministry, check-
ing the caves were empty. Have some coffee.'

'Or he was keeping you away from the paintings.'

'Paintings? . . .'

'The Byzantine ones in the caves; we're cleaning some up
and writing a book about them. The boys are supposed to
guard them for us. There are hundreds of them . . . look . . .
like this.'

And he picks a photograph off a table to show me: an old
haunted face, thin and sallow, with high cheekbones and
deep sunken eyes that dream between sin and heaven, and
round it a pale glowing halo.

'Jesus!'

'No. St Michael actually . . .'

There should be more like this: groups of the young and
enthusiastic who want to reclaim the essence of south Italy

before it disappears for ever. Just a small one in every town would do, and it would soon be alive again, proud and pleased with itself. All it needs is a spark or a seed or a germ to set it off – or love – and then energy to spread it. And then Lagopesole might get a visit, and the magic lakes of Monticchio, Pertusillo, Cecita and Ampollino; and the ruins of Egnazia could parade their ghosts, and the Sila its forests, and Cannae its warriors, and Lecce Cathedral all its ornaments; and you could sit on the crust of Sybaris and watch for its dancing horses and pet dwarfs, and listen for the bells of all the drowned Greek cities as they toll them under the sea ... It will come, in the distant years as far away again as the past is, when the world finds another set of values.

There are about ten people at the nucleus of La Scaletta, most of them just out of university. One helps in his father's ceramic factory, another works on a paper, a third is a doctor; there is an artist too, who won the Prix de Rome, a teacher in a school, a man from the council who keeps agrarian statistics, and one of them owns a shop, and the girl is a teacher too and is going to marry one of the others. Slowly and uphill they are moving Matera back on to the map, without money or anyone's interest; the paintings they try to clean are defaced and chipped by the children, who hate ugly mysteries from the past; and when the painter wants to record them for the present they spit and tear up the drawings. 'They're afraid,' he says, 'ashamed of seeing themselves as they really are – misshapen, ugly, underfed, like little gargoyles. They're frightened of anything they can't understand; it must be evil.'

Grandiose schemes are afoot, they say, for the rebuilding of Matera; but they too laugh at it, with confused embarrassment, caught in the vortex between progress and antique tradition, with their own hearts closer to the past. And in the morning they show me. First the old sun-god that no one knows the date or meaning of, his cheerful face cut into stone, with curling flames for hair and mane; then out of town to the narrow Bat Caves, where the late Dottor Ridola made a lot of his neolithic finds; then on further to the maze of rock-chapels, scattered for miles and bored into stone by the monkish beetles of Byzantium between AD 800 and 1300, riddling their way to safety and oblivion like weevils into iron-grey nuggets of ementhal, with crypts and cupolas and apses and recessed frescoes and weird cross-vaulting – all smoothed with years of devoted labour – and whole walls washed with pale technicolour Christs and archangels, Marys, Adams, apostles, crucifixions, and enough sacred saints to fill a calendar. Some are as fresh as yesterday, others raddled by damp and image haters, and all are morose and mournful, with the hopeless eyes of misan-thropes bearing a joyless world on their shoulders.

Perhaps that's the reason for Materan sadness: living on top of these melancholy ghosts all weeping over some guilty past. There is no joy to be seen in Byzantium, however sublimely passionate those artists were; it is all doom and gloom and exquisite wretchedness, harrowed by discontent, tormented by self-accusation. After an hour of it one is desperate for laughter.

And that comes in the evening, in the *cantinas*. For not all the caves are sacred – far from it; some of them, older than Byzantium, are robustly secular. And tonight is Satur-day, the 'night of the lamb', and some are already ringing with merriment and soaked in wine-fumes, the black walls are gleaming with diamonds of damp. We have bought our supper in the square, tightly packed among groups of men waiting excitedly for their turn at the shop door, where the air is rich with hungry muttering and the tempting smells of grilled meat, and the night sky flares with the belching flames of furnaces. Tonight is the weekly feast-night for Matera's young men, most of them in from the fields, who are stamping in mealtime impatience and expectation along the Via delle Beccherie, watching skewered lumps of flesh spit and bubble in the heat, and pacing out their anxieties as they sniff hungrily at the air till they are called to take their packet. Then off they run down the alleys, clutching it to their chests, crying *'Murt' e c'te murt"* – Curses on your ancestors – only pausing for seconds to buy a handful of herbs or celery or radishes from an open door.

Then it is our turn; and off we rush too, warm packets on the chest, tumbling down hundreds of steps in the dark, hugging round cliff corners and crouching through tunnels, till we step into a cavernous grotto with cathedral ceilings out of sight, and steam-engine bulges of mammoth vats along the walls. There are long yards of wooden tables stretching to infinity, lit by pale candles where shadowy figures are already seated in the distant gloom. Down we go, on to benches to scramble at our greasy packets as jeroboams of dark wine arrive with a stack of glasses; we all sink into a moment of banquet silence as mouths are filled and washed away, while more shapes come to circle and take up the tables. Great bat-shadowed men are thrown huge against the walls like Eisenstein giants that swoop and cower, and the surf-like roar of speech starts back and forth, then booming to the ceiling. And if you want to be heard you shout, and to be heard properly shout louder still, and if that doesn't work you can start to sing – because that stops the talking and you can sing anything you like and get away with it, from bantering leg-pulls to dangerous insults. So everything is bedlam as purple wine bubbles out by the glassful, and hunks of hot lamb are torn apart to chew, and everyone shouts, and pandemonium roars to the roof and back again, and no one can hear a thing in the total happiness; till a *stornello* starts in a darkened corner and a standing figure in the distance lets out a cello bellow:

'Let me see your sister again, the one with dark eyes.'

'Don't be stupid; she could eat you.'

'If she's hungry I'll bring my donkey. He's big enough to please her. Then I'll carry her off exhausted.'

'You couldn't pick a chicken up.'

'She'll do that for me on all fours on the floor.'

'She'll blow you over with a fart.'

'I've changed my mind, now you've admitted your sister smells.'

'You should be used to stinks like that.'

'I'm not loose-bummed like your family; we're strong enough to pick paper off the floor.'

'And in the street! I've seen you doing it, hopping about like a trouserless toad . . .'

Harmless unromantic scatology, as someone sings out an opinion and a challenger accepts; then another starts in a different corner, and as the wine flows and inhibitions fade three or four competing antiphons echo out and chase each other in a verbal wit-pit – while the cheroot-smoke curls upwards in the dark, and glasses brim over and dribble down chins, and there are snorts and bellows to soak up more, and the sawdust round your feet darkens. Into the candle-mist of fetid centuries darkening the walls, stale bouquets of wine and wood-musk swirl, and hollow murmurs of half-lit faces swim in a timeless sea.

'How many ages hence shall this our lofty scene be acted o'er?' they might have said – warriors of Justinian or Belisarius, or the steely Lombards carousing after bloody sacks and mountain battles, roaring their conqueror's oaths, or the barbarous Turks of Byzantium soaked in gore, or two lots of hell-raising Saracens, and then the wild-fighting Norman knights. They too must have clamoured their victory choruses to this smoky roof, and spilt blood and wine together on this floor. And might not the homesick songs of crusaders have drowned the squeaky birth of travelling brats? And war-lording Angevins and Aragonese drunk fearsome healths between these very walls? Anything is possible in this Seven Sleepers land of chimera and fancy, where these lean, swilling men, home from the murderous sun, sway through the guttering candles like ghosts of old charcoal brigands.

La Scaletta is proud, and has energy and vision, but no great support. No one is interested in the folk memories of old peasants (hundreds of them stored away on tape), or how the invading Lyki from Anatolia gave it the name Lucania, or how the Byzantine governor Basileus changed it to Basilicata. No one cares where St Francis preached in 1218, or which local recluse has a collection of paintings by Solimena and Breughel. And does anyone want to know about the cures and curses used by *inciarmatori*, or who wears badger-hair and abracadabra amulets, or who believes in the magic of menstrual blood? One *mago* has just been put away for curing two girls when they had their first pains of ovulation by getting them pregnant. It is all on record, noted, filed, indexed, cross-referenced, as are the paintings in the caves – pallid faces, symbols, bodies – ripening the faded blues back to gleaming azure, dead gold into harvest sunshine, anaemic vestments back to iridescence, lighting their way by midnight moons of haloes that peep through the dusty patina of age.

Then they take me to Matera Nuova, the new town, all of them caught in the equipoise of uncertainty: the painter, who is a Communist, violently in favour of tearing up roots and smashing a way into an ideal world; while Daniele the journalist knows more about human nature and is ruefully cautious, his heart in tradition and his mind on progress; and Tortorelli the headmaster is cynical but committed; and the girl Antonietta is confident that it will all work in the end, and probably with half an eye on one of the new apartments where she can start a family.

Up on the plateau and miles back from the caves, shining new villages are being constructed with great tower blocks of apartments, as incongruous as rashes of eczema. To these the troglodytes are heaved out, piecemeal, on government orders, their belongings transported by the cartload to the fourth or fifth floor, complete with animals, vegetables and children. As there is nowhere to house the livestock and no place to plant the vegetables, after a week of growing tomatoes in the bath they fill it with coal instead, then creep stealthily away by night, back to the womb of the *sassi*. Slowly and relentlessly the roundabout circles on, amid grumbles and frustration; the bulldozer-dust is choking, the roar of drills pandemonic, the paint starts to peel, the concrete cracks, and busy men rush around clutching important briefcases to put things right. Meanwhile someone says the engineer in charge of rebuilding Monte Scaglioso Abbey wasn't qualified, so no wonder the floor slopes; and what happened to the fifty million lire given by the government towards the Monastery of Cristo Re? because the walls are cracking, the bells are too heavy for the tower, and the foundations are forty centimetres deep instead of four hundred. 'A minor oversight that defied the laws of gravity as well as all the other laws,' says my informant.

'Why the hell are they doing all that building anyway?' ask the cave-men. 'It is only so their whores can walk up and down the roads without getting their shoes dirty. Whose idea was it?' Which is a good question, as no one is quite sure of the answer, except that all the best architects in Italy were invited to submit plans for new villages, and most did so without ever coming here. It is Roman *paternalismo* again, say the cave-men, painting more hammers and sickles on the walls, as another tap runs dry or the electricity fails; while up on the plateau arguments get louder and tempers shorter about the finishing touches. Asphalt or gravel? Play area, car park or lawn?

We go round three of them, sometimes proud, sometimes horrified: Rione Venusia, with its half-finished streets of grey rubble, skeletons of anglepoise cranes and lorries belching dust clouds over cubes of concrete; then Serra

Venerdi – a prize-winning satellite – with strings of apartments at different heights so the outline looks like a fort, and the open spaces watched by all the windows; and Spine Bianche, finished throughout in dark terracotta, and every entrance anonymous. The inhabitants slouch, looking lost and out of place, foreigners in an alien land, while officials throw blame in the air like showers of confetti, and wag their heads and wave their hands about, and hunch their shoulders in outraged dudgeon.

Then there is La Martella, an island of New World gloss stuck out in an ocean of rocky fields, with its own custom-built avant-garde church that nobody uses. Its inside is filled with sparkling innovations, peacock-tail ceramics of vibrant blue and green, radiating a kaleidoscope of breath-taking Kandinskyesque designs, shapes that are surrealist and sacred. It shrieks with outrageous beauty, bursts with colour, clamours with light and energy; its daring touches the spirit, as rays of watered sun stream through the windows to make powdery translucent rainbows.

But nobody comes. It is an incongruity to God, an exclamation of profanity. The visiting priest cannot bear to hold a service in it, and has nailed some plastic madonnas and Woolworths crucifixes in appropriate places, and always covers the godless ceramic decoration with sheets or spare altar cloths. The small handful of locals detest it too; they let weeds grow along the paths, and sometimes they throw stones at it and break the windows. In 1959 they built a rough grotto of concrete beside it, and inside they put a figure of Mary standing on some rocks, her eyes piously distant and her ashen face sunk in dyspeptic torpor; and here they kneel on Sunday and hold their services.

There was an outcry of course: the futurists cursed the traditionalists, and vice versa; it only ended when the Archbishop of Taranto said that on holy ground worshippers could place any religious images they pleased. So the modernists gave up, and crept silently away. And so did

UNRRA CASAS* after financing and organising the creation of a whole new village – because no one could agree about the finishing touches: grass or gravel, neon or tungsten, palms or geraniums, bus stops or playgrounds. So none of it happened at all: the puddles filled, weeds grew, bins overflowed; the doctor didn't come, nor did the postman or the shops or the buses; the school didn't open. Then someone said it was all too far from Matera anyway, and it would be better to build another village somewhere else much closer . . .

Meanwhile the lonely madonna smiles on, half hidden by invading vegetation, and the last few remaining inhabitants try to steal away back to the caves, and the archbishop closes his part in the history of Matera. 'There was only one thing wrong with La Martella,' he wrote in a letter to the newspaper, 'it was built *fuori della realtà* – beyond the bounds of reality.

* United Nations Relief and Rehabilitation Administration, Comitato Amministrativo Soccorso ai Senzatetto

NINETEEN

Matera 2

A day at the seaside! I have been wrested from the isolation of my *pensione* by the welcoming committee of La Scaletta, who want to show me Metapontum. It is only twenty miles, they say. Just as I was deciphering a linguistic enigma too, on the back of the bedroom door, informing me that if my identities are doubtful, my dactyloscopic and anthropometric details will be taken. Off we go instead then, in somebody's car, and hurtle out of Matera as if hounded by Beelzebub – Tortorelli the headmaster, Daniele the journalist, Palumbo the financier, Antonietta the teacher, and me – squashed into medleys of contiguous malformations as we dive bumpety-bump, shouting with glee and discomfort, down our near-vertical descent which loops round absurd mountain corners scattering goats and dust, and leaps over gaps in absent asphalt, and gives rubbery howls of indignation throughout, swaying us like squids in springtime intimacy, with the frenzied engine smelling freedom and sniffing for the magnet of the sea. And there it is, Gissing's Ionian – a smudge of translucence all smoky and silvery blue, darting and dodging behind obscurant hills, then peeping out in V-shaped patches here and there, streaked with sun, to grin for half a blinding second like Tantalus – as olive and eucalyptus trees whizz past the windows beyond stone walls, scattering like running refugees, and the hot wind whips through the car's conversation, and no single face watches the caterpillar road tipping down ahead except mine. Whitely.

And there it is again, closer: a rolling land mass of browns and purples and greens, ghostlier than Greece itself and even more vanished, as if its marbled wonders had never existed. Darkened by clumps of trees, it sweeps down to an azure sea where the waves still lap gently at it after two thousand years. This is where the glories of Magna Graecia were, stretched out in colonnaded cities with temples, *agorae*, warm-water baths, marble fountains, theatres, statues, armies, gold- and silversmiths. This is where Gissing dreamt that he was back in ancient Croton, and described its wonders; where Lenormant begged passionately for the uncovering of Sybaris; where Ramage got a lighthouse-keeper drunk. And this is where everything vanished, with barely a trace: an expanse now of nothing, swept by wind and bleached by sun, where delirious ruin seekers come to hear the ghosts of dead ages as they sleep, locked away together in miles of warm oblivion all along the long lost milk-and-honey curve between the heel and toe of Italy. Where Pythagoras taught, and sheep grazed, and great cities were built three miles across, and fleets of triremes littered the sea, and Sybarites dined off oysters and slept on rose-petals, and the rich were so profligate and the luxury so wanton that half the Mediterranean glowered in jealousy ... Such stuff is for visionaries and poets, and for another age that may seek true civilisation.

Down slide the hills more gently, to mile after mile of barren strand cut by dried-up river-veins between mounds of hillock, all sprinkled with anarchic clumps of trees and giant bullrush where the earth is hard and sandy, and grass struggles. Then we scurry along a new asphalt road, over a level crossing into a sudden dark night of trees, where a freshly planted seashore woodland hides a Disneyland of tucked-away holiday houses crouched among thickets of pine. Welcome to Marina di Matera, the up-and-coming resort built on old Metapontum, where the motorised and moneyed mountainfolk rush at weekends, joined by holiday hordes from Ferrandina, Pisticci, Ginosa and Bernalda, limpetly astride their phutting Lambrettas or sweatily bursting

from stretched Topolinos, breathless to murder the innocent sea and hack the beach into shreds of flesh.

It strains the eyesight in each direction: giant leagues of
naked sand, with a backcloth border of guardian pines that
dwindle to nothing, and beside it a world of endless blue
acres stretching beyond vision to touch the sky. Years ago I
swam here in abandoned isolation – me and the sun – then
four old matrons swathed in black came out of the woods
to paddle, and fled when they saw me, screaming back to
the undergrowth as if I were a spawn of Neptune. Where
are they now, I wonder, those cackling harridans from
another age, encased in everlasting midnight? And where
are those pillared temples with their statues of bronze and
gold? And those languid rulers wrapped in white togas being
fanned by ebony slaves? Slaughtered, massacred, ruined,
powdered to irrecoverable dust by man's preordained cycle
of love and hate, creation and destruction.

A bad attack of 'Ruinenlust', I fear: a touch of the
Macaulays, a bout of Gissing's romantic gloom. I have
caught his germ of 'immemorial desolation' and of nature
triumphing 'over the greatness of forgotten men'. And why
not? Today's poetry is in pylons; its magic is the taste of a
hot hamburger; its vision is Ferraris on the moon; it dreams
of death by modern megatons, Mammon and Midas
extinguish the last breaths of beauty, the sirens sing only of
wealth, and we murder the innocent babes of emotion – the
last fountains of inspiration.

There are scratchworks of excavation here and there
beside the pineta where they think they have found the
market place; a network of foundations has been uncovered,
but the space is bare and unattended, swept over by breeze
and dust. Not far away off a track there's an earthen hollow
with a dozen mutilated tombs, lids off or askew, mourned
over by waving grass and bushes of mulberry, eucalyptus
and bright green myrtle. And a mile beyond that the only
real sign of Greek Metapontum: the fifteen Doric columns

that stand stately on a little hill and are called the Tavole Paladine as a curious by-product of the Charlemagne legend, of his knights in battle with the Saracen king, Agolant of Calabria. Some randomly call it the Temple of Pythagoras (as does the guidebook) with the same sheepish uncertainty that Cicero expressed when he came here and was shown the house where the great philosopher had lived and died and preached his political theories.

Metapontum was five miles round in those days; its land was fertile, its harbour splendid, its horses famous and its people rich. But the whole coast had been colonised by different Greek races, and no sooner did each city prosper than it grew jealous of others – and so they destroyed each other: Spartans, Achaeans, Dorians, Euboeans, 'like spiders trapped inside a bottle'. Every city fell, then raised itself, then fell again: Locri, Siris, Croton, Taras, Medma, Brentesion, Policoro, Metapontion, Herakleia, Pandosia, Thurii, Kaulonia, and darling Sybaris with its hundred thousand swooning hedonists.

So now it is ice-cream among the pines, or would I rather have a can of Coke? And over there will be a hundred-room hotel; and next to it a fast-food pizzeria with pinball games and juke-boxes while-u-wait; and that area there will be blocks of holiday apartments; and beyond that a football field; and the open area at the edge of the trees will be for tents and caravans; and won't it be fun when thousands come here in the summer? I mean, just look at that beach – isn't it better than anything you've seen at Ostia or Viareggio or Rimini or Forte dei Marmi? – and aren't the flowers lovely, the azaleas and oleanders waving a welcome, and the honeysuckle climbing mad, and the tamarisk weeping, and that carpet of gladioli and iris and columbine and peeping scilla? . . . Isn't it going to be wonderful?

A few days ago, I am told (we are back in Matera), there was an invasion by a group of American Valkyries who stopped here for refreshment on the final leg of their annual pilgrimage. A coachload of transatlantic matrons circled the square like beagles, my informant says, baying with excitement and making clouds of energetic dust before being sped off into the blistering sun, their noses aquiver for a scent of the approaching goal. Can I guess? he smiles, so I ponder. Hannibal? No . . . Pythagoras? Unlikely . . . A missile site? Doubtful . . . So how about Antony and Cleopatra? But he shakes his head. No, it was none of them. They were the Rudolf Valentino fan club from Cincinatti, Ohio.

This I must see, the birthplace of a bronzed Apulian *bambino* claiming the hearts and minds of a blue-rinsed horde from thousands of miles away, desperate to the point of paroxysm. Where is the shrine, I ask, this Mecca of a semi-silent Hollywood, where the graven image of a mournful spaniel with soup-bowl eyes gazes out reproachfully from the suffocating folds of a collapsing wigwam? I too will make the hadj to witness this wondrous thing that is come to pass, where imagined figments of lissome adolescence can stir antique breasts enough to cross an ocean and bring rays of romantic twilight into flatulent old age.

I hurry away southward in the direction of Taranto, through the chalky dust and the slowly flattening landscape along a serpentine road that will bring me to Castellaneta. When it emerges over a ridge, it seems no more than a group of bleached houses as white as desert bones strung along a single street. A few aboriginal olive trees lament disconsolately round the edge of it, and there are drooping tassels of asphodel between the rocks, fighting their exhaustion.

And no sooner am I among the houses, sticky with sweat, that I am whirled up into another village wedding, taking up the whole street, where everyone is bounding along with celebratory mirth, a spongy infection of happiness that sucks up spectators and passers-by, and wandering dogs and

chickens, into a cyclonic reel of Bacchanalia. Flowing movement mills around in chaos colours of white and grey and
blue and brown; and any old peasant suit will do if it is
jabbed with a red carnation; and everyone is welcome; and
any dog may bite the mingling shins; and any car can toot
its horn in affirmation of love's agreement. So everyone
claps their hands, and some shake tambourines, and two
jigging men wheeze along on conflicting concertinas, and
children skip past throwing flowers, and we all dissolve
into mobile smiles and swim along together in a musical
sweat of happiness. *'Auguri, auguri,'* and Gather ye rose-
buds: off I go joining in; a flagon of wine is thrust at me by
a dancing girl whirling past on the hoof, and away for a
moment goes crabbed northern sanity and cold reserve; I've
caught the epidemic of exuberance.

Later, when the storm of matrimony has subsided breathless into a field, I ask the priest for information, but his
mind is elsewhere; his cheeks are crimson and his voice as
dishevelled as his sacred garb, for this connubial-bliss business has gone to his head, and he has been tippling like
Falstaff ever since he authorised it. 'Castellaneta is only
important for one thing,' he mumbles, 'the night in 1503
when the garrison of French soldiers went on a carnal
rampage and violated every female in the village' – so
touched by the incident he almost overbalances with the
effort of shutting the details from his mind – 'but in the
morning the menfolk slaughtered the lot of them.' Then he
puckers his brow so the sweat gleams. But Valentino? No
. . . the name doesn't ring a bell, he says, sorry . . . was he
one of the French soldiers perhaps? And he tries to scratch
his head through the rebellious folds of his tangled cassock,
and forgets which hand his empty glass is in, so wriggles in
disarray back into the throng holding both out.

It isn't far in fact, for the wedding is beginning to
evaporate beside a farmhouse at the end of the lane, and
there are unusual sounds audible: the unsteady pounding of

old machinery and descant bursts of busy chatter. On the wall outside, a bronze plaque is hanging. RUDOLF VALENTINO it says, A NAME THAT IN A DISTANT LAND MEANT THE ART AND THE BEAUTY OF ITALY. THIS PLAQUE WAS LAID BY MEMBERS OF THE RUDOLF VALENTINO CLUB OF CINCINATTI, OHIO. Above the inscription is a relief of a young man clutching a mask and leaning forward as if to kiss a naked woman who is leaning back on a bed and holding a harp out towards him.

I wonder what the members' thoughts were this time? And what about the inside? The bedroom upstairs where he was born is a storehouse filled with sacks of nuts, and the downstairs is a workshop where they are shelled and ground, first by a row of chattering girls seated at a bench and popping the kernels expertly into their aprons (for which they are paid not for the thirteen hours they work each day from 6 a.m. to 7 p.m. but for the weight of kernels each of them produces in the time), then by a hammering machine that pulverises them to a pasty dust before tipping it away into sacks.* They smile at the name Valentino, and nudge each other. Yes, of course they've heard of him – and they laugh with bright earthy eyes alien to pangs of romantic infatuation, which know exactly when a spade is a shovel. He was lucky to get so much of it, is their view . . . they wouldn't mind that kind of luck either. No, he wasn't their type – too soft and effeminate. But then in America . . . They're all a bit weird over there . . .

A lucky man, then: from the nadir to the meridian in thirty years, the son of a veterinary surgeon who had moved down here from Foggia, and who sent the boy back there to study as soon as he was old enough. His subject was cows – something he had always been interested in around Castellaneta as a child, and which doubtless proved useful later

---

* This entire occupation has an interesting local name: *il lavoro del cazzo.*

on in his amorous career, when he was just one more of those thousands of southern emigrants hoping for a new life. He found it with little trouble, and began a triumphant passage through celluloid history as soon as he discovered that bovine passion within incinerator eyes could move ranges of emotional mountains. And they are still moving; that is why an anonymous wreath arrives here each year on the anniversary of his death, and is placed reverently against the wall of the nut factory.

As a result Castellaneta has something of a problem. Should it or should it not erect a statue in his memory? The debate has gone on for some twenty years, but never been finally resolved, as local elections are frequent, and any incoming administration has always cancelled all previous decisions at a stroke. But at last it seems that unanimity has been achieved, and a statue has actually been ordered; so very soon a memorial to him will stand in the square. Though by then it may be a little late, as the granddaughters of the Cincinatti fan club will never have heard of him.

Nothing matters now: I have smelt the sea. It was there at Metapontum, sparkling smiles of it, and now I can sniff its scent again, just beyond those last few ridges, a waiting sheet of lapis lazuli. Its air is in my nostrils, bright and clean and cutting the dust, up here on these hills where the two worlds met, and where the naked tribesmen scowled down from their lairs in atavistic uncertainty at the disembarking Greeks – the Bruttii, Lykani, Oenotri, Iapygi, Peucetti and Dauni – hugging the remoteness of their forested crags and fearful of things that came out of the sea. They've always been like that, frightened by it: three sides of them surrounded by water and one by the Pope; so staying in the mountains they're safe from both.

So I push on unsteadily to Massafra, glittering untidy white on one of the last ravines before the land falls gently away to the Ionian. It is caught up in the same uncertainty, for waves of progress are creeping up into its inland sleep and forcing transformation on it. And not all of them creep: some of them are more hurried. For Massafra is built on the side of a cliff, and the motoring clubs of Taranto have discovered its snaking circuit of narrow roads, curves, inclines, hairpin bends, precipitous corners and impossibly winding streets, and have found them irresistible. First it was motor cycles and then it was cars, and now it is anything that can make a noise loud enough to boom and roar and echo off the walls, to scream at corners, smell of smoke and rubber and keep everyone out of the way. The Massafrans have welcomed it – they are famous at last – and they all stand out after mass on Sunday when the priest gives an open-air blessing, then press back against the walls shielding their eyes, or lean from windows or stand in the bars with shirt-collars open, gazing in pleased amazement as the bits of coloured metal roar past faster and faster. For noise is fun, and noise brings people, and people become crowds, and crowds spend money – so all the bars and shops and stalls are open, with ice-cream, cakes, Coke and beer, and people want pizzas and sit-down spaghetti and a bottle of wine in the sun, and the children want flags, balloons, sweets and toy Bugattis. So everyone is happy and knows all the ratios of camshafts to overhead valves.

'You ought to come in September,' says one of the spectators leaning against the wall, 'it is better then: we have the championships all weekend.'

'Marvellous,' I answer.

'Yes, it is *festa* week. Famous drivers come from Foggia, Bari and Brindisi.' He shouts it out, beaming proudly as a Lancia hurtles by within a foot of us.

'*Festa?*'

'Yes, it used to be horses, a parade of them all dressed up, but the Bourbons stopped it. Anyway, there aren't many left now. So we have tractors and racing cars too. Times change, *signore* . . .'

They most certainly do, I tell him: the birth of the motor

car and a man landing on the moon, all in the space of a single lifetime – but philosophy doesn't interest him, so I wander off towards the back streets where there may be shade and silence. One worship is as good as another, I suppose, if it keeps people content and out of mischief, and doesn't cause offence and bloodshed. We all need something to idolise and fill our time with.

Nothing moves once the noise has gone: the streets are quiet and deserted, almost Pompeian, just a few hens pecking in the dust and the occasional sleepy dog stretched like a corpse. I can hear my own footsteps as they pad along in the ghost town. Then round a corner is a man, bending down almost motionless by the wheel of a cart, caressing it slowly with his wrist and arm, touching it delicately with streaks of paint. There are three more cart-wheels against the wall beside him – old ones, like fossilised starfish. '*Bello*,' I say, watching as his fingers creep the little brushes steadily along each radiant, turning them into bright firework patterns of gold, crimson and blue, with tendrils of vine leaves and twists of serpents and heads of birds and sweeps of fishtail, carefully dabbing out all his gleaming minutiae with enormous love – each petal, each scale, each tiny feather, giving birth to a rainbow.

'*Bellissimo*,' I say again, fresh colours everywhere.

'Five,' he answers. 'That's all this year. Five . . . Nobody uses carts now.'

'They're beautiful.'

'There was a line of them right down the road once; years ago. I had to work on Sundays.'

'Today *is* Sunday.'

'I know. It is the only day I do it now, away from that noise of machinery. When I was a boy in Sicily it was all carts: twenty or thirty a week sometimes.'

'Times change.'

'True . . . and the paint is so rotten now it fades in a week.'

I watch him as he pencils in a line of gold along the rim and under the leaves, stoically resigned to the passage of time, not really caring any more. 'There's no *bellezza* now,' he says, 'that is the problem. No more *bellezza* . . .'

Precisely. Profit and persuasion and the harsh consumer scythe chopping it all down to the ugly stubble of progress. Beauty is not commercial; only professional victims want beauty, so forget them. If they've got souls and sensitivity they aren't really part of today's world.

It is the same with Massafra's caves; there are nearly as many as Matera, and well over a hundred paintings. Where are they? I ask, but three people shake their heads. 'Down there, perhaps,' they say, 'or there . . .' watching for more cars to pass. Who knows? they shrug.

It is nearly evening, so it doesn't matter. I wonder if anybody ever will know.

TWENTY

Taranto

'*Spintriae* . . . Aren't they lovely?'

'Beg your pardon?'

'Tiberius' little fishes.'

'Oh . . .' I turn to look at him: old and lined with blubber lips and a drip shining on the end of his blue-veined nose. He must have come up behind me very quietly on soft shoes.

'I knew you were English,' he says, staring down over the wall at the water, his eyes hooded like a night bird, the visible bits pale and watery blue, big lids fluttering. I hadn't noticed the swimmers till then, but was looking across at the other side, stripping away the houses and seeing an ancient Greek landscape with lots of green pastures and plenty of sheep and perfect peace, looking for '*molle Tarentum*'. He had crept up on sandals, and his clothes were loose on his spindly frame, and he kept moving his lips like a pair of worried worms as if he was chewing on his tongue all the time.

'Parson's Pleasure,' he goes on.

'Oh yes? . . .'

'You at Oxford?'

'No.'

He gives a sigh, and chews some more, staring downwards. 'Aren't they pretty?'

So I look down at the sea below the wall where the kids are swimming, trying to get his drift; then one of them climbs out on to the rocks, laughing and shaking the water out of his hair, and I think I get it straight away. The boy has got nothing on; the lips are going harder now, as if his tongue might be escaping, and his eyes are fixed.

'Beautiful,' he whispers. 'Isn't he lovely? Bye-bye, dear boy, I must pop down and meet him.'

Taranto is warm and soft, its light a flow of golden honey round a pool; and as well as that it is aloof, proud and gently decadent. What is more, it doesn't care. It just lies like a basking serpent curled round its sea, old and unrepentant.

I must be wrong, of course – probably the sun. Gregorovius called it 'stinking', and Hare said its population was 'miserable, filthy and scrofulous', and Swinburne couldn't believe his eyes: 'Without doubt the most disgustful habitation of human beings in Europe' was his opinion (though he did stay long enough to describe it all in considerable detail). Pity: I need something sleazy and depraved at the moment; it is strange how seductive water is after days in the mountains, warm and tempting as it touches old fibres and makes forgotten bits tingle. And the sun makes you want to look at it for ever, to enjoy all the swells of contentment.

They're ruining it round the edges, though, over to the west: palls of smoke vomiting out of chimneys, sheets of flame leaping from furnaces, a scarecrow skyline of phallic gargoyles stabbing upwards out of miles of megamuck where the sooty air is so thick the sun never shines. It is all factories and foundries and oil refineries and hydro-some-things and blasting steelworks, combusting all day, lowering their shadows and belching a rumble that sighs across the city like dragon's breath, deromanticising everything. All that is out on the broad flat land towards Metapontum, before everything narrows back towards civilisation and to the point of a triangle that juts into the sea. This is where the city is, at the apex; it reaches across a stretch of water to another protruding tongue of land half a mile away, where more of the city is: stretched out like Michelangelo hands on the Sistine ceiling, two fingers encircling an inland sea. That new part is the nineteenth-century Borgo, square and elegant, with gracious houses and long avenues shaded by palms, an almost-Regency town with pillared façades, classical pediments and lawns all along the sea front, broken by red-blazing beds of salvias. There are real people, too, sitting on park benches and staring out across the water, or wandering along in loose conversation, and the odd lady exercising her poodle.

Between the points is an island, joined to each tip by a narrow bridge, so you can walk or drive right across – straight from the industrial unromantic smut on to the medieval island and then over into the spa. And behind it all is the inland sea, the Mare Piccolo, of which Napoleon said, 'This place is more valuable than Gibraltar,' and where the *cozze* and oysters are, and the shells giving purple dye. Then turn round, and there is more of it – the real sea, stretched for miles – and Taranto sits there enjoying both of them, sun-soaked and parchment-yellow and sucking it all up on each side like a delighted overfilled sponge.

Not bad for a bunch of Dorian bastards, to start all this after they'd been kicked out of Sparta in around 700 BC for inciting rebellion. All they had to do, with Phalanthus leading them, was to deal with a handful of Iapygi fishermen on the beaches, and take over the Daunian settlement of Satyrion with its outlying farms, then Greekify it a bit: sow grain, plant fruit trees, graze bigger herds, catch more fish, improve on the Messapian pottery, shake hands with the locals, start a little trade. It was all very friendly at first – though legend has it that before long they exiled Phalanthus to Brindisi for being too autocratic. Then when he died there an oracle told them to have him back, so they deified him as their founder and put him on their coins riding on a dolphin.

Not much is known for a while after that, except that the other Greek settlements stretching along to Sicily and up to Naples all fell out with each other regularly, and ate one another up like spiders. Also the natives weren't always friendly, so there were battles with the Daunians, and the

273

Peucetti, the Bruttii and the Samnites, from time to time over the next five hundred years. A bloody period for Taras, say Polybius, Livy, Silus Italicus, Strabo and other commentators, telling us it had three hundred thousand inhabitants at one time, and was the third largest city in Italy. Most of it is now buried under the Borgo, or still to be uncovered, out towards the south-east. For a brief period it dominated the land as far north as Naples; and under Archytas, who rescued Plato from the Sicilian tyrant Dionysius, was famous throughout the Mediterranean for its wealth, magnificence and luxury. Unwisely, however, after that it invited Pyrrhus to help it curb Rome's expansion, and later did the same thing again when it supported Hannibal and the Carthaginians. When the consul Fabius Maximus finally overcame it in 209 BC, he collected thirty thousand slaves and took away as much treasure and as many works of art as he could; these included Lysippus' seated Herakles (though not the sixty-foot-high bronze of Zeus), and – according to Livy – eighty-three thousand pounds of gold (a mistake, in the view of modern scholars, who think he meant three thousand; four hundred tons seems rather excessive).

Its reputation, however, lived on for some time; for rumours had long spread as far as Egypt, Persia and Numidia of its extravagant life-style: public nudism, women with painted nipples, young girls in diaphanous garments, men wearing giant dildos in the street, captured prisoners having to join in orgies before being killed, obscene plays and exhibitions in the theatre and the worship of indecent statues. 'A golden bride, wanton on the blue gulf' was what Caesar called it, as the scandalous ways of the southern Bacchus worship spread up into Rome (those 'vile and alien rites', as Livy called them). Horace was a good deal more tolerant, and preferred the sad remnants of 'peaceful Tarentum' to the roughness of 'queenly Rome'; he sat in its remaining glades and mused on its vanished glories – its three thousand villas spread along miles of lotus-eating shore, basking by a limitless sea under a cloudless sky, and its acropolis, its temples, its Olympic arena, its huge theatre, its farms, honey, flocks of sheep . . .

And that is possibly why it perished in the first place. It was luxuriantly lazy, and so dedicated to pleasure that none of its men would join the Army or go to war: they would rather pay mercenaries to do it for them. Archytas had been the only exception, during its most prosperous period; Duty and greatness first, was his dictum, lust afterwards. One wonders what the young moralist Cato must have thought when he arrived with the victorious Fabius Maximus and saw the result of all that evil, the folly of all that carnal pleasure, the ultimate consequence of always gratifying sensual passions. *

Pan suppressed can be Pan volcanic. He is still here, tingling, languid, whispering suggestions in the warm winds that slide in off the sea with immodest caresses and proposals of most pleasant misbehaviour. There is something alluringly feminine about Taranto – or is it perhaps something Hyacinthine and androgynous?

I am resisting temptation in the turbulent medieval quarter of the crowded island, where the houses are piled on each other in indiscriminate heaps, and there is a wide, fish-smelling waterfront looking out on to the Mare Piccolo, and somewhere behind among the bedlam of roof-tops bubbles up the cathedral of San Cataldo. This is where everyone believes in being close and intimate, like currants squashed together in a bun. I must have a drink to overcome this sunny bewitchment, to allay those lurking devils. This

* Cato was so well known for his puritan disapproval of things unseemly that during the Floralia celebrations in Rome the festive crowds would actually stop undressing the women as he walked past, waiting until he had gone.

is a most simple matter, as the number of *osterie* and *taverne* along the quayside is legion, and any doorway that isn't bucolic is a congestion of unoccupied ladies raucously drying their sweat off in the sun.

These *taverne* are dark and open-mouthed, and the stone floors make them cool; the wine they serve is purple, nearly black, and is dealt out in large flagons. No mealy-mouthed sippers here: two innocently thirst-quenching mouthfuls and the spiderish transportation starts, barely perceptible, inch by subtle inch away from reality, and with such smoothness one does not notice the broad squares of sand-stone jetty out there blur for a moment, and a passer-by wobble; nor does one feel the vapour stealing upward and lightly tapping the brain cells, puff by innocuous puff; nor even notice that those tottering towers of criss-cross lobster pots baking in the sun outside may be thinking of multiplying.

Innocently one takes a couple more swallows, and asks for some *salsicce tarantine* to help absorb it, and perhaps overcome the powerful, slimy fish effluvia wafting in through the open door, where the rowing boats seem to be bobbing happily on the blue like corks, and there's a seated fisherman mending a net who is occasionally becoming one and a half fishermen. The sausage will help settle things, you think, so away it goes followed by another mouthful to wash it down, and all is well for a moment; then just at the prime second of regaining normality something awful happens: the innocent sausage bursts half-way down your throat, releasing a nest of hornets round your tongue, and the Sahara is scorching your epiglottis to cinders and you can't get at the wine quickly enough to drown the pain of hidden peppers: violet, purple, ultramarine, darkest cyanin – no matter so long as it is liquid and can be gulped at ravenously.

And that's when the lobster-pot towers start to sway more recklessly, quadruplets of identical fishermen form, the boats bob out of the sea into the sky or sink completely into empty water, and everything starts to go wrong because try as you may you can't get sober again. As fast as you grab iron-fisted at reality it slips away, and you're high and dry in a private cloud of time, lapped at by silly little waves you'd like to kick, surrounded by a murmur of old gramophone voices that won't go away. Then the world becomes overcrowded with elusively important problems. What on earth makes the women so hairy – so much robustness wrapped in a tangle of blackened cobweb, such ranks of cactus arms? And what a filthy fish-smell – shrimp-stink, winkle-waft, eel-reek. And why no cats then? – didn't the Tarantines introduce them into Europe? Swinburne says they weren't averse to a slice of well-fed cur, but nothing about cats. (Oh my God! He's back again, looking in all the bars.) What was an Irish monk doing here in the eighth century founding their cathedral? Great travellers the leprechauns. And who was that Archbishop of Taranto who said in the middle of a conversation with someone, '*Mon chat veut chier*,' and popped him out of the window? And what was Choderlos de Laclos up to down here – or down to up here? All extremely important.

'Hello, dearie . . . Thought I might find you.'

'Yes.'

'Let's have a little drink.'

God, he is old! His restless lips keep writhing and munching, his face is bony and lined, his half-sealed eyes are bluey-wet, almost babyish. The problem is, I can't move: no legs. He looks like a vulture, moving his head about on a long white neck, inquisitive and guilty; a skinful of old bones.

'No thanks. I've had enough.'

'Oh dear . . . He was lovely, exquisite,' and he waves a floppy hand vaguely for a drink, and licks his lips till they shine like soft roes.

'Who was?'

'Enzo. He's perfect. A little god. I'm meeting him again this evening.' Munch, munch.

Then I have a thought: if he means what I think he means, then the police will arrive at any minute and we will both be arrested. Accessory, accomplice, aiding and listening . . .

'Look: I don't want – ' and his eyes narrow.

'Don't be so bloody fey,' with an edge of petulance, 'I saw you peeping over the wall this morning at those little brown bottoms.'

'I was thinking of Horace – purple dye – Greece.'

'Poppycock. You're a hypocrite, repressed faggot. You were on a beezie hunt.'

' "Beezie hunt"?'

'Boys, you bloody fool . . . That's all people come here for, stupid. Here, and Naples and Sicily . . .'

'Oh.'

And he takes a wine glass, rakes his lips out angrily and sucks it down greedily. I think I ought to leave, risk staggering away into daylight. 'Why are you here then? Enjoying the sun?'

'Quite . . . Thinking about a book. Roman roads . . .'

'Italians love the sun . . . specially the boys. Been to Taormina?'

'No.'

'Lovely. They can't wait, cocks like wine flasks, used to go there on a yacht every summer. Same in Bali.' I'm steadying the lobster pots outside: they're getting better. Then they fade again. Dare I stand up? 'All sun worshippers . . . stayed in a hotel. Ruined by bloody Americans now: made them put clothes on. Boys used to do naked sun-dances . . .' And his eyes go dreamy, big hoods fluttering.

Bloody liar, I think. This isn't really happening; everything will be all right in a minute. Have a long blink. But he's still there, sucking at his wine and going on about Germany before the war – Isherwood days, tea-stirring times, swimming pools and camps full of hungry two-way queers. *Nackttanzen*. The poet in Rome had a friend like this – obsessed – round and round the world like Casanova, prick's progress, scrotums of hope . . .

'Oh,' I say, into a silence, hearing something about teaching English, and having to pay the little darlings. Then I jump at a shadow in the doorway, but it looks round and goes away.

'Worried, dearie? Don't be silly. Nobody minds it here. All queer as coots. Like the Arabs. Do it to melons. Seen the Sleuh dancing boys?' This is gruesome, like a shopping list, a magic-lantern show. Time to stand up. But he is scrabbling in his pocket for something, pulling out a crumpled envelope, tipping it on to the table. 'Look,' he says, letting cobwebs of fluff drift over the plastic. Christ almighty! Not another pubic magpie and mini-depilator – more tonsured cocks. What does he do with the stuff? Frame it? He fingers the tuft of downy hair, lips chewing.

'Jesus!'

'Enzo, this morning,' he says, 'very sweet. I've got more in my room . . . and photographs.'

'Bloody hell!' standing up. 'Doesn't it bother you, going on and on doing the same thing?'

'Silly bugger,' he says, eyes narrowing. 'Don't be so romantic. Always room in my heart for another one . . . Do pay for my wine, would you dearie? Haven't got a bean – not after this morning . . .'

Great gulps of dizzy air again, breathing in fish-smells under a standstill sky, miles of little waves lapping. I must have dreamt it. Shock can be very sobering, specially in this sheet of phosphorescent sun as I make my way over the unsteady slabs to a jungle of market stalls, where the stench is of sickly sweetness and everything glints in a torn tapestry of silver bodies and shredded dots of scales. They ooze and flop in dead convulsions, filling a waist-high flood of barrow trays with the dance of their silver-black bodies, still or sliding at angles, glittering bellies up in oblong shapes. Swinburne counted forty-eight species of fish in the market, and could have found more. And there are chain-loads of exhausted black mussels hanging like bracelets for Hercules, and the squelching of owl-eyed squid turned mucously inside-out but breathing stickily, and the final mortuary paroxysms of stranded lobsters dreamily crawling forward to death with one last claw-struggle. Everything is garnished with rococo ribbons of green seaweed, even the old tin basins of dark-shelled drowning oysters and the deep pink piles of twitching shrimps. What a carpet of sea-harvest, alive and pungent on the thick-scented air. Who-ever could consume such a fishy feast? Perhaps the evening cooks will soon be out for a sunset bargain: the rest will then be hawked round the *trattorie*.

What language too! A most jovial repertory of all things unprintable, and spiced with the same laughter Ramage heard when he turned up in their midst caked with mud. And plenty of French thrown in – '*Oie, venez qui*', '*Voulez poisson*', '*Avete besoin*', '*Achetez mo*''. What might not the sea have to do with all this exuberant happiness? I wonder. There are roars and calls and deafening yells competing for air room, and lungfuls of exuberant discord clashing, as if they have sucked in some frivolous spirits from the wind and waves and are shouting them out again.

I swim through the piscatorial jigsaw, past towering condoms of swinging lobster pots – soaring to heaven like domed carillons of undersea torture chambers – and more rippling bowls dark with the sulking triangles of Lucullan oysters, air filled with the bawl of irreverent fishmonger interruptions riding on it like thunderbolts – '*Fic' alla Madonna*', '*Fa' un cul' al Santo Spirito*' – those datelessly masculine thoughts that the old seafarers had in the Ionian days of Archytas, spilling the same oaths but with other perils to dare.

An hour or so further on, and the town peters out into unloved, soggy scrub, crossed by cart tracks, with an occasional boat skeleton decomposing in the mud, and one or two scattered white buildings. There's no sign of a river, just swampy mess and a few trees labouring to grow. But no one knows where that limpid rustic river of the *Odes* is, 'rich with the sweetest of Hymettus honey and where grazing sheep would shed their wool', and whether it flowed into the Inland Sea or the outer one. The locals point vaguely to a stream out there somewhere called Citrezze; or, if you ask them often enough, they say it used to be Galiatrezze once, and tell how romantic travellers would sometimes sit there for hours, lost in a pastoral haze. The modern plans of Taranto even call it Galeso.

I stumble on it eventually: a mile-and-a-half length of still water only inches deep, resting on a bed of weed and silt, where shoals of minnows scatter at the move of a shadow, and frogs plop gently into the mud. Above it there's a cathedral of guardian trees with slender branches arcing to the dappled sky, the silver-green leaves ringing in the breeze as if all the baby bells of heaven were shaking with laughter, and there's sunlight streaming in veils of fairy haloes like light bursting through a butterfly's wing; you listen for heathen whispers of Hellenistic Gods – Nike, Aphrodite, Eros, Artemis, Apollo, Orpheus, Herakles, Dionysius – and look for the fruit trees and the lilies, poppies, roses and hyacinths, and thirst for the taste of pears and plums and almonds, and dream of a golden shore spread with gardens, pastures and orchards. But nothing's there: it is just nostalgic appetite feeding on vague evaporations, trying to link a stupendous past with an unlovely present and stretching itself back vainly into limitless deserts of time.

Outside the imagination nothing stirs, until I reach the shallow spill where it widens to meet the Inland Sea; here there's a single creeping fisherman wading out to his thighs, then crouching low to watch the water, poised with a leaded lasso-net called a *sacco*. Suddenly he hurls it out and skywards, billowing like a web in the air before plummeting hawk-like to explode flat on the water and sink its meshes in a greedy trap. A pouch is slung at his hip above rolled-up trousers, and he fills it with his puny catch each time he pulls the net in, slow hand over muscled hand, unlacing each wriggling silver icicle with loving care, while behind him on the sandbank is a scattering of unwanted bodies, growing warts of blue flies in the evening sun.

Taranto Museum is a place of unsettled habits: everything seems to move and nothing is where it was yesterday. Perhaps they have little else to do. Nor is the official guide much help, as nothing corresponds. '*Mi dispiace*,' they say, with the usual platitudinous shrug: '*riparazione*,' or '*in restauro*,' as if they'd spent most of yesterday smashing up the amphorae. Or else it's '*un po' di riorganizzamento*', which is their way of extending chaos a little longer. Where on earth is all the stuff? you ask – five hundred years of Spartan civilisation; over a million tombs; ship-building and temples and potters and smiths; millionaires, kings, generals; as many holidays as days in the year; a star-studded cast of gods and goddesses; a golden wealth to rival Sybaris'. '*Beh* ...' and they wave their hands – what Lawrence calls 'dripping spaghetti' – and look sheepishly around at a gallery of dusty plinths and cabinets lurking against the walls.

The sooner they get this show on the road the better, you think; it needs a Getty or a Guggenheim. Then you want to see something by Lysippus, or the forty thousand terracotta figures found, or all the variously shaped Horsemen of Tarentum found on coins, or the fabulous silver treasure they dug up in 1896 from under a pavement – decorated cups, bowls and boxes with intricate reliefs of masks and flowers, a ribbed cantharis, an incense burner and a hoard of diobols and staters – but the shrugs go wobbling on and no one seems to know. Or if he does he's away for the day – 'Sta fuori città,' or 'impegnato,' or some such rubbish – till someone suggests you might try the museum at Bari or Brindisi, or aren't they building a big new one at Policoro for all the things they're finding at Heraclea? In the mean time, *signore*, we do have a little gold . . . Step this way . . .'

And this is pure ravishment: gleaming and intricate, fat as butter or thin as hair – yards and yards of it, rolled into serpent bracelets with eyes of amethyst; earrings of hanging godheads or elegant swans; necklaces made of golden roses dripping with buds and masks and beasts; chains and clasps and pins and brooches – an endless display of exquisitely crafted bullion, woven into a galaxy of delicate shapes as if made yesterday. Cellini would have had a fit. Rings for your fingers, and coronets for your hair, and sceptres to hold in your hand, its fine-spun radiance pin-pricked with the flash of coloured jewels, all of them weeping their leafy tears for another world, the last extant ounces of golden Taras lying on its fabled shore.

There are some Dionysiac shapes, too, if you ask to see them: little men with grotesquely equine penises waving about, just to prove that inferiority complexes are nothing new; orgiastic dancers with the vile leering grimaces of demented satyrs enjoying the coarseness of their gestures; and some shameless women too.* Shreds of these heathen customs are still left today, if you can find them – wild dances performed at certain times of the year, out in the sun-baked fields of the Messapian promontory – suffering a little from two thousand years of laundering. The tarantella is the most common, though that too is disappearing – a

* The *crissa*, I'm told, was a Tarentine dance performed competitively by girls and involved 'the wanton undulating of the loins'. The winner was the girl who produced the most erections in the audience.

paroxysm of female carnality usually limited to unmarried girls between fifteen and twenty-five, and attributed to the bite of a harvest-time spider, though in fact the local arachnid, *Lycosa tarantula*, has long been proven harmless. Spectacular accounts of its devasting power abound however: in 1695 Baglivi saw a multicoloured one with eight red eyes on its head and back; the Normans met some in Sicily that made them fart; Pigionati saw a man bitten, who then danced so obscenely his hands had to be tied behind his back; another account advises that children should not be present during the 'licentious Bacchic movements and poses'; a simulated version was arranged for Swinburne, who found it 'far from pleasant'; Ramage saw a modest version called *la pizzica*, in which a circle of young girls threw coloured handkerchiefs at possible male suitors; Lear heard of a southern bishop forbidding women to dance at local *festa*s because their movements were becoming too explicit. It is all the rustling of dead leaves in the folk memory, as innocently pagan as the maypole dance. The same ancient tremors even appear as far away as Catalonia in *il ballo dels aranyons*.

The popular definition is that a girl working in the fields in summertime will be bitten by a spider, and will then fall into a coma from which she can only be roused by certain music. An embellishment is that it must strike the exact rhythm of the insect's movements before any cure can start. Then at a certain moment in their playing, which may have to go on for hours, she will get up as if in a trance and begin to dance frenziedly round the room, whereupon the spectators who have gathered start to throw or wave coloured handkerchiefs, shawls or scarves at her. Eventually she will rush at one of the coloured items, seize it and trample it on the floor, as if to death. The performance is then over: she falls exhausted, and when wakened has come out of her coma.

Naturally there are certain problems, and not a little

confusion among those who have witnessed it. Some say it happens in the dark; others, in front of the family; yet others, before the whole village. It can take two hours, or sometimes go on for three days. Bagpipes are needed, say some; fiddle and tambourine, insist others; drum, flute and castanets, says a third group. Then who pays for and feeds the musicians? Do married women ever suffer from it? Can it recur? The incidents are so varied no one is sure.

'*In questo paese l'amore si manifesta cantando e ballando*' – love manifests itself singing and dancing – just as it did for the Greeks under another name, an ancient *cordax* spiced with some Dionysiac spirit and human passion strong with summer sensuality. It is probably the closest we shall ever get to what life was like once upon a time when the pagan ladies of Taras had little shame. And for a sight of it, I suggest a visit to the barber at Nardo: Signor Stiffani is also a talented violinist and has been known to arrange performances.

The fisherman took me out in his boat this morning, standing up at the back to row with one oar, bobbing us past the protruding wooden staves, all coated with garlands of daisy-chain mussels, boring down to the sea bed like giant skewers. A calm porcupine sea for a hundred yards.

'Look down there,' he says pointing. 'Can you see them?' and hands me an old square tin with a sheet of glass glued in the bottom, and makes me lean over; but there is a fog of dusty brown under the blue, and I can't see a thing. 'No matter,' he smiles, 'we'll try at night sometime. That is when you see them best.' There are liquid eyes of pale jade shining on the sea bed, he tells me, best seen on clear moonlit nights when the water is still, but no fish must be caught then or they'll be moonstruck, and send you mad if you eat them. They're the eyes of the Three Wise Men, who fled here from Bethlehem; but Herod ordered them to be drowned in the bay, and from that day to this they've never stopped staring in amazement at what they had seen. And *signore*, be careful of wandering alone on the banks of the Mare Piccolo, as you may meet Lauro and make him angry and then all your photographs will be blank, and your winebottle will turn to vinegar – but of course you may not notice him at first because he's less than a foot high and wears a tiny pixie hat, the *capello pizzuto* of the Calabrese, and he can move like lightning. He steals into houses at dead of night through the gaps under doors, and he kills new-born babies because he's jealous; he sprinkles powder on food to bring bad dreams; in the daytime he likes to call sheep away from their shepherds and make them wander off and disappear in the hills. You'll have to look carefully for him though: he's coloured green.

All inventive fantasies, making little gods out of superstitions. It is easy to see how it started, with such creative genius at work in this teeming cradle of inexplicable wonderment. All the poetry of abstract invention, pouring tirelessly out of fertile minds into myths, magic and beautiful mumbo-jumbo, all whirling away like little dots to get lost in the milky way of time. Copertino is not far away; I'm probably on the flight path of the Flying Monk immortalised by Douglas. There is a story in the paper today about a woman who went to see a *mago* because her husband was very ill, and when she'd described the symptoms the wizard told her to go home and unpick all the knots in the wool inside her husband's mattress. The poor fellow died the next day of chronic asthma.

I've been drinking that wine again, after the boat-ride – in a different *cantina* this time, hidden round a corner, rationing myself to fried sardines and bread and cheese. They still don't know if there was or wasn't once a bridge across the narrowest point of the Mare Piccolo, a distance of about seven hundred yards; they've been arguing about it since Polybius and Strabo. Oh God! That bloody man has got the nose of a ferret.

'Hello dearie, anything in the paper?' looking round and munching before pulling up a chair. No answer. Furious. 'Oh well, be like that . . .' and he leans over to pinch a sardine with bony fingers, then chews it with disgusting relish: 'Juicy,' and smacks his lips. 'Sulking are we, then?'

'No. Look, I – '

'Selfish bugger. I hate English people like you: repressed, intolerant, hypocritical, bloody do-gooders. Kicked me out last year – having some fun with some Boy Scouts near Brighton when the bloody police arrived. Interfering idiots – had to skip . . .'

'Huh,' and I try to finish the sardines before he does. He waves for an extra glass.

'Shall I tell you about Wystan?'

'No, I'm not inter – Wystan who?'

'The poet, stupid. Ever so lovely. Used to send me all his schoolboy poems. Such a big one too. His mother hated me, silly woman.'

'Christ! Where are they?'

'What. Oh, threw 'em away, lost . . . old suitcase some-where. Can't keep things when you're always moving.' His eyes fade for a moment. 'Dear Wystan. Ever so naughty. His stupid mother found our love letters.' Pause for digestion.

'More wine?'

'Thought you'd never ask . . . I almost like you. Getting interested, eh? Big on vicarious thrills? Bit of English voyeurism?'

'No. Just don't believe it . . .'

An angry snort, and he leans forward a bit: 'Want a catalogue then? Getting greedy? A list of cocks from Cairo to Cape Town? So you can write them up in your bloody book?'

'No. Why don't you write one?'

'Humph,' he grunts, thinking about it. 'No time, really . . . not yet, anyway. Do buy me some sardines, dearie, I'm starving.' And his lips reach out into the wine, sucking at it like a stranded turbot, pumping with his Adam's apple. 'Humph,' he goes again, licking it off his lips. 'Remember Augustus John? . . .'*

It is time to leave after that. If I walk he'll catch me up, so a bus must be found as soon as possible, heading east. There is quite a choice, but no central fount of information, nor even a timetable: each route is operated by a separate company and each starts from a different terminus; no lines know what the other ones do, nor do they care. I could end up in Galatina, where St Paul landed, or at Toricella where he also landed, or at Santa Maria di Leuca, where he did it again. One of them has a famous statue of him, reputed to have such miraculous powers that according to one traveller it regularly attracts 'a devilish inferno of screaming, shouting, pleading and gasping people, all leaping and twisting in the air'. To be avoided, obviously.

Here I sit, stunned, watching other passengers mount to join me. The label said SAN GIORGIO, FRANCAVILLA, ORIA, and the driver agreed, so hurry up. Did I dream it then, all those fairy tales – cock tales: Boy Scouts in Brighton, bollock-naked in Battersea Baths, commis waiters, pages in hotels, long ones in Lagos, male brothels in Beirut, Japanese jism, after-school buggers' ballets at Sadlers Wells? Must be rubbish. People like that don't exist. And Wystan too? . . . My God, now this I do not believe! A schoolboy has got on, and the driver has got a ruler out to measure him. Everybody is watching and listening to the argument. The driver is insisting and the boy is standing there acquiescent. Oh, thank God – it was only his height after all. He had paid half-fare and was being checked for size, and now he is paying up for being too tall.

Then the bus moves, and it is Farewell Taranto and those

---

* He did write a book eventually. In fact, I am told, he wrote two. I believe he died in Malta some years ago; or perhaps it was Gozo.

three days of extended anchor in the sun. That amount of sea is a bit like a virus – catching. I could live here, I think – wafting along in light clothes, sucking figs, drinking Falernian wine – and die here too, like Choderlos de Laclos, who turned so atheistic he wouldn't even utter the word 'God' on his deathbed. It had got to him as well.

I hope this is the right bus, racing out eastward through the blistering flatness, past rolling sandbanks of burning earth and scattered armies of charred olive trees stretching their dark green helmets to the horizon like a serrated sea. Broken stone walls in all directions, sagging donkeys ear-twitching in pools of shade, bent peasant bodies hooped low in calcified bum-jutting shapes nursing an inch of earth, scarf-headed leathery women stooped double in balloon-bag skirts, a leaning, dreaming, ghostly shepherd stuck under a tree in armless drapes pondering mindless sheep . . . All this was sun-scorched Messapia, wooed by the Cretans and Greeks long before the dolphin-birth of Taranto, where there are still Minoan and Mycenean remains going back forty centuries, where the ghosts of swarthy Ulyssean sailors stormed ashore like Mafia pirates greedy for spoil, and flitted through the writhing olive-trunks to die whimpering between the sunburnt thighs of Salentine goddesses.

Sticky sweat trickles; windows open to buffet in gusts of oven comfort; and when we're not roaring with dragon fury and snorting hate at a dawdling cart, we're hissing with suppressed resentment at having to evacuate or suck in a passenger. The driver must be a reincarnated charioteer with the shouts of the crowd in his thirsty ears, as foam-flecks of houses dart in and out of sight between the trees, and we growl through narrow channels of white-hot villages almost touching us with their silent shoulders of stone.

TWENTY ONE

Oria

Janet Ross has written a warm and engaging book about the Salentine Peninsula, digging into its remoter corners: somewhat refined and botanic, but full of 1880s charm and innocence, and most violently anti-Bourbon. She enthused over everything, loving the people, adoring the views, praising the flowers, chatting to anyone, and obviously quivering along the promontory in eager and artless purity. She certainly never heard the women swear.

When Apulian women do that it is quite an experience. It seems they have more to complain about than their menfolk, and when touching on matters physical are a great deal more imaginative. Their Rabelaisian outlook, moreover, has a multilingual richness to draw on – Greek, Turkish, Moorish, French, Spanish . . . – which I am discovering in a fig-packing factory, where the bus has drawn up, in Francavilla. The fruit itself may be pertinent, and perhaps I shouldn't have asked them what they were doing: the life-cycle of the *fico* has set them off.

I have sought shade a moment in the open brick shed beside the road, where a beetle-scrum of them is squatting on their toad-haunches low on the concrete floor, cackling blackly together over wicker baskets running amok with swollen green fruit. They are tenderly removing each half-ripe pod, examining it, then caressing it into a layer of soldier rows in a cardboard box, my question barely interrupting their speed and nimbleness.

'Madonna figs,' they cackle; then Eve figs, Mother-of-Jesus figs, Spanish figs, Roman figs, figs enjoyed by the Holy Ghost, their employer's mother's fig . . . all variously occupied; then moving on to the more deadly area of ancestral figs, which is where the business becomes serious. That you or your sister are unprintable means nothing; that your deceased great-grandmother may have been is more grave, and can be a duelling matter. For in south Italy you do not speak lightly of the dead: their departed spirits are sacred, and to be revered with all the solemn passion their Greek forbears had for honouring (or sometimes dishonouring) their ancestral corpses. They provide some simulated examples to pass the time: his great-grandfather was the sperm-dust of an unmarried eunuch and his buttocks were open like barn doors; her grandmother's fig was so ripe everybody tasted it, even dogs and donkeys. Such words are dangerous, and can have dire consequences; they are curses with a long way to go. Ten minutes in their company and I have learnt quite enough about saints, physiology and the pedigrees of local sinners.

Francavilla is very clean, and looks extremely pleased with itself; it is white, brilliant with desert heat, and the houses appear newly washed. It is also called Francavilla Fontana – because a noble duke was out hunting one day, and raised his gun to shoot a stag drinking at a pool in a wood; his gun would not fire, so he went to investigate, and at the bottom of the pool he found . . . a statue of the madonna. (Someone will count them all one day; it would be an entertaining thesis, a life's work.) Visible a short distance to the south is Oria, an easy walk away, rising up on a small mound, its castle towers breaking the hardened cake of worrying flatness all around – leagues of ominous monotony where the highest point is barely five hundred feet above the sea and the horizon's dwindling edges are roughened by the tops of olive trees.

Janet Ross says Francavilla is 'famous for its pyrotechnics', but I have found no sign of them, nor do any of the elderly gentlemen enjoying the sun know what she could have meant – though one or two of them might well have seen her when they were four or five years old. 'Ask him,' they say, shrugging uselessly, and point to where Francavilla's doctor is drinking coffee under a tree. 'He knows everything . . .' But the doctor is as mystified as they are; in spite of being a local, he has recently graduated from Padua University, and has already become cynical.

'We're a hundred years behind down here,' he says; 'it is as if Garibaldi had just landed,' and cannot understand what I am doing in the area anyway.

'No patients today?' I ask, it being little more than ten o'clock.

'They prefer San Cosimo to me,' he answers. 'They think splashing about in a holy well will do more than I can with penicillin.'

'No injections then? Typhoid? Vaccination?'

'That is Devil's work. Ask a priest, see the *mago*, but don't touch the doctor. If a snake bites you, cook a snake and eat it, same with a scorpion, and for a dog bite wear some dog-skin. There's a saying: "*Ogni male, vul' medicin uguale*" – Any illness needs a kindred cure. Hopeless.'

'What about having babies?'

'Worse,' he laughs. 'If you haemorrhage, drink goat's urine; don't brush your hair on Friday or the baby will die; and if you dream of horses you'll have a miscarriage . . . Once I thought I could do something, but they think I'm from another world.' And he sighs ruefully.

He finds the matter of the pyrotechnics equally baffling, and thinks it must have been something to do with unification, and freedom, and local elections. 'Have you ever seen an election meeting in the south?' he asks. 'Everybody clamouring, shouting, telling lies, making promises, arguing – *that* is fireworks for you – car-horns, bands, flags, speeches, loud speakers crackling like fried bacon, pandemonium everywhere, they love it. They know it doesn't mean anything being told how *serio, competente, onesto* they are, because they know it's not true anyway; or how their "*potere locale*" must unite with the "*potere centrale*"

sapphire saucers of clematis — as if a swarm of tropical butterflies has just arrived to pay homage. Through a gateway is a wooden-balconied loggia, piers decked with oleander and all swathed in ivy and bells of columbine, where Juliet should be standing, or a Tudor courtier strumming his lute, or a white-frocked Yolanda from Jerusalem anticipating her royal nuptials. Day-dreaming. There it is again:

'Would you like some wine, *signore*?' She is standing just behind me with a jug in her tiny hand, wide-eyed and apprehensive, but watched by her mother, arms akimbo in a doorway. 'Please have some . . . Mamma says . . .' and out comes the glass from behind her back on to the bench, her hand straining at the earthenware pitcher as she starts to pour — a joyous waterfall of salmon pink, sparkling and gurgling to the brim. Then she watches studiously as I drink in case there are problems; but there are none, except that the glass is empty. Was it Lacrimae di Gallipoli, or Malvasia, or the rosé of Cerignola which is soaking up dust so perfectly, a hydrant to the toasting void, an ice-floe to the smouldering pyre of my stomach? It doesn't matter; it disappears as if into blotting paper. So does the second glassful. Where on earth can it be going? Her politely wondering eyes consider its disappearance thoughtfully before she races off with the empty jug to hold her mother's skirts: We have a hollow man sitting on the pavement out there; what shall we do? He's magic, like one of those swallowers at *festa*-time, who eat flames and glass and Coca-Cola cans and live lizards. *Aiuto* . . . and she hugs closer. But mother smiles.

'*Mo*,' she calls then — Now then — waving a hand in a gently dismissive shoo, which in fact means exactly the opposite, and is a polite summons: '*Mo . . . voulez manya?*'

'But madam, madam . . . this is all too kind,' I say. 'I will find a *cucina* or *trattoria*; how much do I owe you?'

She thinks a little, then smiles. 'Ten minutes,' she answers, brushing her daughter off her skirt as she turns away, leaving tiny Terpsichore balleting up and down on tiptoe in eight-year-old elastic excitement.

It is not ten minutes of course, it is nearly an hour, and interrupts some serious fairy-tale-telling on the pavement: Sleeping Beauty (transposed into Oria castle for today) versus Pinocchio; followed by the wicked Folletto, who buried a pot of gold at the foot of one of the towers and no one has ever found it, so I promise we will go and dig for it afterwards. And finally *il pranzo casalingo*; what difference can an hour or two make in this roasting life under the same sun that has been going on for thousands of years? None whatsoever.

So welcome, stranger, to a home-made, hydra-headed, rainbow salad of tomato, olives, lemon, asparagus, mushrooms, chicory, anchovies, almonds, onion, melon, lettuce, artichoke, pepper, beans, ham and grapes; and when you've done with that we will start our meal. Take your time. The young coal eyes watch every mouthful over the edge of the table, sea-deep with wordless questions, following each swallow, each tear at mahogany bread, each sigh of growing repletion; until *pranzo* itself arrives. Gnemeriidde – a Salentine speciality – which is slivers of lamb stewed in oil with onion and cheese and parsley, and should have been part of Belshazzar's feast; and yet another jugful of soothing pink.

Such miracles call for an explanation, which she gives, half proudly but also shyly in case I should doubt her. Once, she tells me, she was cook up at the castle, and ever since leaving has longed to try her skills again, and this very morning was remembering one of the dishes she used to prepare, and thinking how nice it would be to have guests again. Then she looked up and saw a stranger sitting outside her door, *'veramente come un angelo, grazie a Dio'*, with a fervent cruciform across her breast.

Thanks indeed! Nearly two hours of it, and not finished yet: almost stupefied, sipping an *amaro di San Domenico*,

astride the final pinnacle or in the deepest trough, sun
slanting through the window, I know I shall never get to
Brindisi. What matter? Oria will do. *'Una femina ex Uria'*
said Petrarch mysteriously: Hannibal's woman again, hovering in the imagination with melting curves and radiant
smiles, a Salentine succubus . . . How light and cool the
breeze is coming through the window, how friendly the
cicada-chat, how musical the voices, how heavy the eyelids,
how swims the room . . .

This will never do! I must to Manduria and Pliny's Well.
Five miles? Six miles? Seven? 'Of course you will get there,'
she assures me, 'and back again, for supper.' But what
madness, in this heat. Do I have to? Oh very well. I had
better take her husband's Vespa. It is outside. Is it a Sicilian
Vespa? No, and she misses the point, but says he is
gardening up at the castle – safely asleep under a bush by
now, or chatting up a new servant.

Mercifully I remember little. I went. Heat blew. Roads
bumped. Fat olive trees tumbled past. Walls subsided. I got
there. Terpsichore was on the back when I started and still
there when I arrived. She had aunts and uncles to see in
Manduria, she said, and was as happy as a limpet – wouldn't
they be surprised?

I forget where we parted company; on a corner somewhere. One minute there, one minute not. It was too hot,
and enthusiasm had evaporated; the land had become a
spillage of monotonous sand seared by a blinding light.
Even the walls were ghastly: three miles of enormous
debilitation crawling pointlessly round in an exhausted
circle. Sorry we're in the way, they say, trying to hide.
We're just as bored as you are, we're anachronisms. It is the
same with Pliny's Well: now tedious, comatose, covered in
a layer of dust down a tunnel – silly fellow didn't know
there was a feeder cistern somewhere which always kept it
at the same level – a hollow of everlasting somnambulance
with a peppering in the clay of deep-water fossils, from

those lost millennia when the sea washed over everything. I shall dig one or two out with a knife and pretend to Terpsichore that I have been to the seaside.

She wasn't interested, though. I found her somewhere in the Mandurian dust watching her male cousins playing a game of bellicose marbles.

'Look,' I said, 'a seashell . . .'

'Look,' she answered, as there was a whimper of anguish from the loser, kneeling expectantly on the earth and awaiting his sentence. It was forfeits. Anything goes. Luckily they were only eight or nine years old, but there was already malevolence in the punishment, a streak of cruelty, humiliation. No fun at all. 'Hold your right ankle up in your hand behind you,' he said solemnly. 'Now hop down to the end of the road and back again, and shout "*Stupido*" all the way.' Nice people. Already that imp of frustrated power is lashing its tail inside their overheated breasts.

'You know about the Italians, don't you?' says the *signora* at suppertime, feeling her years at the castle have given her some special insight. Know about the Italians! Where on earth does one start? 'Well, you see, it was St Paul,' she goes on. 'He landed at Capo di Leuca with his followers, after the shipwreck; then began walking up to Rome. Not far from here they passed a man lying in a ditch who was bleeding and badly wounded – he'd been robbed by thieves, but he was just lying there, not making a sound. "Shall we stop and help him?" asked the followers, but St Paul said, "No, leave him where he is." Then further on they passed another one in the same state, but this one was screaming and shouting, making an awful noise. "Quick," said St Paul, "go and help him." Then later on, the disciples asked him why he'd left one and helped the other. "It is very simple," St Paul answered; "God was looking after the first one, I could tell: he was silent, obviously a foreigner. But the second one was Italian – you could tell by the noise he made – and God wasn't looking after him at all . . ." That's us,' she says; 'that's why we make all the fuss.'

Perhaps that is what Janet Ross meant by pyrotechnics. She wouldn't be the first one. Plenty of fireworks and lots of talk is all they want, a friend told Henry James. Barzini knew it too. 'The show is many times more important than reality,' he said, meaning people don't come to Italy for the depths of life, just for its surface, and what it all looks and sounds like.

TWENTY TWO

Brindisi

Brindisi is best at night; it is silver then, and goes to sleep early. The sea laps in on ripples of moon, sardine stars flash diamonds of phosphorus under the oily surface, and fat boats rest on the swell like giant gulls. There is a sigh of trees round the edge of the harbour, and a whisper of old ghosts. In a gap between waterfront houses, and up some steps it stands: a sudden lone column, greyish-white, unannounced, surprising, and perfectly calm. Slender and pettily proud, it tries to be grand among the dwarfing *palazzi*, and is as poignant as a furled sail put away for numberless seasons – but restrained, also, standing there knowing infinite things, dreaming wistfully of the sea, of clarion trumpets and ancient armadas.

It is terribly alone bereft of its twin, which is shorn off at the stump – an ankle-bone is all that's left, broken and crooked. An earthquake tumbled it in 1528, and it lay around awhile until the Spanish Viceroy ordered the pieces to be given to Lecce in 1695 during a plague – some say in return for a supply of sausages – so they could put a statue of St Oronzo on it for having saved a few of them from the pestilence.

Life hasn't been easy for this column either, elegant now in naked isolation, marble-smooth and reaching hopelessly for the stars to share an ocean of memories with them – of emperors, poets, priests, prophets and kings, laughter and death. They took it down at the beginning of the last war – not to preserve it, but because the Mayor of Brindisi lived next door, and didn't wish to be crushed if it fell. But unfortunately there was a storm on the very night the last section was safely lowered, and the crane and all the scaffolding collapsed on to his house instead. 'Serves him right,' says my companion; 'he should have shown more respect for the past, but he was just a Fascist. If I remember rightly, didn't Lord Carnarvon have a sad accident at Luxor?' Probably. My guide is the Brindisi town librarian, pleased at a chance to abandon work and show me round, after I had surprised his whole staff by asking if they had a copy of Cluverius. Once, they said, but it had long since disappeared. 'And that's not all,' he goes on. 'When they put it back again after the war, they forgot to put the locking studs in, the dowels that hold the sections together. I've got them in a drawer at home with some other pieces. In the mean time they're just balancing, strapped together with steel bands, but if a really good storm comes – woomff! away goes another piece of history.'

I like the librarian: he is mildly sardonic, distanced from events, and views things with a certain detached humour; the contents of his library must have revealed most human foibles to him, as has the behaviour of the borrowing public. He is the only official I have met who refuses to be co-opted on to committees. '*Chiacchieroni*' he calls them – chatterboxes – and would rather go fishing.

We wander over to inspect a plaque on a nearby wall. 'One of Mussolini's two legacies,' he informs me, and reads it out. '"Here landed two thousand years ago the greatest poet of nature and of the Empire, Virgil, to greet his homeland with love, and then to die", et cetera. They've rubbed the date off now, and the Duce's name from the bottom.' He turns round. 'There's the other one – that concrete rudder stuck on the harbour wall – a memorial to Italian seamen. Did you ever see anything so completely hideous?' I take his point: it is hardly what maritime families might expect as an obsequy; but didn't he say art and beauty made the Italians soft?

The librarian has suggested that I should leave my *pensione* and stay with him for a couple of days, which I do with pleasure. Anything to escape the buzz of German tourists, swarming over everything with recent sunburn and discontent at everyone's inefficiency – no newspapers, no ferry timetables, no tickets, the booking office never open, no porters, in fact no useful information at all. They retaliate by strutting round loudly like swollen flamingoes, then shunt their Mercedes from one possible departure point to another along the quay in fits of exasperation. All their heated energy is gazed at sourly by phlegmatic onlookers leaning against walls, who spit shreds of tobacco off their lips, not quite in anyone's direction. Another Aryan tribe, the hard-heeled *Jugend*, all creamy-haired and bronzed to the hilt of their rolled-up shorts, are staggering up from the station, bent like avalanched Atlases under boulders of rucksacks – their flags of discomfort in the pursuit of pleasure. All eyes are turned towards Greece.

'*Poco amato*,' says the librarian with a sigh – 'an unloved city', the exact words of Osbert Sitwell. One wonders why; it looks happy and busy enough now. Swinburne didn't stay long: the harbour was silted up, people were dying from the plague, and the cathedral officers were allowed 'the ancient custom of having handmaids'; Ramage complained of the 'pestilential effluvia' and found one-tenth of the population had just died from malaria; Keppel Craven saw 'large black snakes' and 'low melancholy-looking houses', and heard prisoners 'clanging their irons' in the castle dungeons; Sir William Hamilton went even further: 'doomed to speedy destruction' was his view.

It was Caesar who started the rot, apparently. Before he tried to block up the harbour entrance and so trap Pompey's fleet, it had been a thriving port for a thousand years, and much used by the Messapians, who called it Brentesion – Stag – on account of the two channels that split like antlers from the entrance. The stakes and the rubble that Caesar put in were still being pulled out as late as 1800, according to Pigionati, who then had the job of clearing the harbour to make it usable again. Other blockages had occurred from time to time before that: the Venetians had to be kept out, so had the Turks, and various others who saw its geographical significance. The best way to prevent invasion had always been to seal up the harbour entrance – with disastrous long-term results, of course, as the water very soon became putrid, and those who hadn't died in battle were soon finished off by disease. And so it remained until the nineteenth century, when the much-maligned Bourbons began a programme of reclamation, which has now been going on for over a hundred years, in an effort to get some of the harbour's energy back. Progress is slow, but things are already better: there are comings and goings of little boats, and bustles of excitement; the port is filled with high emotions, golden opportunities and a flood of changing faces, as the gulls bob up and down on the water watching. It is not inward-looking like Taranto, scorning the international scene, but tries to be more like Naples – expectant and adventurous, where something new happens every few hours, or if it doesn't will soon be made to, just to keep everyone's spirits up.

Pigionati, the Bourbon engineer in charge of reclamation, was more than just that, so the librarian informs me: he was something of an antiquarian, with an interest in folklore, and he found traces of the Appia Antica at Lapani, four miles away. He also observed women afflicted by *tarantismo*, recording instances of sufferers who danced for ten hours non-stop, girls who looked so ugly afterwards they could never find husbands, and unscrupulous practical jokers who would repeat the music later in the hope of inducing another fit. Being Neapolitan, he took the phenomenon very seriously and wrote various treatises on it – not convincing enough for Swinburne, however, who thought his arguments had little weight, and dismissed it all as lower-class temperament, female hot flushes and pagan folk-memory.

*

'We shall go fishing,' announces the librarian, pacing the floor of his smart off-the-peg apartment in one of Brindisi's senior suburbs – indicative of how the town has spread out crabwise since the war, into a clutter of nudging satellites where pale apartment blocks jostle together – 'and look at history.'

There is not much of it left in the town, he decides, after the Appian Column and part of the castle: an odd church perhaps, and then the cloisters of San Benedetto . . . he shrugs. Well, what can you expect, is his view, after disease, wars and everlasting battles? The back door in and out of Italy – ravaged, pirated, stormed, starved to death, '. . . and bombed by the English in 1943,' he adds smiling. Then he remembers an English battery commander giving his men target practice outside the town. 'Go on,' he told them, 'just break up that old bit of barn over there.' So they fired a couple of salvoes; but when the smoke cleared nothing seemed to have happened, so they went to look . . . it was a lump of Roman aqueduct, and the shells had been bouncing off it.

We drive out to the north over flatland skirting the town, past the stony site of Tancred's Fountain, where the crusaders are supposed to have watered their thousands of horses; then we head off seawards along a narrow track through scrub and over dunes. 'Just a word with the coastguard,' he says, drawing up by a gate with a barking dog; I see lots of handshakes and nods of intimate knowledge, which, he tells me, was just a precaution, as we drive on cheerfully over the next ridge . . . on to a curving mile of empty yellow beach. A smooth rim of half-cooked pastry lies ahead, curling round a dish of cornflower blue that slowly darkens to ink as it deepens in the distance: blinding beams of sunlight that scald the eyeballs with a dance of white-hot stars. On it bobs one tiny rowing boat, nose in the sand.

'You think it is beautiful?' he asks, smiling wryly, which I confess I do.

'Yes,' he nods, 'and a graveyard ... Brindisi's cemetery, an underwater necropolis, like the Tiber in Rome. We'll go and see.'

Two youths row us out, swarthy and comfortable, sliding us over a milky blue which turns to pale gossamer as the powder clears under the half-glass hull; the shelf of sand deepens inch by inch over half a mile ... one foot, two feet, then three ... and even a mile out you could stand with your shoulders in the sun. They row steadily for twenty minutes; single flecks of weed pass underneath, and grey arrows of darting fish, as the water darkens to mystery blue with scollop-shapes of sand scudding away underneath, the wrinkles losing themselves in roughness then forming again, then breaking up altogether as the boat starts to ease. The youths breathe in slowly to fill their lungs, then slide snake-like over the gunwale to disappear, wandering below us in leg-waving handstands to the sea bed, clawing at it slowly as they hover upside-down. Then they burst up again suddenly with a muscled kick, and flick spray from their hair, each holding half an amphora. 'No,' says Dottor Bruno, 'that won't do,' but he takes them; so down they sink again with a gulp of air, and we drift on past them slowly, scavenging at swallowed history.

'It was running away, this one,' says the librarian. 'Most of the amphorae are whole: the ship had to raise speed quickly, so everything got thrown overboard. Ah! That's better,' and he leans over to take one.

Soon we are filling: six of them pulled out of twelve feet of water, and two small lecythi, and a broken krater. 'Brindisi's history,' he smiles, waving his arm, 'miles of it: triremes, galleons, men-of-war, slave ships, privateers, cargo boats, barges – anything you want. Two hundred wrecks we already know of: canons, swords, amphorae, jewels, vases, bronzes, coins, bones ... Plenty of bones: skeletons in chains, some in armour. A whole load of tanks for Ethiopia ... an English battleship ... casks of wine ...'

'Don't people take them?'

'Tch,' and he shakes his head, '*vietato*.'

'And these, then?'

'Ah. These are different. I have a permit; and I told the coastguard you are an English archaeologist. He knows me, anyway.'

'But surely other people . . .'

'The police are watching all the time. So is the coast-guard. Sometimes in summer the holidaymakers try, but the police come out and arrest them.'

'Ah. Then what happens?'

'They fine them, and confiscate the vases. Later on they sell them.'

Brindisi itself is not known for its miracles – unless you would call its survival a marvel in itself – but there are plenty in the area. Apart from some Knights Templar seeing the Devil's grey cat here, there are madonnas who get washed up after storms, and at Monopoli one even came floating in on the crest of a wave. At Otranto she is said to have scowled, which was enough for the invading Turks to flee or sink; and at Modugno she caught most of the Spanish canon balls – a feat repeated by Santa Trifone against the Austrians at Montrone. The Archangel Michael was in evidence a lot, winging his way up and down the coast to help, and one of his battalions is reported to have saved Molfetta. But nobody came to save Brindisi at any time – though Frederick of Hohenstaufen had a part to play, after Louis IX had unwisely allowed the blessed Host to fall into the hands of Sultan Saladin during a crusade. (He actually gave it to him in return for his own release from captivity.) The furious Frederick sent Louis scurrying back with three thousand gold ducats to redeem it with; and when it did eventually reach Brindisi again it was too heavy to carry into the town, and a white horse had to be found to transport it. Its joyous home-coming is celebrated every year on the day of Corpus Domini by the Bishop of Brindisi going through the town and celebrating communion astride a white donkey.

Frederick did more than that in the area. Always seeking for ultimate truth through experimentation, he cast doubts on St Francis of Assisi's vows of chastity, and slipped a naked girl into his bedroom at night, then (it is reported) watched through a spy-hole. All he saw was St Francis raking some red-hot coals from the fireplace to lie on, and then asking her to come and join him. There is a plaque on a wall not many miles away commemorating the incident.

It is hereabouts too, they insist, that Frederick had a brief affair with his chief minister's wife, Signora della Vigna, but in the fairy-tale song the children sing about it, all ends happily. He went to her bedroom, pulled the clothes back, but dropped his glove in his excitement; so that explanations could be made to the offended husband next day he gave a banquet, where the fable says the following exchange was made:

Wife: I have always been una Vigna, but now am
               not loved.
               I want to know why I am out of favour.

Husband: You have always been una Vigna, but you
               are not loved,
               Through the King's favour you have lost my
               favour.

King: I went to see the Vigna, and I lifted the
               sheet,
               But by the crown on my head, I took no
               favour.

which is sweet and romantic, and very innocent – unlike most tales – and shows what can happen to history through the years (since it was Pietro della Vigna who fell under suspicion for something in the end – whether of poison plots, deceit, betrayal, or an illicit love affair, we do not know – but he died most unpleasantly).

A priest has been watching me solemnly as I photograph the column. *'Bello,'* he says, coming over, then continuing the conversation in German, which I find offensive. *'Ich bin Engländer,'* I tell him, but he carries on unperturbed, one occupying force being much the same as any other to his way of thinking, and far more concerned by the present than by any past resentment. They have this facility, a great many Italians: complete forgetfulness – except in the vendetta. *'Giove, Nettuno . . .'* he says, pointing upwards to the plinth, then sweeping with his hands to indicate that a chain may once have hung between the pillars with a brazier suspended as a light to guide in the Roman ships. I don't disabuse him, though no one knows for certain whether there was or was not; scholars are divided, as they are about whether there were statues on top of the columns.

A crowd starts to gather: women in doorways, faces at windows, people stopping on the pavement to watch, interrupting the photographs. Damn, I think; what price solitude? and wish they weren't so inquisitive – to the priest, hoping he might take the hint, but it passes him by completely and he starts to philosophise.

'It is living *all' aperto,'* he assures me, 'seeing what is going on, like curious children . . . eager to know. Everyone is friendly.' Which is something at the moment I could do without. Like children, says this one; like animals, said the older and wiser one at Eboli; at the moment half Brindisi is being bovine, everyone gazing at me stupidly, with cowshed eyes in blank faces, and not a thought among them. Hopeless! But of course this is Sunday evening: ramblingtime, vacant, stupefied with idleness, totally brainless. So I pack everything up; and as soon as they see the show is over they turn their backs and drift away; the moment I start to leave, the little piazza is empty again – not a soul anywhere; even the priest has vanished. That is the hell of

Italy: nothing stays the same for a moment, it all churns like a millstream; if something is there for more than half an hour it is boring, old hat, not worth bothering about. That is why they keep changing their governments, and don't like their old buildings – they've all been there too long.

Monaco's is the answer: a little wine shop I have found in a back street where the house brew is *sedici-gradi* and tastes more bitter than that potent lubricant in Taranto. Giuseppe, the owner, says it has been in the family since his grandfather's day, which would take it back to the Risorgimento and the days of that odious little red-shirted comedian who even Tennyson said possessed 'divine stupidity'.

'*Bwenyo*,' says Giuseppe, putting the flask down, rich and red, standing to watch as I take a mouthful.

'*Chi beve vino dopo la minestra,*
Vede il medico dalla finestra,'

he chortles. In that case I'm safe, I assure him; I'm doing my drinking first, a private celebration, me and me. Dinner is at the librarian's house, later. A little *festa*, or something, before I leave tomorrow. It will be sad, yet happy. There are times when one has had enough; memory is just a saturation of half-lost impressions, folding over each other like waves trickling on to the beach. How I wish I had seen it when Frederick was building that castle, or even when Augustus landed, or when they garroted the Doge's son on the headland in full view of the Venetian galleys. All gone. What a pity the crusaders drew no pictures (nor did Sandys or Fynes Morrison or Nugent). Everything is left to the imagination, until they unearth some old dusty parchments in someone's forgotten archives.

More drinkers come in, nodding at me in my corner – me and my rosy flask, nearly empty – wallowing in my self-indulgent nostalgic appetite and getting nowhere. Beauty or knowledge? Where does it get you, digging it up, turning the clock back? Didn't Beckford hate them for plucking the trees and bushes off the Colosseum, and even D'Annunzio said unification produced a 'blizzard of barbarism'. Just one more flask then . . .

Nice people in Brindisi: friendly, almost cosmopolitan, and used to strangers; but dignified and private too, settling down to play their cards and wrinkle up their weather-beaten old faces in concentration. 'A land without shadows, full of fantastic knotted shapes', somebody said. But Brindisi is nearly brand-new, bubbling over – prosperous even – things in the shops from Paris, London, Rome . . . A whole lifetime away from those bodies sweating in the thankless fields back towards Oria.

Sweating bodies . . . there are moments when I understand it – almost. Such a sensual land, stretched out like a human form, palpitating and tickling away at unmentionables, tumescent-tempting in lubricant heat, quickening the lower pulses, waking the boneless lamprey. Who called Italy a 'beautiful naked body'? Someone did, probably Frederick, pulling that sheet off the beautiful della Vigna. First of the Renaissance princes . . . Just time for one more glass . . . And Goethe wanted to call his book *Erotica Romana*; he didn't exactly behave in the south, one gathers, Germanic goat. 'No petticoat left unturned', Barzini says. Can you blame him? Give yourself wholly to passion here, was Lady Burgoyne's advice, sensible woman. I wonder what she got up to? How on earth can this seat of Christendom be so totally pagan? It stinks of it. Don't get behind me yet, Satan, old bedroom-breath; license my roving thoughts a bit. Voluptuousness transcends the dirt and ruins . . . winds and whispers from light-fingered Aphrodisia. Was she born from these waves? I wonder. Horace would say so – another goat, another dreamer, another beautifier of things past. All the pains of unassuaged nostalgia, moaning for the ones that got away – me, Frederick, Horace, Goethe and all the other *Weltschmerzers* – what a miserable bunch, and all backward-looking except Frederick. Different types of visionaries, Utopian dreamers seeking ghosts of times past, seeing spectres of things to come.

Nearly finished, landlord. Flagon's empty. And what's in the future then? Nothing but problems ... One, getting back to the librarian's; two, getting his present of two amphorae back to England; three, what about the two left in Terracina?; four, there's bound to be a fourth somewhere. Oh well, does anything matter? Sufficient unto the day ... *Domani, crai, crai,* and *bis-crai* ...

'*Ciao, Giuseppe, grazie ... domani Inghilterra.*' Sanity, fog and cold. The room stops and I'm standing up. '*Ciao,*' and we shake hands, almost for a minute. 'I did it,' I tell him, 'all the way.'

'*Sì, sì, bravo,*' he smiles, '*bravissimo,*' and the room applauds; or perhaps they're just playing cards and dominoes again.

The night air hits me like a wet flannel.

'*Trecento lire,*' he says, taking my arm a little more than gently.

The pillar watches, half-silvered in the moon, hugging its old cold dreams in stony silence, while the same stars peep. Pythagoras' ...? Pompey's ...? the unconceived ...?

Vale Brundisium. Your dreams are richer than mine.

Postscript

It was strange going back after thirty years. Here again! I thought, older and wiser perhaps, much confused, and not believing half of what I had written, cowardly with embarrassment. But walking is myopic, tunnel-visioned into small meetings, tiny incidents, limited scenes and impressions. It is not a broad brush, just a self-indulgent private squint at pinheads of experience. Now I felt pleasure at many of the changes, and pain too that much of old Italy had gone for ever, shredded by motorways and tractors and telephones. Only one donkey between Rome and Brindisi, slowly crossing the traffic lights at Venosa and holding the cars up, side-satchels heavy with sticks; and not a single upright Amazon woman striding along with a massive pitcher on her head. It had to happen. Though the north goes on grumbling and calling the south a running sore, as if it were nothing but desert and the people vampire bats. 'We produce and they destroy,' they tell you. 'The south sucks our blood.' While plenty of southerners are anxious for separation, and freedom from the interfering compulsions of the north. 'We're their captive market,' they complain, 'second-class citizens; we should organise a boycott.' Garibaldi is not over-popular.

Rome is its usual hell, of course: politics, noise and traffic, and roads blocked by strikes. Nowadays the capital is neatly scalpelled out by a nose-to-polluting-tail ring road of massive proportions and baffling signs, which casually slices the old Appia cleanly in half as if it didn't exist, leaving the severed outer end to worm away lonely and pine-lined towards the Castelli in the distance. Some of it is other-worldly still, half-romantic shades of magnificent old dramas tucked away behind dark trees, dim echoes of triumphant processions and marching legions sounding somewhere beyond the picnic spots and heaps of litter. Eventually it comes to a ragged end, blocked by a row of boulders that suggests it would be unwise to investigate further into the sheds of shanty town beyond. Somewhere just further on, the built-up Appia Nuova roars four-laned to the Castelli, barely mentioning Ariccia till you've passed it – the sign to Il Paradiso is still there – and then at an uncertain crossroads saying Nemi is both right and left. Left is preferable; and finally a slender lane, barely visible, slides down to the water's edge near the boat museum – where rumour has it there may be a third hulk still sunk in the mud – to circle three-quarters of the lake till it bumps up into civilisation again among the eaves of Genzano on the crater's rim. Diana has not abandoned it yet: the shell of her temple is there, and you can sit in the tiny Fiocina Tavern near the end of the lane, and watch the poplar leaves dance as she passes while others sing her an endless song.

Afterwards, on to distant Terracina across the teeming marshes – now prosperous and busy, rich in their luscious green and stabbed with yellow houses – all along the dead-straight Appia. It is built up and bustling nearly all the way, criss-crossed by canals or racing them beside the road, till enormous new signs have carved a glossy tunnelled *superstrada* round Terracina and under Monte Anxur, so Naples can be reached in nearly an hour. It is worth pausing by the sea a moment, if only to find the Grand Palace Hotel has long been completed, but inexplicably closed for the last five years, and then as night falls to watch the ghost-eyes of floodlights come on in Theodoric's Palace as if beamed from the sky. They restored what was left of it in the '70s, replacing much of its ancient magic with cement; now there's a road up to the top, and a car park, and a *trattoria* (in season), and you can stand there on polished stone above acres of level sea, gazing at the dome of Circe's hump, and marvel that Trajan's clean-cut road hundreds of feet below has become an anachronism.

Fondi, a little way inland past the lake, is much less visited, still square-cut like crumbling chocolate into narrow, shabby decumani and cardines wedged with strolling people, where behind the shoulder-to-shoulder shops one of the inner courtyards hides the Gonzaga Palace, its stone-balustraded stairways bleached by the sun and strewn with heavy-scented jasmine. A small *trattoria* blinks in a shaded corner, where an ancient serving lady says she can just remember being in swaddling clothes and seeing the great Countess Giulia pass by years ago.

Somewhere up in the hills and farther from the sea scowls Sessa Aurunca, forever glowering over its forgotten greatness and the vast unwanted space of its sunken amphitheatre once lording the valley beyond the escarpment wall; gnarled olive trees mark the central arena, and all around the edges untidily stepped allotments creep forward for space, each ridge of buried rubble tumbling with Hottentot wigs of matted ivy and cascading swags of morning glory. Da Nicola's is still there too, and so is the serpentine Roman bridge a mile away, with its switchback of flagstones sagging on the mammoth arches rising from a time-lost river bed teeming with luxuriant vegetation and drowned in bird-song. Alone in such a carelessly growing Eden, bursting with all things ripe and green, one senses the old abundance and procreant fertility that made it Campania Felix and strewed the rich plains of Capua with such opulence and wealth.

Not today, though. Below the sweep of the Auruncan hills New Capua is joined to Old Capua, and Old Capua is joined to Caserta, and there is barely a blade of grass or daylight between third-world shanty-town barrack buildings that shade the twenty-odd miles of road with meanness and menace, locking themselves tight in mess and mayhem. For the Camorra is still at home here, cankerously grafting, choking out the sun, raddling a queen of cities to a pock-marked slum and strangling it into one of the poorest regions of Italy.* This new breed of mountain brigand has turned a Bourbon favourite into an outcast, where the myriad splendours of Caserta Palace stay unsung and languishing among streets of squalor, and the treasures of Capua Museum are sunk in damp shadow cold as stone. There are no guidebooks, photographs, postcards – no helpful indications – and the old director is long since dead.

'May I photograph the Mater Matutas again?' I asked.

'No you can't.'

'Do you have any pictures of them?'

'No.'

'Will you take one if I lend you my camera?'

'No. It's forbidden.'

'Do any new things come in from excavations?'

'No. Not for ten years.'

I'm not surprised: straight to private collectors and auction-rooms. But at least he unlocked the store-room door to show me all the unloved mothers, lonely and cold and never seen; one wonders why they were ever unearthed in the first place. At which point a vengeful Campanian cloudburst sent water deluging through the museum ceiling like an open tap; but not one of the three attendants moved a muscle. For all they cared everything could have washed away. 'And that is the Italian Civil Service,' said a friend, 'a job for life with pension; off at two every day to a second job for cash. The museum's not theirs; it belongs to the state.'

It is the same at the twelve-hundred-roomed (only forty on view) Royal Palace, where cavernous ceilings and mile-long walls dance with passionate swirls of colour, and there are marbled and mirrored visions of regal banquets, and echoes of stately fanfares in giant halls, and the water gardens cascade triumphantly past throngs of admiring and abandoned Grecian statues. There are as many staff as visitors,

* Fiona Pitt-Kethley calls Caserta 'revolting'. She is right.

and no guidebooks or pictures, and there won't be any till the Director signs the order, but unfortunately he's had to resign . . . and yes, that huge crib is a fake; the real one disappeared one morning five years ago. We still don't know how it went without being noticed. But then funny things happen here . . . We all eat in a certain restaurant or lose our jobs . . .

Everything is tobacco after Caserta, hanging in all the house-yards like ropes of dung to dry in the sun, and the houses themselves piled along the road in ribbons all the way to Benevento, as if any planners had only wanted to block out the rolling hills behind – spectacularly ridged with interleaving folds and dipping valleys as they reach their sweeps of smoothness to the sky, still hiding the Caudine Forks somewhere in their battered rib-cage, endlessly perplexing scholars.

Perhaps Carlo Poerio would be happier now if he could see some of the things happening in the south. Benevento isn't falling down any more, but is just difficult to find, surrounded by a labyrinth of motorways rushing in all directions. Like the Romans, you can obviously get anywhere from Benevento nowadays. The mighty work of Trajan's Arch looks on from the ancient axis, still straddling the tiny Appian square, thighs wide apart in magisterial stance as if for ever the centre of a striding Roman world, and sullenly enduring an army of cleaners and a slow return to a second-century blaze of icing white. The witches, however, have all upped and flown. People laughed when I asked about them: '*Leggende, leggende,*' they smiled, shaking their heads at such Rip van Winkle enquiries. Even Lydia is married with three children. 'Just going shopping,' she said. Though there are traces of them down in the old town on a *trattoria* wall (Antica Taverna), a series of mysterious drawings by an itinerant artist who has sensed the ancient lore still lurking in the valley and has caught the sorcerers at their unearthly rituals.

*

What a change after Benevento! As the motorways and major roads circle north, east and west, the old Appia heads off quietly through San Giorgio, past new excavations at Aeclanum, to worm along southward and undisturbed towards Melfi. Rocky outcrops of little mountains start, all indiscriminate and mongrel-shaped like a litter of wrinkled piglets swimming in sun, some pale and treeless, others dark with firs, and the patternless terrain broken here and there by jagged points where tiny buildings cluster. This is earthquake country, ravaged in 1980 and still only partly rebuilt, bringing cries of outrage from the press and politicians scouring the ten-year rubble of Conza and Sant' Angelo dei Lombardi for the scandal and woe and tales of *malavita* which abound in plenty. But work goes on, inch by tedious inch, among venom and insults; and settlements of prefabricated houses sent by Scandinavia and Germany have turned into rows of flower-strewn and washday-permanent homes; and sledgehammers ever so slowly level crumpled walls; and by the roadside well-planned, gracious groups of bright new pink-roofed villas reminiscent of Forte dei Marmi have sprung up in surprising places.

Deeply hidden in a narow valley below Frigento still bubbles the ancient cauldron of Mephitis, small, grey and permanently evil, sourly popping its swollen octopus eyes and belching out wafts of sulphur; while yards away, just off the charred terrain, sheep bells ring and a static shepherd watches nothing as white dogs circle, baying angrily. Gallo has gone, Pasquale the hermit is dead, and the *padre* has moved to a distant parish and is now a *monsignore* guarding a fervent gaggle of brides of Christ.

'Everything is in Avellino Museum now,' he said, smiling. 'No one is interested any more; though some students did a dig at the temple years ago then covered it up. Remember not to breathe in if the wind's in the wrong direction.'

More little hills run beside the road, fold on fold like

swathes of fallen curtains rising and dipping, then rolling away into dark green curves and even darker valleys, where impudent cockatoo hillocks spring into sunlight from the shadows to vaunt their crests of old castles. Lines of mountains fill the sky, right and left, near and far – a chaos of land-locked dolphins chasing over waves to the distance, where plough-men have made new landscape patterns with paint-brush tractors in sweeps of rich brown earth. And among them in a sudden dip is Bisaccia, pig- and chicken-less, but full of builders at the core, where new doors shine on all the house-fronts, and sills are freshly painted, and drains are at last being laid. There's only one pig breeder left, the barman told me, and he lives on a modern farm a mile away where all the nice new houses are . . . But it's taken ten years for anything to happen.

Things are much the same at old Calitri, perched hazardously on its rocky pinnacle, while the flat land below has spawned a rash of new homes trailing out like a dishevelled skirt, each one elegant and pin-bright with pride at its clean paint and balustered balcony overlooking a flowery garden, leaving the ancient hilltop buildings to fester on the peak: an ant-heap of another age, where old dames still wear the costume and balance on the rampart wall to gaze down on the hairpin valley. It is cut by a new road now, a fast one but hardly used, and quickly becoming thickly wooded as it follows the wandering Ofanto river. This could be England, you think: high roadside banks, trees, more trees, running water, gentle curves, glimpses of speckled dales and fells stretching away to the skyline. And no cars either – someone must have forgotten to put it on the map – until after an hour of peace and loneliness you come to Monticchio.

So does everybody else. For the lakes have been discovered, and in these sumptuous tree-lined craters matted with oaks and elms and beech – thick as bubbling treacle, all splashing palettes of vivid and hybrid colour, their branches whispering a long-lost heathen creed and the ghostly moans of old anchorites – the banks are being filled with hotels and restaurants and 'camping's and playgrounds ... and everything flat is a car park or picnic spot, and nature's litany is vanishing under the inexorable plough of progress, and the green man flees to the peaks from the new barbarians. Even the monastery has been restored and redecorated in startling white and glows luminous in the awesome, dark solemnity.

Not far beyond, over a rise, sits Melfi on its bulging mountain-top, and if Professor Cassota were to return from Rome he might be pleased at last, for the *comune* has bought the castle from the Dorias and it is being massively restored – not quite as Frederick of Hohenstaufen might have approved perhaps – and all those unloved treasures in the dark, reviled thirty years ago, now gleam from splendid display cabinets in a museum on the ground floor. And breathtaking exhibits they are too: every age, every shape, every fashion. And as if to companion Minerva's owl the falconers have come back to roost; they have arrived from all over south Italy with cages of hooded birds for their annual convention, and every morning and evening they race and wheel and hover over the sweep of low hills surrounding Melfi, which has at last become loved again. What a change, what a change! John Julius Norwich and Georgina Masson on sale in the bookshop to revive past glories, and behind the castle like a sculpted gravestone the dark triangle of Monte Vulture rises to a sacred point from which, at sunrise, you can see the new day sparkle into silver life on the Adriatic Sea beyond Bari.

Something has happened here, off the beaten track: smiling, animated faces and courteous people eager to help, pleased to find you here, and girls with bright vivacious eyes that are fully aware of life, as if the southern world around them is waking up and growing busy and proud again. (Perhaps they remember that the south gave ten times more in wealth to the union of Italy than the north ever did.) Vitality is even stronger in Venosa, where a sparkling new hotel commemorates the Guiscards, and there are blocks of apartments growing out in lines north of the old town – still hugging its narrow contorted alleys to its heart and guarding its grave-faced Horace. Ancient houses crouch there in cram-jammed packets, one on the other – bulging, bending, bursting at seams, tortured into incoherent shapes, crook-backed, wizened, dehydrated, a pattern of Beelzebub grotesques, yet monstrously magic; while tree-lined avenues spread from this Gordian centre and from the castle, now being restored and made ready to house Dottor Bricese's collection of antiquities. Here a most courteous guide will show you round it, and just where the Appia passed, and where medieval knights let their horses drink at fountains, and will tell you what the prisoners scratched on the walls in the Del Balzo dungeons. Unfortunately La Trinità is mainly closed – for repairs, they say, or perhaps for excavation: the old *guardiano* isn't sure as he looks into the wire enclosure where nothing is happening, and mumbles something about finding a tessellated pavement covered in figures and offers to show you round the new excavations in the Roman town instead, which he considers far more interesting than an unfinished abbey. They are on both sides of the road now, and more extensive than I remember them – dimly – with the pharmacist, who alas, is dead (it was his *fegato* the hotel proprietor told me).

And the *cantine* are all dead too. Nowhere in Venosa can you see the *frasche* displayed as an invitiation to step down into the welcoming cool of a cellar and have a drink. 'The young people don't like wine, only beer,' I was told. 'That's why they're closed; no demand!' Which is a sorry state of affairs if it's true – though I rather doubt it, not wishing to believe that any young Venusian could have such appalling taste, or that those benchfuls of crusty bronzed patriarchs sunning themselves peacefully by the castle no longer have a sacred place to retire to for their evening tipple. The real reason, I fear, is that shame has crept over progressive Venosa, as with an air of finger-cocked refinement it blushes at the earthy, vulgar elements of its recent past and skips down the genealogical table to something more appropriate. Even the exuberant Stone of Friendship has disappeared, metamorphosed into a marble doorpost. Which is a pity, considering that next year Horace will have been dead for exactly twenty centuries, and they are planning a little festival in his honour – and if any warm-blooded human would have enjoyed a merry evening in a *cantina* with his arms wrapped round a daughter or two of Venus, he would.

Beyond La Trinità Abbey the road south skirts the avenue of caves and winds down to a sun-scorched plain, stretching out like a prairie beside a spine of mountains to the east. They are worth crossing, briefly, for the awesome sight and might of Castel del Monte blazing white in the sun after its restoration and cleaning. One wonders what Gregorovius would think of the polish it's had, and the hollow feel of its vaulted rooms stripped of marble. But the power is still there: the adamantine force of Frederick breathes from the massive weight of walls, and his visionary genius is stamped on its size and shape and muscular omnipotence, as it vaults the surrounding land, and like a majestic eyrie or Ozymandias gazes on a far-flung kingdom that stretches from eyesight into haze on all horizons, and commands a vastness of unspeakable space. And this was only one of his castles.

Afterwards the road to Gravina is unerringly straight, and suggests the determined might of old Rome ruthlessly cutting through the land; but I barely recognised the town on arrival, and only found out where the caves and the Church of Purgatory were by asking a passer-by. It has all grown up and away from where the old town is, through an archway and perched over the ravine, where the congested, shapeless houses tumble down from anarchic joints, and eager urchins emerge from corners wanting to guide you to the skulls. Their broad-shouldered mothers stand gossiping in steep-ledged doorways and laugh happily about Zia Rosa. *'Muerte,'* they say, '. . . no more taxes to pay, lucky woman. *Ma si mangia bene . . .'*

There has been digging too at Gravina. Someone has found a vast mausoleum outside the town and new graves are being opened almost daily. 'It's very important,' said my informant, 'because now we know that the Romans were here. Of course, your Signor Perkins from England told us a long time ago; now we believe him. But the *tombaroli* know more about finding graves than the archaeologists do; they can pinpoint every one.' And he took me aside discreetly, to show me the bronzes he had in a cupboard – a grey-green shape of prancing horses, a discus thrower, a chariot, two wrestlers, a dancing girl . . .

Altamura similarly is much enlarged (or larger than I remember), and has big industrial suburbs that sprawl halfway back to Gravina; in its narrow centre, up the hill, the walking talking crowds are thick and slow-moving as they amble past the scaffolding over the cathedral door, where a small team of workmen are standing on planks and washing down the darkened stone to the music of transistors. Professor Gatti, long retired, now does part-time work for the Belle Arti in Matera, his enthusiasm unabated and his fund of local knowledge at last being appreciated by the Soprintendenza.

There are no caves left in Matera today, or so they will tell you; above its two empty troglodyte valleys, the ragged rock-face still wormed with a hundred sockets of unused eyes blinded by time and sun, it has grown and grown and is still expanding. But La Scaletta is always there, down tortuous steps descending the ravine into the old town where an arched doorway bursts into whitewashed *palazzo* rooms that are now a centre for art students. Every year it initiates or produces new books and publications – *Traditions of Basilicata, Cartier-Bresson in Matera, The Paintings of Carlo Levi, The Crypt of San Nicola dei Greci*. Nearby is the Ridola Museum, where hopeful boys lurk, inviting you on a tour of the empty *sassi* afterwards, insisting they know more than the official custodians. On the outskirts, Rione Venusia looks smart and prosperous, all white with radiant street-lamps, well-kept lawns and a car in each driveway; La Martella has become a thriving reality at last, in spite of the archbishop, inhabited by office workers, civil servants, bank clerks and one or two farmers, and they can all drive to work in ten minutes.

'The worst thing is the heat in the summer,' said Daniele the journalist, 'but they love it all the same; the town is only a mile away with all its activity and expansion. Never mind what the north says about us; they'd soon fold up if we refused to buy from them.'

'And the caves . . .?' I asked.

'All shut. One is done up as a showpiece for tourists, but the farmers don't live there any more; they've got houses or flats in town and drive out every morning, then they jump on a tractor and do a day's work in ten minutes . . . The problem is though' – he paused – 'can the south cope with the rapid progress? It's an avalanche: computers, mobile phones, a new business starting every week . . . and I'm not a journalist now by the way; I'm Press Officer for the new industrial consortium.'

And I'm schizophrenic; half glad, half sad; still whimpering over history's autumn leaves as they blow away, nervous for the fulgent rites of every spring that no icicle hand can stop. 'Is the Mafia here yet?' I asked him.

'Yes, getting closer,' he said. Then I asked why La Scaletta didn't start an ethnological museum of south Italy.

'We'd like to,' he smiles, 'but no one has the drive to do it.'

Someone has begun, in Castellaneta down the road.

Rudolfo Valentino is firmly in pride of place and is so livid and alarming I assume he is a joke, and wish the few angry shots fired at him after his erection had been more effective. He shimmies on the pavement, hugged in a mantle of vicious royal purple-blue that would poleaxe a peacock; his right hip has a jaunty thrust, and his skirt is neatly slit at the back. How could the burghers of Castellaneta have done it? you wonder. Or was it the ceramicists of Grottaglie exacting a feudal revenge? Or some mischief maker's gesture to those love-sick grandmothers in Ohio? And you leave amazed at this purple patch of progress saluting distant Hollywood.

But the road onward is excellent: straight as a die towards Taranto, past drawn-up armies of olive trees on either side, bent with age, and along wide, burning tarmac where huge new industrial complexes and factories sit back behind fields, and the white towers of Massafra glint high up in the sun. The blossoming sea town sprawls and sprawls further inland almost daily, frantic with new wealth and energy, till in the midst of all the activity the road wheels off to the left to sever the Salentine Peninsula, leaving the dark smudge of oil refineries far to the right. Then at Grottaglie the two-lane highway ends, as if acknowledging that the rush is over and life can now become more peaceful and staid – which it does immediately, suggesting it is time to drink and think. Not easy, however: Chardonnay di Puglia is dry and soft and soporific, and the Airport Restaurant (nowhere near the airport) is clean and welcoming. It all makes the onward road seem dull and tiresome, the land barely visible in dismal flatness, until the mound of Oria Castle rears up ahead. Here warrens of age still circle the fortress for safety, white and narrow and on the tilt, with a new surprise round every corner: stairways, balconies, arches, massive gates linked in punch-drunk sloping mayhem – the paradoxical accretions of history woven into the castle skirts. Count Martini has opened a small museum inside, and is happy for you to walk on his ramparts and climb his towers and think about jumping into his garden. Just visible is the inflexible line of trees that marks the road to Manduria, still bound by grey heaps of Messapian wall, behind which Pliny's Well crouches in a vegetable garden. The boys have put a notice on the gate saying CHIUSO: IN RESTAURO, so that they can open it for you with mini-Mafia smiles of expectancy, and then lead you underground to hear the incessant drips.

Finally Brindisi, approached by a massive four-lane highway that dives straight into ragged suburbs, down a shrunken road car-jammed with ambling bodies that force you to snail-pace it for miles to the sea. And suddenly the waft of oil and the gull-cries come, and lights on the mastheads roll and blink, and the fresh sea sparkles darkly on its way to Greece. And it is still there, all watched by a lonely white column unaware of passing time, where everything in the world has been seen before, and, whatever may seem to change, life will always be just the same.

It was smaller than I remembered it.

Select Bibliography

Acton, Harold, *The Bourbons of Naples*, London, Methuen London, 1959

The Last of the Bourbons, London, Methuen London, 1961

Addison, Joseph, *Remarks on Several Parts of Italy in the years 1701, 1702 and 1703*, London, J. & R. Tonson, 1767

Barzini, Luigi, *The Italians*, London, Hamish Hamilton, 1964

Douglas, Norman, *Old Calabria*, London, Martin Secker, 1915

Eustace, Rev. John Chetwode, *A Classical Tour through Italy*, London, J. Mawman, 1815

Forsyth, Joseph, *Remarks on Antiquities, Arts and Letters during an Excursion in Italy in the years 1802 and 1803*, London, John Murray, 1816

Gibbon, Edward, ed. J. B. Bury, *The History of the Decline and Fall of the Roman Empire*, London, Methuen & Co., 1909

Gissing, George, *By the Ionian Sea*, London, Chapman & Hall, 1901

Graham, Maria, *Three months passed in the mountains east of Rome during the year 1819*, London, Longman, Hurst, Rees, Orme & Browne, 1820

Hawthorne, Nathaniel, *Transformation*, London, George Bell & Sons, 1906

Hibbert, Christopher, *Garibaldi and his Enemies*, London, Longman, 1965

The Grand Tour, London, Thames Methuen, 1987

Benito Mussolini, London, Longman, Green, 1962

Keppel Craven, The Hon. Richard, *A Tour through the Southern Provinces of the Kingdom of Naples*, London, Rodwell & Martin, 1821

Lampedusa, Giuseppe di, *The Leopard*, trs. Archibald Colquhoun, London, Collins Harvill, 1960

Lear, Edward, *Journals of a Landscape Painter in Southern Calabria*, London, Richard Bentley, 1852

Levi, Carlo, *Christ Stopped at Eboli*, London, Cassell, 1948

Links, J. G., *Travellers in Europe*, London, Bodley Head, 1980

Macaulay, Rose, *Pleasure of Ruins*, London, Thames & Hudson, 1984

Martin, Selina, *Narrative of a Three Years' Residence in Italy, 1819–1822*, Dublin, W. F. Wakeman, 1828

Masson, Georgina, *Frederick II of Hohenstaufen*, London, Secker & Warburg, 1957

Matthews, H., *The Diary of an Invalid*, London, John Murray, 1820

Moens, W. J. C., *English Travellers and Italian Brigands*, two vols, London, Hurst & Blackett, 1866

Origo, Iris, *War in Val d'Orcia*, London, Jonathan Cape, 1947

Ramage, Crauford Tait, *The Nooks and By-ways of Italy*, Liverpool, Edward Howell, 1868

Revel, Jean-François, *As For Italy*, trs. Anthony Rhodes, London, Weidenfeld & Nicolson, 1959

Ross, Janet, *The Land of Manfred*, London, John Murray, 1889

Swinburne, Henry, *Travels in the Two Sicilies in 1777, 1778, 1779 and 1780*, London, T. Cadell & P. Elmsly, 1790

Index

Index

Index

Index

Also available in Minerva

HENRY MILLER

The Colossus of Maroussi

'*Colossus* was written from some other level of my being. What I like about it is that it's a joyous book, it expresses joy, it gives joy'

When Henry Miller visited Greece with his friend Lawrence Durrell in 1939, his experiences amounted to a complete rebirth. For Miller it was the paramount adventure of his life and it moved him to write what is in the opinion of many his finest book, certainly one of the great travel books of this century. No other writer about Greece has captured its visual splendour and pinned down the spirit of place with such inspired felicity. But this is not the only quality that brings *The Colossus of Maroussi* close to the heart of Greece. Like the Greeks themselves, Henry Miller's chief concern is with people; his classical landscapes are never without their teeming and fabulous human figures, chief among whom is the poet Katsimbalis, the Colossus himself, a monumental portrait of heroic proportions.

'Unlike anything else ever written about Greece' Edmund Wilson

'No other modern author has the same power to make you feel good to be alive' *Guardian*

V. S. NAIPAUL

India

'It is literally the last word on India today, witness within witness, a chain of voices that illustrates every phase of Indian life . . . with a truthfulness and a subtlety that are a joy to read. Something like love enters the narrative – a real feeling for the land and its people'
Paul Theroux, *Literary Review*

'Brilliantly enjoyable . . . I loved the old Naipaul for his sardonic wit. The new one is to be loved for his sweetness of nature, amounting almost to sanctity. Everybody should read him'
Auberon Waugh, *Sunday Telegraph*

'He represents probably the nearest available equivalent to a contemporary Dickens . . . his persistence and penetration, his sharpness of outline and urgency of feeling, his ability to make sense of a chaotically unravelling world in the mirror of his strange, exhilarating, disturbing and yet oddly reassuring books'
Hilary Spurling, *Daily Telegraph*

'There are descriptive passage which are among the finest things he has written . . . an exceptional portrait of India'
Ian Jack, *Independent on Sunday*

'With this book he may well have written his own enduring monument, in prose at once stirring and intensely personal, distinguished both by style and critical acumen'
K. Natwar-Singh, *Financial Times*

PAUL RAMBALI

French Blues

Traversing memory, encounter and anecdote, *French Blues* is a foray through the supermetro tunnels and graffiti-tagged suburbs of a France that can no longer recognise itself; where the *nouvelle* literature is the comic book and the most popular setting for romance a computer network.

Paul Rambali dines with *couture* king Christian Lacroix, dives into a limo with sex symbol Beatrice Dalle, explores Paris with veteran photographer Robert Doisneau, discusses Hyper-reality with Jean Baudrillard and attends a rally with 10,000 *Front National* supporters.

Revisiting the France of his childhood, the author discovers a quite unfamiliar country. Exotic, iconoclastic and enlightening, his unsentimental journey lays to rest outdated myths and recounts the stuff of new ones.

'A jazzy, sceptical portrait of modern urban France . . . Like a series of video-clips, naively provocative and steeped in a flashy, youthful cynicism, yet it does contain insights . . . He asks many of the right questions and arguably comes closer to the real France than many a romantic, rural Francophile' *Sunday Times*

'The first book for a long time to evoke a truly recognisable France. Rambali is a fine contemporary *flaneur*' *City Limits*

PETER CONRAD

Down Home

Tasmania is a strange place to be born – the offshore island of an offshore continent, regularly omitted from maps of Australia; a sad, lonely, savagely beautiful place which, in trying to forget its past of penal brutality and aboriginal genocide, has convinced itself that it's a demure little England, an Isle of Wight adrift twelve thousand miles from London. Peter Conrad grew up there, left in 1968, and after almost two decades went back to see the home he had lost, with its wild rivers, impassable rain forest, marsupial monsters and historical scars. In the process he discovered a small world he had never known: a Lilliput of wonders and oddities – his own home and the secret, forgotten birthplace of Australia. The result is an extraordinary book combining travel, autobiography and history, by a supremely versatile and penetrating critic of contemporary culture.

'A rich achievement'
Colin Thubron, *Independent*

'Erudite, imaginative, wide ranging'
New Statesmen & Society

'Here is a work of real distinction, marked by Conrad's aboriginal cunning, which he nearly junked forever in leaving home'
Sunday Times

'A personal and literary triumph'
Literary Review

A Selected List of Titles Available from Minerva

Fiction

☐ 7493 9026 3	**I Pass Like Night**	Jonathan Ames	£3.99	BX
☐ 7493 9006 9	**The Tidewater Tales**	John Bath	£4.99	BX
☐ 7493 9004 2	**A Casual Brutality**	Neil Blessondath	£4.50	BX
☐ 7493 9028 2	**Interior**	Justin Cartwright	£3.99	BC
☐ 7493 9002 6	**No Telephone to Heaven**	Michelle Cliff	£3.99	BX
☐ 7493 9028 X	**Not Not While the Giro**	James Kelman	£4.50	BX
☐ 7493 9011 5	**Parable of the Blind**	Gert Hofmann	£3.99	BC
☐ 7493 9010 7	**The Inventor**	Jakov Lind	£3.99	BC
☐ 7493 9003 4	**Fall of the Imam**	Nawal El Saadewi	£3.99	BC

Non-Fiction

☐ 7493 9012 3	**Days in the Life**	Jonathon Green	£4.99	BC
☐ 7493 9019 0	**In Search of J D Salinger**	Ian Hamilton	£4.99	BX
☐ 7493 9023 9	**Stealing from a Deep Place**	Brian Hall	£3.99	BX
☐ 7493 9005 0	**The Orton Diaries**	John Lahr	£5.99	BC
☐ 7493 9014 X	**Nora**	Brenda Maddox	£6.99	BC